Secrets of Meat Curing and Sausage Making

.

FIFTH EDITION

SECRETS OF

MEAT CURING

AND

SAUSAGE MAKING

HOW TO CURE

HAMS, SHOULDERS, BACON
CORNED BEEF, ETC.

AND

HOW TO MAKE ALL
KINDS OF

SAUSAGE, ETC.

TO COMPLY WITH THE

PURE FOOD LAWS

PUBLISHED BY
B. HELLER & CO.
MANUFACTURING CHEMISTS
CHICAGO, U.S.A.
December, 1922

INDEX

2

H

I

J

K

9

L

M

S

T

V

W

Z

B. HELLER & CO.

PREFACE

ADOLPH HELLER

Adolph Heller, the father of the members of the firm of B. Heller & Co., was a scientific and practical Butcher and Packer and a Practical Sausage Manufacturer. He studied the causes of failure in the handling of meats, with the aim of always producing the best and most uniform products that could be made. He was so successful in his business that his products were known and recognized as the best that could be made.

His sons were all given practical training in all departments of the business, from the bottom rung of the ladder to the top. The problems of the Packing Industry were kept constantly before them in their school and college days and influenced them in the investigations and study which developed into the present business of B. Heller & Co.

Under these circumstances, the Science of Chemistry naturally claimed the sons of Adolph Heller. Naturally, too, the Chemistry of the Meat Industry overshadowed all other branches of the fascinating profession. With their habits of study and investigation, they soon discovered that one of the great causes of failure in the curing and handling of meat products was the lack of materials which were always uniform, pure and dependable. This led to the founding of the firm of B. Heller & Co., whose aim has always been to furnish to the Butchers, Packers and Sausage Makers such materials as could be absolutely depended upon for purity and uniformity. They also early found that even with good materials to work with, the lack of fixed rules and formulas contributed largely to the lack of uniformity in the finished goods. This led to the publication of ''Secrets of Meat Curing and

18

Sausage Making,'' in which definite rules were given for handling all kinds of meats and making all kinds of sausage.

The enactment of the National Pure Food Law, the National Meat Inspection Law and the various State Pure Food Laws has made a great change in the Butcher, Packing and Sausage Making Business. The use of Chemical Preservatives is now prohibited under these various food laws, making it necessary to preserve meats and manufacture sausage without the use of many agents which were in general use.

The firm of B. Heller & Co. anticipated the enactment of the various food laws, and already had completed investigations which enabled them to assist packers, butchers and sausage makers at once by giving them curing agents which were free from the Antiseptic Preservatives which these laws prohibited, and yet would produce cured meats, sausage, etc, of the highest quality without the use of the Antiseptic Agents. The underlying principles for handling meats and making sausage with the antiseptic agents and without them are very different, and it became absolutely necessary that the firm of B. Heller & Co. should furnish their friends and customers such information as would enable them to cure their meats and make their sausage so as not to incur losses from goods that would not keep, and to turn out goods of fine quality and appearance. This book is the result. In its pages are formulas and rules for the handling of all kinds of meat and the manufacture of all kinds of sausage which are the results of many years of experience as Packing House Experts and Chemists who have made a life-time study of the business in all its phases. If the directions and rules are followed, anyone can produce the finest of cured meats and sausage, whether they have had previous experience or not. Furthermore, the products made according to these directions will comply with the requirements of all the Food Laws at present in force in this country.

Hoping the following pages will be found instructive and helpful and thanking the Butcher Trade for their support and patronage in the past, we beg to remain,

Very respectfully,

B. HELLER & CO.

BENJAMIN HELLER

ALBERT HELLER

JOE HELLER

EDWARD HELLER

HARRY HELLER

PACKING-HOUSE EXPERTS

ANALYTICAL AND CONSULTING CHEMISTS

We have been Consulting Chemists for the Large Packers for many years. Our advice in the handling of meats has saved Packers many thousands of dollars. We offer our advice free of charge to our customers. We make a specialty of both Analytic and Synthetic Chemistry. Our large clientele will always find us prompt in our services as heretofore.

Analyses Given Careful Attention.

General Syntheses

a Specialty

B. HELLER & CO.

PRIVATE OFFICE
of
BENJAMIN HELLER

PRIVATE OFFICE
of
ALBERT HELLER

VIEW IN GENERAL OFFICE

VIEW IN GENERAL OFFICE

The Board of Food and Drug Inspection of the Agricultural Department, at Washington, has permitted the use of certain Curing Agents, by not objecting to their use; but, at the same time, has ruled out, for curing purposes, such chemicals as come under the heading of Antiseptic Preservatives. As a consequence, certain chemical preservatives are prohibited in meats and meat food products if they are to be sold in the Territories or are to be shipped from one State to another, or from any State or Territory into any other State or Territory.

For that reason, we have changed some of our former preparations and have also placed on the market several preparations that will take the place of some of our former products. These new products are Freeze-Em-Pickle, "A" Condimentine and "B" Condimentine. They contain nothing that has been ruled out by any of the rulings or regulations under any of the Food Laws in this country.

The Antiseptic Preservatives that have been ruled out are: Borax, Boracic Acid, Fluoride of Ammonia, Formaldehyde, Benzoic Acid, Sulphurous Acid, Sulphite of Soda, Salicylic Acid, Abrastol and Beta Naphthol.

CHICAGO. U. S. A.

The use of some of these Preservatives is considered by many high authorities of the world to be harmless. However, as the majority of the Food Commissioners of this country object to their use, and have recommended to the State Legislatures and the Congress of the United States that the use of these Preservatives be prohibited by law, and the State Legislatures and United States Congress have passed laws to this effect; these laws are now in effect and it is, therefore, the duty of every citizen of this country to obey these laws, strictly and to the letter.

In this book we are giving to the Butchers and Sausage Manufacturers the results of much study and experiment, so as to enable the Butchers and Sausage Makers and Packers to produce goods which will meet the requirements of the various food laws and yet avoid the danger of loss from turning out meat food products that might not keep the necessary length of time. Our methods are original, and will produce most excellent results.

It must be remembered that meat must be handled at the proper temperature and according to certain rules, which must be followed to the letter if the Butcher desires to turn out products of the best quality and of appetizing appearance. No detail mentioned in this book is too small to merit strict attention.

All the materials mentioned for use in these pages are in strict accordance with the various food laws. Nothing is recommended or suggested that would come in conflict with the application of the regulations under the existing food laws.

We invite the correspondence of our customers and whenever they are in any doubt it will afford us much satisfaction to hear from them and to give them full information concerning any feature of their business upon which they desire our advice.

BEGIN CURING OF MEAT IN THE PEN.

Thousands of pounds of Hams, Shoulders and Sides are spoiled annually before the hog is killed. Overheated hogs, or hogs that are excited from overdriving, should never be killed until they are cooled off or have become perfectly quiet. When the temperature of a hog is above normal, the meat always becomes feverish. This is especially true of large fat hogs, and when the meat becomes feverish, it will never cure properly, but nine times out of ten will sour. The meat of feverish hogs can never be chilled as it should be, and unless the meat is properly chilled, it cannot be properly cured. Before hogs are killed, they ought to be driven into a cool place and if necessary, sprayed with cold water until they are thoroughly cooled off. This precaution is necessary only in hot weather; in winter, they simply need plenty of rest.

If it is necessary to hold the hogs for several days in the pen before they are killed, they should have an abundance of water and also a little feed. This prevents shrinkage and will also keep them from getting nervous from hunger.

CHICAGO, U.S.A.

CURING PORK THE YEAR AROUND

Up to a comparatively few years ago, all Pork Packing was done in the winter. Packing Houses would fill their plants during the winter months, and in the spring would smoke out the meats. In this way, most of the meat had to be sold over-salted, the shrinkage and loss to the Packer was greater and meats, therefore, had to be sold at a much higher price, besides, they were of very inferior quality.

At the present time, due to improved methods, packing can be done all the year around, and meat can be sold as fast as it is finished. In this way, cured meat can be produced at a much lower price, the money invested in it can be turned over four, five or six times a year, and the meat will be much better, taste better and more of it can be eaten because of the fact that it is more wholesome and more easily digested.

HOISTING HOGS IN A LARGE PACKING HOUSE, WITH A HOG-HOISTING MACHINE.

Great care should always be exercised when hogs are hoisted before sticking. When hogs are hoisted alive to be stuck, very often when a very heavy hog is jerked from the floor, the hip is dislocated or sprained, and blood will be thrown out around the injured joint, so the Ham will be spoiled. Great care should also be exercised in driving the live hogs, as hogs are the heaviest and weakest and easiest injured of all animals.

Special pens should be provided for them, so they are not crowded, and so they have plenty of room when they are driven to the killing pen. They should be handled very carefully, and piling up and crowding should be avoided as much as possible. Many hams are injured by overcrowding the hogs in the killing pens, for when hogs smell blood they become excited and nervous, and unless they have plenty of room, they will pile upon each other and bruise themselves so that

MACHINE USED IN LARGER PACKING HOUSES FOR HOISTING HOGS.

there will be many skin-bruised hams, and the flesh will be full of bruises. Men driving hogs should never use a whip. The best thing to use in driving hogs is a stick about two feet long, to the end of which is fastened a piece of canvas three inches wide and two feet long. By striking the hogs with this canvas, it makes a noise which will do more towards driving them, without injury, than the whip which will injure and discolor the skin.

STICKING HOGS IN A MODERN PACKING HOUSE.

(Copyrighted; Reprint Forbidden.)

Men sticking hogs should be sure to make a **good,** large opening in the neck, three or four inches long, in order to give the blood a good, free flow. It is very necessary to sever the veins and arteries in the neck, so as to get all of the blood out of the hog. The man who does the sticking must be careful not to stick the knife into the shoulder, for if the shoulder is stuck, the blood settles there, and the bloody part will have to be trimmed out after the hog is cut up. In large Packing Houses, there is a report made out every day, of the number of shoulder-stuck hogs, and the sticker must sign this report before it is sent to the office.

HOW HOGS ARE STUCK IN A LARGE MODERN PACKING HOUSE.

This shows the sticker the kind of work he is doing and makes him more careful. In small houses, most butchers stick the hogs on the floor and let them bleed there. Those who can possibly do it should hoist the hog by the hind leg before it is stuck or immediately after it is stuck, as the case may be, so as to allow the hog to properly bleed. When the hog is properly hoisted by one hind leg, alive, and then stuck while hanging, it will kick considerably and the kicking and jerking of the hog will help in pumping out all of the blood, making a much better bled carcass than if the hog is first stunned with a hammer and stuck on the floor. The better the hog is bled, the better the meat will be for curing.

SCALDING HOGS.

(Copyrighted; Reprint Forbidden.)

It is impossible to give the exact temperature one should use in scalding hogs, as this will vary under different circumstances. In winter the hair sticks much tighter than in summer and requires more scalding and more heat than in summer. Hogs raised in the South, in a warm climate, will scald much easier than those raised in a northern climate. A butcher will soon learn which temperature is best adapted to his own locality and the kind of hogs he is scalding.

SCALDING HOGS IN A LARGE MODERN PACKING HOUSE.

In a Packing House where a long scalding tub is used, the temperature depends entirely upon how fast the hogs are being killed. If the hogs are killed slowly, so each hog can remain in the water longer, it is not necessary to have the water as hot as when they are handled fast and are taken out of the water in a shorter time. It is, however, universally acknowledged that the quicker a hog can be taken out of the scalding tub the better it is for the meat. The hog is a great conductor of heat, and when kept in the scalding water too long, it becomes considerably heated and bad results have many times been traced to the fact that the hog was scalded in water which was not hot enough, and was kept in this water too long in order to loosen the hair. Overheating the hog in the scalding water very often causes the meat of fat hogs to sour and Packers wonder why it is that the meat has spoiled. We therefore wish to caution Packers against this, and to advise the use of water as hot as practicable for scalding hogs.

To make the hair easy to remove and to remove dirt and impurities from the skin, we recommend Hog-Scald. This preparation makes scalding easy, it removes most of the dirt and filth, cleanses the hog and whitens the skin.

In many localities, where the water is hard, Hog-Scald will be found of great value, as it softens the water and makes it nice to work with; it cleanses the skin of the hogs and improves their appearance. It is a great labor saver and more than pays the cost by the labor it saves, as it assists in removing the hair and leaves the skin more yielding to the scraper.

The skin of all hogs is covered with more or less greasy filth, which contains millions of disease germs and these extend down into the pores of the skin. If this germ-laden filth is not removed, and if it gets into the brine when the meat is being cured, it injures both the meat and the brine in flavor, and also spoils the flavor of the lard if it gets into that. Hog-Scald removes most of this filth and cleanses the skin, and for these reasons alone, should be used by every Packer and Butcher. Hams and Bacon from hogs that have been scalded with Hog-Scald are, therefore, cleaner and will be much brighter after they are smoked than when the filth of the hog remains in the pores of the skin.

Those selling dressed hogs will find Hog-Scald very valuable, as hogs that have been scalded with it are cleaner and look whiter and much more appetizing.

The use of Hog-Scald is legal everywhere. It does not come under the regulations of the Food Laws, as it is simply a cleansing agent. Hog-Scald costs very little at the price we sell it, and everyone can afford to use it. Butchers who once try it will continue its use.

SCRAPING HOGS.

As much of the hair as possible should be scraped from the hogs, instead of being shaved off with a sharp knife, as is often done. If the hog is not properly scalded and scraped and the hair remains in the skin, such hair is usually shaved off with a knife before the hog is gutted, and sometimes after the meat is chilled and cut up. After the meat is cured, the rind shrinks and all the stubs of hair that have been shaved off will stick out and the rind will be rough like a man's face when he has not been shaved for a day or so. Hams and Bacon from hogs that have been shaved instead of properly scalded and scraped, will look much rougher and much more unsightly than if the hogs are properly scalded and scraped. Therefore, Packers should give close attention that the scalding and scraping is properly done. The scraping bench should be provided with a hose right above where the hogs are being scraped and this should be supplied with hot water,

SCRAPING HOGS IN A PACKING HOUSE.

if possible, so the hogs can be rinsed off occasionally with hot water, while being scraped. The hot water can, however, be thrown over the hogs with a bucket.

After the hog has been gambrelled and hung up, either on a gambrel-stick or on rollers, it should be gutted. After it is gutted, it should be washed out thoroughly, with plenty of cold, fresh water. As every Packer understands how to gut a hog, it is not necessary to go into details.

GUTTING HOGS IN A MODERN PACKING HOUSE.

CUTTING THE HIND SHANK BONE.

(Copyrighted; Reprint Forbidden.)

We advise the cutting of the hind shank bone after the hog is dressed, so as to expose the marrow, as shown in cuts A and B. It is the best thing to do, as it helps to chill the marrow. The chunk of meat that is usually left on the hind foot, above and next to the knee, if cut loose around the knee, will be drawn to the ham, and when chilled, will remain on the ham instead of being on the hind foot, as shown in cut A. After the meat is cut, the bone can be sawed, in the same place where the hock would be cut from the ham later. See cut B. The hog will hang on the sinews the same as if the bone had not been sawed, except that the cut bone separates and exposes the marrow so it can be properly cooled. On heavy hogs this is quite a gain, as the chunk that would remain on the foot would be of little or no value there, but when left on the ham, sells for the regular ham prices.

FACING HAMS AND PULLING LEAF LARD
IN A MODERN PACKING HOUSE.

The first two figures in the above cut show two men Facing Hams. The first man faces the Ham at his right hand side and the second man faces the Ham on his left hand side, as the Hogs pass by.

The advantage of Facing Hams right after the hogs are dressed, is this. The knife can be drawn through the skin and through the fat close to the meat, and the fat will peel right off the fleshy part of the Ham. Between the fat and lean meat of the Ham, between the legs, there is a fibrous membrane which is very soft and pliable. When the knife is run through the skin and fat, it will run along the side of this membrane, making a clean face for the Ham. That part remaining on the Ham will shrink to the Ham and will form a smooth coating over the lean meat, which closes the pores and makes the Ham look smooth and nice when it is smoked. It also makes a much smoother cut along the skin. The skin when cut warm will dry nicely and look smooth when cured, whereas if it is trimmed after the meat is chilled, it looks rough and ragged. Facing Hams also allows the escape of the animal heat more readily. If Hams are not faced until after the Hogs have been chilled, this fat must be trimmed off and the Hams will not look nearly so smooth as they will if this tissue and fat is removed while the hog is warm.

The second two men in the opposite illustration are
Pulling Leaf Lard. The Leaf Lard should always be
pulled out of the hogs in summer, as it gives the hogs,
as well as the Leaf Lard, a better chance to chill.
During the winter months it can be pulled loose, but
can be left hanging loosely in the hog, from the top.
In this way it will cool nicely, and it will also allow
the animal heat to get out of the hog. Most of the
large packing houses pull out the Leaf Lard in the
winter as well as summer, and hang it on hooks in
the chill room to chill. Leaf Lard that is properly
chilled, with the animal heat all taken out of it, makes
much finer lard than when pulled out of the hog and
put into the rendering tank with the animal heat in it.

SPLITTING HOGS IN A MODERN PACKING
HOUSE.

(Copyrighted; Reprint Forbidden.)

Splitting can be done in several different ways.
Where the back of the hog is to be cut up for pork
loins, the hog is simply split through the center of
the backbone, so that one half of the backbone remains on each loin. Packers who wish to cut the sides
into Short or Long Clears or Clear Bacon Backs run
the knife down on both sides of the backbone, as close
to the backbone as possible, cutting through the skin,

fat and lean meat; then the hog should be split down
on one side of the backbone. The backbone should remain on the one side until the hog is cut up and it can
then easily be sawed off with a small saw. By cutting
or scoring the back in this way for making boneless
side meat, the sides will be smooth and there will not
be much waste left on the bone as when the backbone
is split and half of it left on each side and then is
peeled out after the meat is chilled and is being cut up.

VENTILATION IN HOG CHILL ROOM.

HOG CHILL ROOM IN A MODERN PACKING HOUSE.

(Copyrighted; Reprint Forbidden.)

Many chill rooms are not properly built. There
should be at least from 24 to 36 inches of space between the ceiling of the chilling room and the gambrel-
stick, or more if possible, in order to enable the shanks
to become thoroughly chilled. The animal heat which
leaves the carcass naturally rises to the top of the
cooler, and unless there is space between the ceiling
and the top of the hog the heat will accumulate in the
top of the cooler where the temperature will become
quite warm; this will prevent the marrow in the shank
and the joints from becoming properly chilled. It is
this fact that accounts for so much marrow and shank
sour in hams.

TEMPERATURE OF CHILL ROOM.

(Copyrighted; Reprint Forbidden.)

All Packers who have a properly built cooler for chilling hogs and who are properly equipped with an ice machine will find the following rules will give the best results. Those who are not properly equipped should try to follow these rules as closely as they can with their equipment.

A hog chill room should be down to from 28 to 32 degrees Fahrenheit when the hogs are run into it. As the cooler is filled, the temperature will be raised to as high as 45 or 46 degrees F., but enough refrigeration must be kept on so the temperature is brought down to 36 degrees by the end of 12 hours after the cooler is filled, and then the temperature must be gradually reduced down as low as 32 degrees by the time the carcasses have been in the cooler 48 hours. In other words, at the end of 48 hours the cooler must be down to 32 degrees.

All large hog coolers should be partitioned off between each section of timbers, into long alleys, so that each alley can be kept at its own temperature.

In the improper chilling of the carcasses lies the greatest danger of spoiling the meat. The greatest care must be given to the proper chilling, for if the carcasses are not properly chilled, it will be very difficult to cure the meat, and it will be liable to sour in the curing. Meat from improperly chilled carcasses, even with the greatest care afterwards, will not cure properly. Therefore, one of the first places to look for trouble when Hams are turning out sour is to look to the chilling of the meat, as it is nine chances out of ten that this is where the trouble started from. We have found by experience that by deviating only a few degrees from these set rules, the percentage of sour meat is surprisingly increased.

It has always been considered an absolute necessity to have an open air hanging room to allow the hogs to cool off in the open air before they are run into the cooler. It has always been considered that this saves considerable money in the refrigeration of the hogs. However, by the experiments made in some of the large Packing Houses, it has been demonstrated that this economy is very much over-estimated. There are certain conditions which must be closely adhered to for

43

the safe handling and curing of pork products, and the most important of these is the proper temperature. In the outside atmosphere the proper temperature rarely prevails. Hogs that are left in the open air on the hanging floor over night are generally either insufficiently chilled or are over-chilled the next morning, depending upon the outside temperature of the air. We feel that it is of advantage, however, to run the hogs into an outside hanging room and to allow them to dry for one or two hours before putting them into the chilling room.

Packers who cure large quantities of hogs must see to it that their chill rooms are properly constructed and have sufficient refrigeration, so the temperature can be kept under perfect control at all times. The cooler should be partitioned off lengthwise, between each line of posts, making long alleys to run the hogs into, each one of which can be regulated as to its temperature separately from the others. The hogs can be run into one of these alleys as fast as they are killed and should the temperature get up above 50 degrees F., the hogs can be run out of this into another. The cooler in which hogs are chilled should never go above 50 degrees Fahrenheit, and a properly constructed cooler can be kept below this temperature.

While the cooler is being filled, the temperature should be held at between 45 and 50 degrees Fahrenheit, and should be kept at this temperature for about two hours after filling. At the end of two hours, all of the vapor will have passed away, being taken up by and frozen onto the refrigerator pipes, and the hogs will begin to dry. When the hogs begin to show signs of drying, or in about two hours after the refrigerator is filled, more refrigeration should be turned on, and the temperature should be gradually brought down, so that in twelve hours from the time the cooler is filled, the temperature should be brought down to 36 or 37 degrees temperature Fahrenheit. If the temperature is not brought down to 36 or 37 degrees F. in 12 hours it means a delay in removing the animal heat, and a tendency for decomposition to set in. If the temperature is brought down lower than 32 degrees Fahrenheit during the first 12 hours, the outside surface of the carcasses are too rapidly chilled, which tends to retard the escape of the animal heat. It is known, from practical experience, that where the meat is chilled through rather slowly, the animal heat leaves the meat more uniformly. Too rapid chilling on the outside seems to clog up the outside of the meat so that the heat in the thick portions does not readily escape.

The first 12 hours of the chilling of all kinds of meat and the removal of the animal heat during this period is the most important part of the chilling. After that period, the proper temperature is of much less vital importance.

Hogs that are to be cut up for curing should never be cut up sooner than 48 hours after being killed, and the temperature of the cooler should be gradually brought down to 28 degrees Fahrenheit by the time the hogs are taken out of the chill room to be cut up. After the hogs have been in the cooler 12 hours the temperature should gradually be brought down from 36 degrees at the end of the first 12 hours, to 28 degrees at the end of 48 hours; that is, if the hogs are to be cut up 48 hours after they are killed. If they are to be cut up 72 hours after being killed, the temperature should be brought down gradually from 36 degrees at the end of the first 12 hours, to 30 degrees F. at the end of 72 hours. This would mean that the temperature should be brought down from 36 degrees to 30 degrees F., if the hogs are to be cut up at the end of 72 hours, or a lowering of six degrees in practically 58 hours; or a lowering of eight degrees, from 36 to 28 Fahrenheit, if the hogs are to be cut up in 48 hours after being killed. This means a reduction in temperature of about one degree for every eight hours. This does not mean that the six or eight degrees should be reduced in two hours' time, for if that were done the meat would be frozen.

In a large Packing House, where the cooler is properly equipped, and one has a good attendant, these instructions can be carried out in detail. When the foregoing instructions are carefully followed, the safe curing of the product will be assured.

While the curing of course requires careful attention, yet, if the chilling is not done properly, the curing will never be perfect.

The floors of coolers should always be kept sprinkled with clean sawdust, as this will absorb drippings and assist in keeping the cooler clean and sweet. If the drippings from hogs are allowed to fall on the bare floor, the cooler will soon become sour and this will affect the meat that hangs over it.

TEMPERATURE FOR CURING MEAT.

An even temperature of 38 degrees Fahrenheit is the best temperature for curing meats. Most butchers, however, have no ice machine, and, therefore, are not able to reach such a low temperature in their coolers; nevertheless, they should try to get their coolers as low in temperature as possible, and should at all times be careful to keep the doors closed, and not leave them open longer than is necessary at any time. The temperature of 37 to 39 degrees Fahrenheit is what should govern all packers who use ice machines; those who are fortunate enough to have ice machinery should never allow the cooler to get below 37 degrees, nor above 40 degrees. Many packers let the temperature in their coolers get too cold, and in winter during the very cold weather, the windows are sometimes left open, which allows the temperature to get too low. This should always be avoided, as meat will not cure in any brine, or take salt when dry salted, if stored in a room that is below 36 degrees Fahrenheit. If meat is packed even in the strongest kind of brine, and put into a cooler, which is kept at 32 to 33 degrees of temperature, and thus left at this degree of cold for three months, it will come out of the brine only partly cured. The reason for this is the fact that meat will not cure and take on salt at such a low temperature, and as the temperature herein given is above freezing point, which is 32 degrees, the meat will only keep for a short time, and then it starts to decompose when taken into a higher temperature. Anyone, who is unaware of this fact, will see how necessary it is to have accurate thermometers in a cooler, to examine them frequently, and to closely watch the temperature of the room. See illustration of our Standard Cold Storage Thermometer on page 282.

The first essential point to watch before putting meat into brine, is to be absolutely certain that it is properly chilled through to the bone. Those who are not equipped with ice machinery for properly chilling meat in hot weather must spread the meat on the floor after it is cut ready for packing, and place crushed ice over it for 24 hours, to thoroughly chill it before it is packed in the salt. This will get the temperature of the meat as low as 36 to 38 degrees Fahrenheit before putting it in the brine. It is necessary that small butchers, who have no ice machines, and rely upon the ice box for a cooler, should use the greatest care to see that the meat is well and thoroughly chilled.

Thousands of pounds of meat are spoiled yearly simply for the one reason that the temperature of the meat is not brought down low enough before the meat is salted. In the summer, hams and heavy pieces of pork should never be packed by persons having no ice machine, unless the meat is first put on the floor for at least twelve hours with broken ice to thoroughly cover it. If our directions are carefully followed and **Freeze-Em-Pickle** is used, such a thing as spoiled meat will be unknown.

CONDITION OF MEAT BEFORE CURING.

(Copyrighted; Reprint Forbidden.)

When cured meat turns out bad, it is not always the fault of the man who has charge of the curing so much as it is the condition the meat was in when put into the brine to cure. Good results should not be expected from a man who has charge of the curing unless the meat is delivered to him in proper condition. Hogs should never be killed the same day of purchase at the Stock Yards or from the farmer. They ought to remain in the packing house pen for at least 24 hours before killing. If different lots of hogs are mixed together, they will sometimes fight, which greatly excites them. Whenever they show this fighting disposition, they should be separated.

THE TEMPERATURE OF BRINE.

(Copyrighted; Reprint Forbidden.)

Make all Pickle in the cooler, and have the water or brine of as low a temperature as the cooler when it is put on the meat. Try to have the temperature of the brine not over 38 degrees Fahrenheit when putting it over the meat. A great deal of meat is spoiled in curing by having the brine too warm when the meat is put into it.

GIVE CLOSE ATTENTION TO DETAILS.

Be careful to do everything right as you go along, for if you spoil the meat you will hardly become aware of it until it is too late to remedy your error.

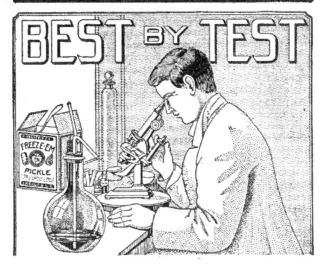

WITH THE FREEZE-EM-PICKLE PROCESS AND "A" AND "B" CONDIMENTINE ANYONE CAN CURE MEAT AND MAKE GOOD SAUSAGE

Bacterial action causes great annoyance and loss to Curers of Meats and Sausage Manufacturers, and, since the enactment of Pure Food Laws prohibiting the use of antiseptic preservatives, the proper handling of meats has become a matter of the greatest importance if good sausage and well-cured meats are to be produced.

We have acted as Consulting Experts for the large Packers and Sausage Manufacturers for many years, and have formulated and systematized methods for the curing of all kinds of meat and the making of all kinds of sausage. We have crystallized the results of our large experience into a plan for the proper curing of meats and the making of all kinds of sausage, which, if followed, will always give satisfactory results.

For curing meat we have combined the necessary curing agents for this Process into a combination which is always uniform and which is known as Freeze-Em-Pickle.

Freeze-Em-Pickle furnishes to the Packer, Butcher and Sausage Maker the proper materials, scientifically

and accurately compounded, and by using it according to the Freeze-Em-Pickle Process, which is set forth in this book, any man, whether he is experienced or not, can get as good results as the most expert packer in the business.

If the Freeze-Em-Pickle Process is followed, and Freeze-Em-Pickle is used according to the directions given in this book, the meats and sausage will be uniform and of fine quality. They will have an appetizing color, a delicious flavor and they will comply with the requirements of the Pure Food Laws.

By curing meat by the Freeze-Em-Pickle Process, the albumen in the meat is so congealed that only a small percentage of it will be drawn out of the meat into the brine, and the natural flavor of the meat is retained, making it far more palatable.

When Freeze-Em-Pickle is dissolved in water with the proper quantity of sugar and salt, the brine will be decidedly sweet and of the proper specific gravity to properly cure Hams, Bacon, Shoulders, Corned Beef, Dried Beef, etc., with a Delicious Flavor, without loss from spoiling. The meat will not be too Salty, but will have that Peculiar Sugar-Cured Flavor which is so much liked. By the use of the Freeze-Em-Pickle Process anyone can make fine cured meats, whether or not they have ever had any previous experience in the curing or handling of meats.

Packers, Butchers and Curers have many difficulties in turning out good, sweet-pickle cured meat, owing to their inability to compound the proper proportions of curing ingredients. Besides, their methods of curing are frequently incorrect and unscientific.

By adopting the Freeze-Em-Pickle Process, the proper ingredients are used and the meat is handled in the right way. That is why the finished products made by the Freeze-Em-Pickle Process are superior to what they are when made in other ways.

In making Bologna and Frankfurt Sausage, if the sausage meat is cured for a few days with Freeze-Em-Pickle and handled according to the Freeze-Em-Pickle Process of curing Bologna and Frankfurt Sausage Meat it will produce Finer Sausage, in both taste and appearance, and will have an appetizing color and will not spoil in hot weather, within a reasonable length of time, and the sausage will comply with the Pure Food Laws.

DIRECTIONS FOR CURING HAMS.

Use the following proportions of Freeze-Em-Pickle, Salt, Sugar and Water to obtain the best results in curing Hams:

Small Hams, 8 to 14 Lbs. Average.

Use for 100 lbs. Small Hams.
- 7 lbs. of Common Salt.
- 1 lb. of Freeze-Em-Pickle.
- 2 lbs. of Granulated Sugar.
- 5 gals. of Cold Water.
- Cure in this brine 50 to 60 days.

Medium Hams, 14 to 18 Lbs. Average.

Use for 100 lbs. Medium Hams.
- 8 lbs. of Common Salt.
- 1 lb. of Freeze-Em-Pickle.
- 2 lbs. of Granulated Sugar.
- 5 gals. of Cold Water.
- Cure in this brine 60 to 70 days.

Heavy Hams, 18 to 24 Lbs. Average.

Use for 100 lbs. Heavy Hams.
- 9 lbs. of Common Salt.
- 1 lb. of Freeze-Em-Pickle.
- 2 lbs. of Granulated Sugar.
- 5 gals. of Cold Water.
- Cure in this brine 75 to 80 days.

First:—Sort the Hams, separating the Small, Medium and Large.

Second:—Take enough of any one size of the assorted Hams **to** fill a tierce, which will be 285 lbs.; then thoroughly mix together in a large pail or box the following proportions of Freeze-Em-Pickle, Granulated Sugar and Salt:

More than 285 lbs. of Hams can be packed in a tierce, but this never should be done, as it requires a certain amount of brine to a certain amount of meat, and by placing 285 lbs. of fresh Hams in a standard tierce, the tierce will hold 14 to 15 gallons of brine, which is the proper quantity of brine for this amount of Hams. If too much meat is put into the tierce, it will not hold enough brine to properly cure the meat.

The Sugar used must be Pure Granulated Sugar. Yellow or Brown Sugar must not be used.

Use, for 285 lbs. of **Small Hams**, 3 lbs. of Freeze-Em Pickle, 6 lbs. of best Granulated Sugar and 21 lbs. of Salt.

For 285 lbs. of **Medium Hams**, 3 lbs. of Freeze-Em-Pickle, 6 lbs. of best Granulated Sugar and 24 lbs. of Salt.

For 285 lbs. of **Heavy Hams**, 3 lbs. of Freeze-Em-Pickle, 6 lbs. of best Granulated Sugar and 27 lbs. of Salt.

How To Cure Hams in Open Barrels

(Copyrighted by B. Heller & Co.; Reprint Forbidden.)

When the tierces or barrels in which these Hams are cured are not to be headed up, but are left open, use half of the Freeze-Em-Pickle, Granulated Sugar and Salt dry by rubbing it over the hams in the following manner:

First:—After mixing all of the Freeze-Em-Pickle, Granulated Sugar and Salt together, sprinkle some of the dry mixture over the bottom of a perfectly clean tierce.

The Sugar used must be Pure Granulated Sugar. Yellow or Brown Sugar must not be used. When adulterated sugar is used, the brine becomes thick in two weeks; but when Pure Granulated Sugar is used it will last quite a while, depending upon the conditions under which the brine is kept.

Second:—Rub each Ham well with some of the mixture of Freeze-Em-Pickle, Granulated Sugar and Salt and pack them nicely in the tierce. Put clean boards over the tops of the hams and weight or fasten these boards down so as to keep them under the brine.

Third:—Take all of the mixed Freeze-Em-Pickle, Granulated Sugar and Salt that is left after the rubbing and use it in making the brine; it will require 14 to 15 gallons of brine, as tierces vary some, for each standard size tierce of Hams. Make the brine by dissolving in about 14 gallons of cold water all of the mixed Freeze-Em-Pickle, Granulated Sugar and Salt that is left after the rubbing. Stir well for a minute, until it is dissolved, then pour this brine over the meat. As tierces vary so much in size, it is always best to dissolve the Freeze-Em-Pickle in a little less quantity of water, say about 14 gallons for a tierce. After this brine is added to the meat, should the tierce hold more, simply add cold water until the tierce is full. The right amount of Salt, etc., has already been added; now simply add sufficient water to well cover the meat.

When curing a less quantity than a full tierce of Hams, cut down the amount of Freeze-Em-Pickle, Granulated Sugar and Salt and the quantity of water, according to the quantity of Hams to be cured, using all materials in the proportions given on page 50.

QUANTITY OF BRINE TO USE FOR CURING 100 LBS. OF HAMS.

(Copyrighted; Reprint Forbidden.)

Five gallons by measure, or forty-two pounds by weight, is the approximate amount of water to use for every 100 lbs. of Hams.

A tierce, after being packed with 285 lbs. of meat, will hold about 14 to 15 gallons of water. When curing Hams in vats, or open barrels, whether in small or large quantity, always use no less than five gallons of brine to every 100 pounds of meat, as this makes the proper strength and a sufficient brine to cover the meat nicely.

THE USE OF MOLASSES AND SYRUP BARRELS IN CURING HAMS.

(Copyrighted; Reprint Forbidden.)

Never use old molasses barrels, or syrup barrels for curing meat, unless they have been first thoroughly scoured and steamed, and cleansed with our Ozo Washing Compound. It is best to use oak tierces, and always be sure that they are perfectly clean and sweet before putting the meat into them to cure.

PUMPING HAMS.

(Copyrighted; Reprint Forbidden.)

We strongly recommend the pumping of Hams, full directions for which are given on page 76.

SHAPE OF VATS IN CURING HAMS.

(Copyrighted; Reprint Forbidden.)

Sometimes, vats of certain shapes require more brine to cover the meat than others, and in such cases, a proportionate amount of **Freeze-Em-Pickle**, Sugar and and Salt, should be added to the necessary amount of water to make sufficient brine to cover the meat.

HOW TO OVERHAUL HAMS WHEN CUR-ING IN OPEN PACKAGES.

(Copyrighted; Reprint Forbidden.)

HOW TO OVERHAUL HAMS WHEN CURING IN OPEN PACKAGES

On the fifth day after packing each lot of Hams, it is necessary that they should be overhauled. This must be repeated seven days later; again in ten days; and a final overhauling should be given ten days later. Overhauling four times while curing, and at the proper time in each instance, is very important and must never be forgotten, especially when curing with this mild, sweet cure. Overhauling means to take the Hams out of the brine and to repack them in the same brine. The proper way to overhaul is to take a perfectly clean tierce, set it next to the tierce of Hams to be overhauled, pack the meat into the empty tierce, and then pour the same brine over the meat.

HOW TO CURE HAMS IN CLOSED UP TIERCES.

Large packers, who employ coopers, should always cure Hams in closed up tierces, as this is the best method known.

HOW TO CURE HAMS IN CLOSED UP TIERCES

FIRST.—

First: — Mix the proper proportions of **Freeze - Em - Pickle**, Sugar and Salt for the different size Hams to be cured. These proportions are given in the table on page 50, under the heading, "Small Hams, Medium Hams, Heavy Hams." If the tierces are to be headed up, use half of the **Freeze-Em-Pickle**, Sugar and Salt for rubbing the Hams, and the half that is left over, after the Hams are rubbed, should be dissolved in the water which is to be used to fill the tierces. Rub each Ham well before packing; put only 285 lbs. of meat in each tierce, and then head them up.

Second: — Lay the tierces on their sides and fill them through the bunghole with water in which the

SECOND.—

half of **Freeze-Em-Pickle**, Sugar and Salt left over after rubbing, has been dissolved.

THIRD.—

Third:—Insert the bung and roll the tierces. This will mix and dissolve the **Freeze - Em - Pickle,** Sugar and Salt rubbed on the meat. Where the pieces of meat press tightly against each other or against the tierce, the brine does not act on the meats; but if the meats are properly rubbed with the mixture of **Freeze-Em-Pickle,** Sugar and Salt before being packed in the tierce, such surfaces will be acted upon by the undissolved mixture, so that curing will be uniform, and no portion of the piece will be left insufficiently cured even if the brine does not come in contact with it. For this reason, it is important that each piece should be carefully rubbed with the mixture of **Freeze-Em-Pickle,** Sugar and Salt before being packed in the tierce.

FOURTH.—

Fourth: — Overhaul five days after packing; again seven days later; again in ten days, and once more ten days thereafter. At each overhauling, examine each tierce for leaks; if any of the Pickle has leaked out, knock the bung in and refill. Remember to overhaul four times during the period of the first thirty-two days.

Fifth: — Overhaul the Hams in closed up tierces, simply by rolling the tierces from one end of the cooler to the other. They ought to be rolled at least 100 feet.

Sixth:—See paragraph on temperature for curing meat, page 46.

DIRECTIONS FOR CURING SHOULDERS.

New York Shoulders:—Have shank cut off above knee, trimmed close and smooth, and square at the butt.

California or Picnic Hams are made from Medium and Heavy Shoulders, well-rounded at the butt, and trimmed as near to the shape of a Ham as possible.

Boston Shoulders are made from Light Shoulders, well-rounded at the butt, similar to California Hams.

California and **Picnic Hams** and **Square Cut Butts,** are cured in the same way, and with the same brine, the only change being in the strength of the brine and the time of curing, which must be made to suit the size of the Shoulder.

Small Shoulders.

Use for 100 lbs. Small Shoulders.

- 7 lbs. of Common Salt.
- 1 lb. of **Freeze-Em-Pickle.**
- 2 lbs. of Granulated Sugar.
- 5 gals. of Cold Water.
- Cure in this brine 50 to 60 days.

56

Medium Shoulders.

Use for 100 lbs.
Medium-Shoulders.
$\left\{\begin{array}{l}\text{8 lbs. of Common Salt.}\\ \text{1 lb. of \textbf{Freeze-Em-Pickle.}}\\ \text{2 lbs. of Granulated Sugar.}\\ \text{5 gals. of Cold Water.}\\ \text{Cure in this brine 60 to 70 days.}\end{array}\right.$

Heavy Shoulders.

Use for 100 lbs.
Heavy Shoulders.
$\left\{\begin{array}{l}\text{9 lbs. of Common Salt.}\\ \text{1 lb. of \textbf{Freeze-Em-Pickle.}}\\ \text{2 lbs. of Granulated Sugar.}\\ \text{5 gals. of Cold Water.}\\ \text{Cure in this brine 75 to 80 days.}\end{array}\right.$

The sugar used must be Pure Granulated Sugar; yellow or brown sugar must not be used.

First.—Sort the Shoulders, separating the Small, Medium and Large.

Second.—Take enough of any one size of the assorted Shoulders to fill a tierce, which will be 285 lbs.; then thoroughly mix together in a large pail, or box, the following proportions of **Freeze-Em-Pickle,** Sugar and Salt:

Use for 285 lbs. of **Small Shoulders,** 3 lbs. of **Freeze-Em-Pickle,** 6 lbs. of best pure Granulated Sugar, and **21** lbs. of Salt.

For 285 lbs. of **Medium Shoulders,** 3 lbs. of **Freeze-Em-Pickle,** 6 lbs. of best Granulated Sugar and **24** lbs. of Salt.

For 285 lbs. of **Heavy Shoulders,** 3 lbs. of **Freeze-Em-Pickle,** 6 lbs of best Granulated Sugar, and **27** lbs. of Salt.

Curing Shoulders in Open Packages.

When it is desired to cure Shoulders in Open Packages, use the foregoing proportions and in every way handle the Shoulders as directed for Hams, on page 51.

Quantity of Brine for Curing 100 Lbs. of Shoulders.

The same quantity of brine should be used for curing Shoulders as directed for Curing Hams, full directions for which will be found on page 52.

Quantity of Shoulders to Cure in Each Tierce.

The same quantity of Shoulders and the same amount of brine should be used as directed for Curing Hams, on page 52. The same remarks with regard to the variation in the amount of brine for each tierce, and how to be sure to have the proper amount of the right strength of brine, apply in curing Shoulders, the same as for Hams, (see page 52). Likewise do not use Syrup and Molasses barrels for Curing Shoulders.

How to Overhaul Shoulders When Curing in Open Packages.

It is important to follow the same directions for Overhauling Shoulders that are given for Overhauling Hams. (See page 53.)

How to Cure Shoulders in Closed Up Tierces.

Follow the same directions for Curing Shoulders as given for Curing Hams in Closed Up Tierces, on page 54.

How to Overhaul Shoulders When Cured in Closed Up Tierces.

Follow exactly the same instructions as are given for Overhauling Hams when cured in Closed Up Tierces, on page 55.

Pumping Shoulders.

Pump Shoulders as directed on page 76.

BONELESS ROLLED SHOULDERS

(Copyrighted; Reprint Forbidden.)

Boneless Rolled Shoulders should be made in the following manner: Take the Shoulders from hogs that have been prop-erly chilled and bone them. If the meat has been thoroughly chilled, so it is perfectly solid and chilled throughout, the Shoulders are ready to cure; but if the meat is not perfectly solid and firm on the inside, where the bone has been removed, the Shoulders should be spread out in the cooler on racks for 24 hours, until the meat is thoroughly chilled and firm.

Small Boneless Rolled Shoulders.

Use for 100 lbs. Small Boned Shoulders.
- 7 lbs. of Common Salt.
- 1 lb. of **Freeze-Em-Pickle.**
- 2 lbs. of Best Granulated Sugar.
- 5 gallons of Cold Water.
- Cure in this brine 30 to 40 days.

Medium Boneless Rolled Shoulders.

Use for 100 lbs. Medium Boned Shoulders.
- 8 lbs. of Common Salt.
- 1 lb. of **Freeze-Em-Pickle.**
- 2 lbs. of Best Granulated Sugar.
- 5 gallons of Cold Water.
- Cure in this brine 40 to 50 days.

Large Boneless Rolled Shoulders.

Use for 100 lbs. Large Boned Shoulders.
- 9 lbs. of Common Salt.
- 1 lb. of **Freeze-Em-Pickle.**
- 2 lbs. of Best Granulated Sugar.
- 5 gallons of Cold Water.
- Cure in this brine 50 to 60 days.

The sugar used must be Pure Granulated Sugar; yellow or brown sugar must not be used.

First:—Sort the Boneless Shoulders, separating the Small, Medium and Large, as the different sizes should be cured in separate barrels.

Second:—Take enough of any one size of the Boned Shoulders to fill a tierce, which will be 285 lbs. Then thoroughly mix together, in a large pail or box, the following proportions of **Freeze-Em-Pickle,** Sugar and Salt:

Use for 285 lbs. of **Small Boneless Shoulders**, 3 lbs. of **Freeze-Em-Pickle**, 6 lbs. of Best Granulated Sugar and 21 lbs. of Salt.

Use for 285 lbs. of **Medium Boneless Shoulders**, 3 lbs. of **Freeze-Em-Pickle**, 6 lbs. of Best Granulated Sugar and 24 lbs. of Salt.

Use for 285 lbs. of **Large Boneless Shoulders**, 3 lbs. of **Freeze-Em-Pickle**, 6 lbs. of Best Granulated Sugar and 27 lbs. of Salt.

Third:—After the Shoulders have been weighed, take for example that one has 285 lbs. of **Medium Boneless Shoulders**, averaging, boned, about 10 lbs., which would make 28 pieces for a tierce of 285 lbs. Now, take the 3 lbs. of **Freeze-Em-Pickle**, 6 lbs. of Granulated Sugar and 24 lbs. of Salt to be used for the tierce of **Medium Shoulders**, and mix together thoroughly in a box or tub.

Fourth:—Rub about ¼ lb. of this mixture in each Shoulder where the bone has been removed, then roll it and tie it in the regular way. After it is rolled and tied, rub about ¼ lb. of the mixture all over the outside, and pack the Shoulders into the tierce. After the 28 **Boneless Shoulders** have been packed nicely into the tierce, put clean boards over the top of the meat and weight or fasten down these boards, so as to keep them under the brine.

The sugar must be Pure Granulated Sugar; yellow or brown sugar must not be used. When adulterated sugar is used the brine becomes thick in two weeks, but when Pure Granulated Sugar is used it will last quite a while, depending upon the conditions under which the brine is kept.

Fifth:—Take all of the mixed **Freeze-Em-Pickle**, Granulated Sugar and Salt that is left after rubbing the meat, and use it in making the brine. It will require between 14 and 15 gallons of brine, as tierces vary somewhat in size, for each standard size tierce of Boneless Shoulders. Make the brine by dissolving in about 14 gallons of water all of the mixed **Freeze-Em-Pickle**, Granulated Sugar and Salt that is left after rubbing. As tierces vary so in size, it is always best to dissolve the **Freeze-Em-Pickle**, Sugar and Salt in a less quantity of water, say about 14 gallons for a tierce. After this brine is added to the meat, should the tierce hold more, simply add cold water until the tierce is filled. The right amount of **Freeze-Em-Pickle**,

Sugar and Salt has already been added, now simply add sufficient water to well cover the meat.

In curing a less quantity than a full tierce of **Boneless Rolled Shoulders**, cut down the amount of **Freeze-Em-Pickle**, Granulated Sugar and Salt and the quantity of water, according to the quantity of Boneless Shoulders to be cured.

Quantity of Brine for Curing Less Than 100 Lbs. of Boneless Rolled Shoulders.

The same directions should be followed in curing less than 100 lbs. of Boneless Rolled Shoulders as are given for Hams, on page 52.

The Use of Molasses and Syrup Barrels in Curing Boneless Rolled Shoulders.

The remarks concerning the use of these barrels in curing Hams apply with equal force to the curing of Boneless Rolled Shoulders, and we refer to page 52.

Shape of Vats for Curing Boneless Rolled Shoulders.

See page 53 concerning the Shape of Vats for curing Hams, as the same remarks apply in curing Boneless Rolled Shoulders.

How to Overhaul Boneless Rolled Shoulders When Cured in Open Packages.

See page 53 and follow the same instructions for overhauling as are given for overhauling Hams when curing in open packages.

Pumping Boneless Rolled Shoulders.

This should not be neglected. See page 76 and follow the directions closely. The Pumping of Boneless Rolled Shoulders is very important, because when they are Boned and Rolled, most of the outside surface is covered with Rind, which prevents the Brine from getting through to the meat. However, by rubbing the inside of the Shoulder with the Curing Mixture and then Pumping them before Curing, good results will always be assured.

SUGAR CURED
BREAKFAST BACON

DIRECTIONS FOR MAKING SUGAR CURED BREAKFAST BACON.

(Copyrighted; Reprint Forbidden.)

Light Bellies.

Use for 100 lbs. Light Bellies.
5 lbs. of Common Salt.
1 lb. of **Freeze-Em-Pickle**.
2 lbs. of Granulated Sugar.
5 gallons of Cold Water.
Cure in this brine 20 to 25 days.

Heavy Bellies.

Use for 100 lbs. Medium or Heavy
Bellies.
7 lbs. Common Salt.
1 lb. of **Freeze-Em-Pickle**.
2 lbs. Granulated Sugar.
5 gals. Cold Water.
Cure in this brine 25 to 40 days,
according to size.

First:—Mix together the proper proportions of Freeze-Em-Pickle, Sugar and Salt, as stated above for every 100 lbs. of Bellies.

Second:—Take a perfectly clean tierce, tub or vat, and sprinkle a little of the mixed **Freeze-Em-Pickle**, Granulated Sugar and Salt on the bottom. The sugar used must be Pure Granulated Sugar; yellow or brown sugar must not be used. When adulterated sugar is used, the brine becomes thick in two weeks; but when Pure Granulated Sugar is used, it will last quite a while, depending upon the condition in which the brine is kept.

Third:—Take half of the mixed **Freeze-Em-Pickle**, Granulated Sugar and Salt and rub each piece of Belly with the mixture and then pack as loosely as possible.

Fourth:—Put clean boards over the top of the Bellies and fasten or weight the boards down so as to keep them covered with the brine.

Fifth:—All of the mixed **Freeze-Em-Pickle**, Granulated Sugar and Salt that is left after rubbing the meat should be used for making the brine.

Sixth:—For each 100 lbs. of Bellies packed in the tierce, tub or vat, add not less than 5 gallons of brine, and pour it over the meat. Five gallons of water by measure or forty-two pounds by weight, will make sufficient brine to cover, and is the proper amount for each 100 lbs. of Bellies.

Seventh:—Before putting the water over the Bellies, dissolve in it the mixed **Freeze-Em-Pickle**, Sugar and Salt left after rubbing; stir it for a few minutes until it is thoroughly dissolved, and then pour this brine over the Bellies.

Eighth:—Bellies must be overhauled three times while curing—once on the fifth day; again seven days later, and again in ten days more. Overhauling must never be neglected, if good results are desired.

Overhauling means to take the meat out of the brine and repack it in the same brine. The proper way to overhaul is to take a perfectly clean tierce or vat, set it next to the tierce or vat of Bellies to be overhauled, pack the meat into the empty package and then pour the same brine over the meat.

PUMPING BREAKFAST BACON.

(Copyrighted; Reprint Forbidden.)

Many Packers pump Breakfast Bacon when it is put into the brine, and we can heartily recommend this, as Bacon that is properly pumped will be cured in one half the time and it will have a uniform cure and color throughout and will be as well cured on the inside as the outside. Great care, however, should be exercised in making the pumping pickle. It must be made according to the formula given on page 76, just the same as for Pumping Hams. The pieces of Bacon should be pumped in from three to five places, according to the size of the piece. Very large pieces, especially if the rib is left in them, can be pumped several times more.

FEW BUTCHERS REALIZE

Few Butchers realize the importance of building up a reputation on good Corned Beef. A good trade on Corned Beef enables the dealer to get higher prices for Plates, Rumps, Briskets and other cuts which otherwise would have to be sold at a sacrifice. Corned Beef cured by the **Freeze-Em-Pickle** Process will have a Delicious Corned Beef Flavor, a Fine, Red, Cured-Meat Color, **will not be too Salty.**

To obtain the best results in curing Corned Beef, it is always advisable to first soak the meat for a few hours in a tub of fresh cold water to which a few handfuls of salt have been added. This will draw out the blood which would otherwise get into the brine. The membrane on the inside of the Plates and Flanks should be removed and the Strip of Gristle cut off the edge of the Belly Side.

If any part is **tainted, mouldy, discolored** or **slimy, it must be trimmed off,** so no slimy or tainted parts will get into the brine. If Plates or Briskets are to be rolled, a small amount of mixed Zanzibar Brand Corned Beef Seasoning, **Freeze-Em-Pickle,** Sugar and Salt must be sprinkled on the inside before rolling them. This will give the meat a **Delicious Flavor** and results in a Nice Red Color and will cure it more uniformly and quickly.

DIRECTIONS FOR MAKING FINE CORNED BEEF.

(Copyrighted; Reprint Forbidden.)

Use for 100 lbs. Plates, Rumps, Briskets, etc.

- 5 lbs. of Common Salt.
- 1 lb. of **Freeze-Em-Pickle**.
- 2 lbs. of Granulated Cane Sugar.
- 6-8 ozs. Z. B. Corned Beef Seasoning.
- 5 gals. of Cold Water.

Cure the meat in this brine 15 to 30 days, according to weight and thickness of the piece.

Retail Butchers who cure Corned Beef in small quantities, and who from day to day take out pieces from the brine and add others, should make the brine and handle the Corned Beef as follows:

To every five gallons of water add five pounds of common salt, one pound of **Freeze-Em-Pickle** and two pounds of granulated sugar. In summer, if the temperature of the curing room or cooler cannot be kept down as low as 40 degrees, then use one pound of sugar for five gallons of water. If the cooler is kept below 40 degrees, use two pounds of sugar. In winter the curing can always be done in a temperature of 36 to 38 degrees, and then two pounds of sugar to five gallons of water should always be used. The sugar must be Pure Granulated Sugar. Yellow or Brown Sugar must not be used. When adulterated sugar is used, the brine becomes thick in two weeks, but when pure granulated sugar is used it will last quite a while, depending largely upon the conditions under which the brine is kept.

THE SEASONING OF CORNED BEEF.

It is simple enough to add Seasoning to the corned beef, but the ability to decide what proportion of just what spices, etc., will produce the most desirable flavor requires ripe judgment and long experience. There are many butchers today who could greatly improve their corned beef if they but knew more about the proper seasoning and the proportions to use. We have worked out this problem for him in our special Corned Beef Flavor. It is a splendid combination of just those spices, etc., most suited for seasoning corned beef, and imparts a most zestful and appetizing flavor. This flavor should be added by tying it up in a piece of cheese cloth and allowing it to lay in the brine which contains the corned beef. This will flavor the brine and thus the corned beef becomes uniformly and thoroughly seasoned without any particles of the seasoning adhering to the meat.

HOW TO KNOW WHEN CORNED BEEF IS NOT FULLY CURED.

(Copyrighted; Reprint Forbidden.)

If a piece of Corned Beef is cut, before or after it is cooked, and the inside is not a nice red color, it is because the meat is not cured through. It is often sold in this condition, but it should not be, as it does not have the proper flavor unless it has been cured all the way through, which requires two or three weeks in a mild brine, depending upon the size of the piece of meat. Corned Beef pickled for four or five days in a strong brine, with an excessive amount of saltpetre in it, as some butchers cure it, **is not good Corned Beef and does not have the proper flavor,** although it may be red through to the center, the color being due to the large amount of saltpetre used in the brine.

The **Freeze-Em-Pickle Process** of curing gives the meat a different and better flavor.

PUMPING CORNED BEEF.

(Copyrighted; Reprint Forbidden.)

We recommend Pumping Corned Beef with a Pickle Pump, before it is put into the brine. In this way the meat is cured in about half the time and it will be cured from the inside just the same as from the outside, and will be more uniform in color throughout than if cured without pumping. If Corned Beef is pumped, it should be pumped with the same pickle as for pumping Hams, formula for which is given on page 76. The pieces of Corned Beef should be pumped in from two to four places, according to the size of the piece of meat. One will soon become accustomed to it, after pumping a few pieces. Pumping can of course be overdone, and too much brine must not be pumped into the meat; otherwise it will puff out too much and become spongy.

GARLIC FLAVORED CORNED BEEF.

(Copyrighted; Reprint Forbidden.)

Many people like Garlic Flavor in Corned Beef, and butchers who want to please their customers should keep a supply of Corned Beef both with and without the Garlic Flavor. We make a special preparation, known as Vacuum Brand Garlic Compound, with which butchers are able to give a Garlic Flavor to any kind of meat, without having any of the objectionable features that result from the use of fresh Garlic.

SOME PEOPLE PREFER

Vacuum Brand Garlic Compound is a powder which we manufacture from Selected Garlic. The flavor given by it is delicious, and the advantages gained by it will be thoroughly appreciated by all who use it.

be thoroughly appreciated by

B. HELLER & CO.

HOME-MADE PRESSED COOKED CORNED BEEF

DIRECTION FOR MAKING COOKED CORNED BEEF.

(Copyrighted; Reprint Forbidden.)

Take fully cured Corned Beef and cut it up into different sizes, and pack it nicely into a cooked corned beef press, sprinkling a little Zanzibar Brand Corned Beef Seasoning between each layer of meat so as to give it a delicious flavor. All Butchers' Supply Houses sell presses made especially for this purpose. After packing the pieces of Meat into the press, screw it up tight; then put the press which has been filled, into hot water, of a temperature of 180 F., and leave it there for one and a half hours, then reduce the temperature to 170 degrees and leave it there for one hour longer. A very large press might require three hours cooking before the meat would be cooked through. After the meat is thoroughly cooked, place the press in the cooler and let it remain there over night. The following morning the Corned Beef will be thoroughly chilled and can be taken out of the press.

In the summer it is a good plan to dip the cake of Cooked Corned Beef, after it is removed from the press, into Hot Lard for a second, or even Hot Tallow. This will coat it so it will not become mouldy, and it will keep much better than without dipping it.

Pressed Cooked Corned Beef is an elegant article, is a good seller and very often women would be only too pleased to be able to buy this from the butcher and would be willing to pay good prices for it if they could only obtain it. Butchers should give more attention to preparations of this kind, as they would help greatly in developing business.

DIRECTIONS FOR MAKING FANCY DRIED BEEF.

(Copyrighted; Reprint Forbidden.)

SLICING CHIPPED BEEF

How to Cure Beef Hams and Shoulder Clots.

SMALL PIECES.

Use for **100 lbs.** **Small Beef Hams** and Shoulder Clots.

- 6 lbs. of Common Salt.
- 1 lb. of **Freeze-Em-Pickle.**
- 2 lbs. of Granulated Sugar.
- 5 gals. of Cold Water.
- Cure in this brine 50 to 60 days.

MEDIUM PIECES.

Use for **100 lbs.** **Medium Beef Hams** and Shoulder Clots.

- 7 lbs. of Common Salt.
- 1 lb. of **Freeze-Em-Pickle.**
- 2 lbs. of Granulated Sugar.
- 5 gals. of Cold Water.
- Cure in this brine 60 to 70 days.

HEAVY PIECES.

Use for **100 lbs.** **Heavy Beef Hams** and Shoulder Clots.

- **8** lbs. of Common Salt.
- 1 lb. of **Freeze-Em-Pickle.**
- 2 lbs. of Granulated Sugar.
- 5 gals. of Cold Water.
- Cure in this brine 75 to 80 days.

The sugar used must be Pure Granulated Sugar; yellow or brown sugar must not be used.

First.—Sort the Beef Hams and Clots, separating the Small, Medium and Large.

Second.—Take enough of any one size of the assorted Beef Hams and Clots to fill a tierce which will be 285 lbs.; then thoroughly mix together in a large pail or box, the following proportions of **Freeze-Em-Pickle**, Sugar and Salt:

Use for 285 lbs. of **Small Beef Hams and Small Clots,** 3 lbs. of **Freeze-Em-Pickle,** 6 lbs. of best Granulated Sugar and 18 lbs. of Salt.

For 285 lbs. of **Medium Beef Hams and Medium Clots,** 3 lbs. of **Freeze-Em-Pickle,** 6 lbs. of Granulated Sugar and 21 lbs. of Salt.

For 285 lbs. of **Heavy Beef Hams and Heavy Clots,** 3 lbs. of **Freeze-Em-Pickle,** 6 lbs. of best Granulated Sugar and 24 lbs. of Salt.

Curing Beef Hams and Clots in Open Barrels.

Follow exactly the same instructions as given for curing Hams in Open Packages, page 51.

Quantity of Brine for Curing 100 Lbs. of Beef Hams and Clots.

Use the same quantity of Brine and the same amount of Beef Hams and Clots as directed for curing Hams, on page 52. The same remarks apply as to variations in the size and shape of vats, and in the general handling, as given for Hams.

How to Overhaul Beef Hams and Clots When Curing in Open Packages.

Overhaul and handle exactly as directed for Hams, on page 53.

How to Cure Beef Hams and Clots in Closed Up Tierces.

Follow the same directions in every way as given for curing Hams in Closed Up Tierces, page 54.

How to Overhaul Beef Hams and Clots When Cured in Closed Up Tierces.

Follow exactly the directions for overhauling Hams when cured in Closed Up Tierces, given on page 55.

Pumping Beef Hams and Clots.

Follow the general directions for Pumping, which will be found on page 76.

Take 100 lbs. of boneless Beef Plates and cure them in brine made as follows:

5 gallons of cold water.

5 lbs. of common salt.

1 lb. of **Freeze-Em-Pickle** and

2 lbs. of granulated sugar.

Cure the Plates in this brine 10 to 30 days in a cooler. The temperature should not be higher than 42 to 44 degrees Fahrenheit, but 38 to 40 degrees temperature is always the best for curing purposes.

The 5 gallons of brine should be flavored by placing in it about 6 to 8 ounces of Zanzibar Brand Corned Beef Seasoning. After the meat has been fully cured in accordance with the above directions, sprinkle some Corned Beef Seasoning on the meat; then roll the meat and tie it tight with a heavy string. The meat should then be boiled slowly.

Rolled Spiced Beef should be boiled the same as hams, in water that is 155 degrees Fahrenheit.

This Rolled Spiced Beef is sold to customers raw as well as boiled. Many prefer to buy it raw and boil it at home. This style of Corned Beef makes a beautiful display on the counter and butchers will find this a profitable way of working off fat plates. Meat worked up in this way brings a good price and is a ready seller. Those liking Garlic Flavor can also add a small quantity of Garlic Compound or Garlic Condiment.

GENERAL HINTS FOR CURING MEATS.

(Copyrighted; Reprint Forbidden.)

Curers of meat, who are well acquainted with us know that we have been in a position to acquire more than the average knowledge in the curing and handling of meats. As is well known, we have been consulting chemists and packing house experts for many years; therefore, the general information which we offer for curing meats are suggested by the results of many years of practical experience.

CHILLING MEATS.

(Copyrighted; Reprint Forbidden.)

Hams, Shoulders, Bellies and other cuts must be thoroughly chilled before they are put into pickle. From one to two days before being packed, depending upon the temperature, they should be hung up or laid on a rack in the cooler, in order to draw out all the animal heat that is in them and to make them firm and ready for packing. Packers, using ice machinery for cooling, can bring the temperature low enough during the warm weather to properly chill the meat; however, it must not be frozen. If the cooler in which meats are chilled is not cold enough to make the Hams, Shoulders, Bellies, etc., firm and solid in 48 hours, it is advisable to lay the meat on the floor over night and place crushed ice over it; this will harden the meat.

CHILLING MEATS

Those using a common ice house can employ the crushed ice method, which is to spread the meat on the floor and throw cracked ice over the meat, allowing it to remain over night. It should always be remembered that if meat is put into brine soft and spongy, it will become pickle-soaked and in such condition will never cure properly. It will come out of the brine soft and spongy, and will often sour when in the smoke house. A great deal of meat spoils in curing only for the reason that the animal heat has not been removed before the meat is packed and placed in brine. When the animal heat is all out of the meat, the meat will be firm and solid all the way through. In order to get the best results, the inside temperature of Hams and Shoulders when packed, should not be over 36 to 38 degrees Fahrenheit. The meat should be tested with a thermometer made for this purpose before it is packed. Every curer of meat should have one. An illustration of same will be found on page 284.

OVERHAULING.

(Copyrighted; Reprint Forbidden.)

When curing Hams, Shoulders, and all kinds of sweet-pickled meats in open vats, overhauling is a very important feature; it must be done at least four times during the curing period. When curing in closed up tierces, the tierces must be rolled at least four times during the curing period. Bellies must be overhauled at least three times while curing in open vats, and if cured in closed up tierces, they must be rolled at least three times during the curing period. This overhauling is very necessary because it mixes the brine and changes the position of the meat in such a way that the brine gets to all parts of it.

HOW TO BOIL HAMS.

(Copyrighted; Reprint Forbidden.)

Heat the water to 155 degrees Fahrenheit. Then place the hams in the hot water and keep them in it from eight to nine hours, according to the size of Hams. Try to keep the water as near to 155 degrees as possible. By cooking Hams in a temperature of 155 degrees, very little of the fat will cook out of them and float on top of the water, and the Hams will shrink very little. When Hams or large pieces of meat are boiled for slicing cold, allow them to remain in the water until it is nearly cold, for by so doing the meat re-absorbs much of the nutriment which has been drawn out during the cooking process. Then put them in a cooler over night, so that they will become thoroughly chilled before slicing. Hams should never be cooked in boiling water, which is 212 degrees Fahrenheit, as this is so hot that most of the fat will melt and run out of them.

USING BRINE TWICE.

(Copyrighted; Reprint Forbidden.)

The Pickle, in which Hams have been cured, but which is still sweet and not stringy or ropy, is the best brine in which to cure light bellies. Nothing need be added to it. It should be used just as it comes from the Hams. While brine in which Hams have been cured can be used once more for curing Breakfast Bacon, it should be remembered that it must not be used a second time for curing Hams or Shoulders.

ICE WATER.

Never use the drip water of melted ice from a cooler for making Pickle, as it contains many impurities, and therefore should never be used.

74

CHICAGO, U.S.A.

PUMPING MEATS.

PUMPING MEATS

We highly recommend pumping Hams, Shoulders and other kinds of Cured Meats. It is a safeguard in Hams and Shoulders against shank and body souring, should they, through some carelessness, be insufficiently chilled all the way to the bone, and is a protection against sour joint, and insures a uniform cure. It is also of great advantage to pump Breakfast Bacon, Corned Beef, Dried Beef, Dry Salt Meats, etc. Packers and curers, who do not use a pump and the **Freeze-Em-Pickle** Process, are suffering losses from sour meats, which during a year's business would mean a large profit to them.

There is a mistaken idea among many butchers and packers that pumping Hams and Shoulders is injurious to the meat. The facts do not warrant such a belief, as the best cured and the best flavored meats are those that have been pumped. When Hams and Shoulders are not pumped, it requires weeks for the pickle to penetrate through to the bone, which is the vital spot of a Ham or Shoulder. If the joints, tissues and meat around the bone are not wholly and thoroughly cured, the entire Ham or Shoulder is inferior and no good; because it furnishes a favorable seat for the development of the germs of putrefaction, which render the meat unfit for human food.

In order to always have a mild cure, sweet flavor at the joints, and uniform color, they should be pumped. Pumping with the **Freeze-Em-Pickle** Process is a safeguard against shank and body souring; it gives the inside of a Ham or Shoulder a delicious flavor, a good color, and insures a uniform cure; it cures the joints

75

B.HELLER & CO.

and the meat around the bone thoroughly, and greatly
reduces the period of curing. The secret and principal
feature in pumping Hams and Shoulders, is to have the
right kind of pumping brine. When common brine, or
ordinary sweet-pickle is used for pumping, the Hams
or Shoulders usually become pickle-soaked, and if the
refrigerator under such conditions is not the very best,
or if the Hams or Shoulders are not thoroughly chilled,
the smallest degree of animal heat which may be remaining in them will start fermentation, causing the
meat to sour next to the joints. It is, therefore, plain
to be seen that pumping, under such conditions, instead of doing good, will in reality result in injury, and
this is the reason why so many who have tried pumping meats have failed. On the other hand, when the
pumping brine is made as shown herein, all of these
objections are overcome, and the meat will not be
pickle-soaked, nor will it become soft and flabby. The
brine will be absorbed by the meat around the bone
and joints so thoroughly as to leave no trace of it
after the Ham is cured; it also gives the inside meat
a fine red color, and a delicious flavor. Hams that have
been pumped with **Freeze-Em-Pickle** and cured by the
Freeze-Em-Pickle Process, will not dry up and become
hard when fried or cooked; when sliced cold they will
not crumble, but will slice nicely and have a delicate
and pleasing flavor.

DIRECTIONS FOR PUMPING.

(Copyrighted; Reprint Forbidden.)

One gallon of pumping brine is sufficient for pumping one tierce, or 285 lbs. of meat. Make the pumping
brine as follows:

½ lb. of **Freeze-Em-Pickle.**
1 lb of Pure Granulated Sugar.
2 lbs. of Salt.
1 gal. of Water.

The sugar used must be Pure Granulated Sugar; yellow or brown sugar must not be used. When adulterated sugar is used, the brine becomes thick and
would spoil the meat in two weeks. Stir the above
thoroughly before using. As this will make a thick
brine which is more than saturated, it will precipitate
when left standing, therefore, when mixed in large
quantities, it should be stirred occasionally. Meats

76

should never be pumped with anything but a solution that is thoroughly saturated.

Pump the Hams or Shoulders just before they are packed, and if it is desired to rush the cure, pump them every time that the meat is overhauled. The pumping solution must be cold when pumped into the meat. Ordinarily, three insertions of the needle in the Hams are sufficient; once at the shank to the hock joint as shown at A, once to the thigh and along the bone, Fig. B., and once from the butt end to the joint under the hip bone and into the fleshy part. Fig. C. Solid lines show needle up to point of insertion and dotted line shows direction taken by needle after insertion. In a very heavy Ham as many as six insertions should be made, and the same with very heavy Shoulders. Three insertions of the needle into a medium size Shoulder are sufficient; one at Fig. D, one to the shoulder joint at Fig. E, and one under the blade from the end, or diagonally from the back of the shoulder toward the end at Fig. F.

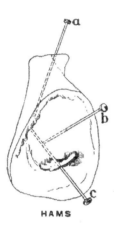

HAMS

More insertions may be made without injury to the meat, but the above are all that are required for good results. One cubic inch of solution is enough for each insertion, and after withdrawing the needle, the hole must be squeezed shut with the thumb to prevent the solution from oozing out. Stir the solution well before starting to pump. The Pumper must be careful not to pump air into the meat. Never allow the Pickle to go below the end of sucker of pump.

SHOULDERS

USE ONLY PURE SUGAR

It will be noted that, in all of our directions for the sweet pickling of meat, we lay great stress upon the importance of using only pure sugar, free from adulterations. The very best and purest of granulated sugar should always be used, if the best results are expected. Sugar, as is well known is a great nutrient and, as a food, possesses practically the same value as starch; it is however, much more readily digested. Therefore the use of pure sugar assists in making meat food products more digestible. In preparing a sweet brine, the one great object sought to be attained is that the brine shall have the highest possible penetrative quality. Any adulterant in the sugar tends to prevent the penetration of the sweet pickled brine and lessens its efficiency in proportion as adulterants are contained in the sugar. It is only by the use of pure granulated sugar that a well-keeping brine can be produced. Many adulterants, even though they are natural adulterants, resulting from lack of proper refining of the sugar, tend to create fermentation in the brine producing a slimy and ropy condition. As is well known to those best experienced in the sweet pickling of meat, ropy and slimy brine is almost always sure to cause meat to sour.

Impurities in sugar used for producing sweet pickle will prevent the proper coagulation of the albumen in the meat uices. Coagulation does and should take place in all well cured meat. The impurities and adulterants, in other words, positively counteract the effect of the curing agents in the brine. Therefore use only the best pure granulated sugar in making all sweet pickle. The general conditions for obtaining pure granulated sugar at the present day are very much improved over those of a number of years ago, prior to the passage of the Food and Drugs Act of 1906. For instance, you can form a good idea of the purity of your sugar by dissolving a quantity in water to make a fairly thick syrup, but not using more than the water will

78

take up. Cork this tightly and place in a dark room over night. We have seen tests made in this way, which in twenty-four hours would show a deposit of blue coloring at the bottom of the bottle, and also a considerable quantity of insoluble salts. This comes from what is known as "bluing" the sugar, but where you purchase one of the well known manufacturers products marked, "pure granulated sugar", these difficulties are seldom met with at the present time. There was a time also when sugar was frequently adulterated with crystalized glucose or as is commonly known "grape sugar." This was a very serious adulterant from the view point of the sweet pickle curing of meat, as glucose tends to ferment in brine very quickly and consequently the brine would become ropy and slimy within a very short time. This resulted in sour and soggy hams, bacon, etc., so that the purchase of cheap sugar containing impurities was never a saving, but proved very costly to the manufacturer who was persuaded to purchase low grade sugar.

It has been a common practice with some butchers in preparing sweet pickle to use molasses or syrup. This method we strongly urge our friends not to adopt. The saving will be many times lost by meat which will have to be thrown away because of ropy, fermented and sour pickle. We cannot urge upon our friends too strongly that they use only pure granulated sugar. Not only from the standpoint of keeping sweet pickle brine in good, clean condition, but from the view point of flavor and thorough cure, the use of pure granulated sugar is absolutely necessary for producing the proper kind of finished meat food products.

Sugar is considered as a natural preservative, but it must be borne in mind that sugar is used in the sweet pickle method of curing meat, not only as a preservative, but also as a flavor. Pure sugar has the property of combining with the other curing agents and by its penetrative property carries the other curing agents into the cells of the meat tissue more thoroughly. This results in the uniform action of the curing agent, producing even flavored meat as a result of the cure. Another peculiar property of pure sugar is that by its combination with the salt used in the brine it has a great tendency to prevent fermentation, thus keeping a clean, clear, sweet, penetrative brine, which will do the largest amount of work with the smallest amount of material, in producing evenly cured meat. To sum up, we will state that pure granulated sugar should take the place of molasses, syrup or any other form of sweetener because it imparts a better flavor and assists in making the brine more penetrative, thus producing best results.

HANDLING CALVES' STOMACHS OR RENNETS

(Copyrighted by B. Heller & Co.; Reprint Forbidden.)

The calf's stomach is divided into four compartments. The first one is known as the paunch; the second as the honeycomb stomach; the third is called the many-plies stomach and the fourth is known as the rennet bag.

The proper way to handle the rennet bag is to remove it from the balance of the stomach, turn it inside out, and clean with fresh water so as to remove the adhering contents. Great care must be taken not to scrape off or in any way remove the mucous membrane (by this is meant the many folds of thin skin) as this is the part of the stomach which has a market value. Of course the stomach must be gently and carefully washed to remove the undigested portions of food which may be contained therein, as otherwise it would very quickly decompose and become putrid. It would then be of no value whatever for any purpose. After cleansing them, dust the rennet bags all over with finely ground salt, and blow them up after having turned them inside out. Then hang them in a dry place in a current of air so that they will dry as quickly as possible.

ROPY OR STRINGY BRINE

(Copyrighted by B. Heller & Co.; Reprint Forbidden.)

Occasionally brine that has been made with sugar will become ropy and thick like jelly, but yet will be somewhat stringy. This is called "Ropy Brine," and can always be traced to either the use of unsuitable sugar or improper temperature of the curing room.

Yellow or brown sugar and glucose sugar will never do for curing meat. It must be Pure Sugar, and the Refined, Granulated Sugar is the best, because the impurities have been taken out.

ROPY BRINE However, even if Pure Granulated Sugar is used and the temperature of the Curing Room is too high, the brine is liable to turn "Ropy" anyway. It is, therefore, absolutely necessary for anyone who intends to cure meat in sweet brine not only to use the proper kind of sugar but also to cure in the proper temperature. Otherwise, the results will not be satisfactory, no matter what kind of a curing agent is used.

In buying sugar for curing purposes, it is advisable to order it from the wholesale grocers or from the manufacturer, and have it guaranteed to be Pure Granulated Sugar put up Especially for Preserving Purposes. This grade of sugar is on the market and is used for preserving fruits, and is the best kind of sugar to use for curing meats.

If brine has become ropy in a curing package and it is desired to use that package again, it is absolutely necessary to thoroughly scald out such package, and it is well to use Ozo Washing Powder for that purpose so as to prevent the possibility of fermentation. Otherwise, the unclean package will cause the fresh brine to turn "Ropy" even though it is made with the right kind of sugar and kept in the proper temperature.

81

BOILING THE BRINE

(Copyrighted by B. Heller & Co.; Reprint Forbidden.)

Boiling the brine improves it some, but not enough to pay for the extra trouble it makes. We recommend boiling the water, if one has the time, as it purifies it. When there is reason to believe that the water is impure, or when it is known to be tainted with vegetable matter, the brine should always be boiled, and the impurities will then float on the surface, and can be skimmed off.

CLEANSING CURING PACKAGES

(Copyrighted by B. Heller & Co.; Reprint Forbidden.)

All curing packages should be taken out of the cooler after the meat has been cured in them, and scalded and washed thoroughly clean with hot water and **Ozo.** Soda or Soda-ash may also be used, but we strongly recommend **Ozo,** which is a thoroughly reliable Washing Powder. When packages have been thoroughly cleaned, they should be put out in the sun and allowed to remain there for a day or two. The sun will thoroughly dry them and the fresh air will sweeten them.

SOME CAUSES FOR SOUR HAMS.

(Copyrighted; Reprint Forbidden.)

Sour Hams are sometimes caused by hanging warm meat in the same room in which the meat is cured. This should never be done. The warm carcasses raise the temperature of the curing room, thus causing the brine to get too warm. Under such conditions the meat is liable to sour in the brine. Furthermore, the brine is liable to absorb the odors from the warm carcasses, which of course is very objectionable.

Many suppose that Hams sour from getting too much smoke, but such is never the cause, as Hams will not sour from over-smoke. Smoke aids to preserve Hams and cannot cause them to sour. When Hams sour in the Smoke House the cause must be traced to the fact that they are not properly and fully cured before going into the Smoke House, and the portion that has not been thoroughly cured, which is generally close to the bone, has not been reached by the brine. In many cases, souring comes from imperfect chilling of meat before putting it into the brine; then again, the meat may not have been overhauled at the proper time and with the frequency which good curing requires.

In order to prevent souring of Hams the various stages of curing must be carried out with the utmost care. In the first place, hogs should not be killed when overheated or excited, and after they have been scalded and scraped, they must be dressed as quickly as possible, washed out thoroughly with clean water and then split and allowed to hang in a well ventilated room until partly cooled off. They should then be run into a cooler or chill room as quickly as possible and the temperature should be reduced to 32 to 34 degrees Fahrenheit. They should be allowed to thus chill for 48 hours. When hogs are properly chilled after curing, the temperature of the inside of the Ham or Shoulder will not be more than several degrees higher than the cooler. After being thoroughly chilled, the Hams must undergo the various processes which will be found in other pages of this book which give directions for the curing of Hams and Shoulders. When these directions are closely followed, there will never be trouble from sour Hams.

83

HAMS AND SUPERIOR HAMS.

(Copyrighted; Reprint Forbidden.)

There seems to exist some doubt in the minds of butchers as to whether one Ham can be cured to better advantage than another, basing their opinion upon the fact that all packers have two grades of Hams, one of which is called of superior quality. Doubt has been expressed as to whether one piece of meat taken from the hog will make any better pork than that taken from another. This doubt should not obtain and could hardly exist in the minds of anyone who has carefully investigated the modern methods of packing. If such a person were to stand by the side of a Ham trimmer in a packing house and examine each Ham as it comes from the trimmer, he would be at once convinced as to the error of his opinion. There would be noticed a vast difference in the quality of Hams, even in their fresh state. Many Hams are of very coarse grain, especially those that come from boars, stags and old sows, while many other Hams are large and too fat. Those that come from poor, scrawny hogs are too small and thin, and this differentiation exists regardless of the grade or the experience in buying different lots of hogs. Perhaps there is no animal which varies so much in quality and condition of meat as the hog, and he fully represents or reflects the quality of the food from which he is made, or the results of wise or unwise feeding. Furthermore, Hams will vary in quality even after they have been graded; some medium size Hams, which is the size usually picked for the finest cure, are of much better quality than others. This will be readily admitted when it is remembered that a Ham may be of proper weight, but it can also be too fat for its weight, it can be too lean, it can have a coarse thick skin, the meat can be coarse in grain or it may be properly graded as to size, but come from an old, worn-out sow. Under such circumstances, it is not only necessary to cull the Hams, but to recull them, until the different grades are divided as to quality.

A fourteen to sixteen pound Ham from a young barrow with a fine, thin, white skin which is not too fat or not too lean, and possessing a nice, fine grained meat is fully up to grade and is taken for the superior quality of Hams. Therefore, a Ham of this description is superior in quality even before it goes into the brine for curing, and it is very easy to understand that when such a quality of Ham is carefully cured, for just the proper length of time, it will be far better than the ordinary run of Hams. Furthermore, the quality of the Hams may be deteriorated in many ways. For instance, the fourteen to sixteen pound Ham is fully cured in from sixty to seventy days, but if a packer has put up a large quantity of better grade Hams which gives him a surplus, he will hold them in the brine from ten to twenty days longer after they have been fully cured, and if they are thus kept in the brine for this additional period, they may become too salty and their fine flavor is lost. Under such circumstances the Hams must be taken out of the brine and smoked, or must be stored in a low temperature for ten or twenty days longer, but the moment they are kept beyond the full curing time they are not as good as when taken out of the cure at the moment they are fully cured. Furthermore, if a large quantity of the superior quality of Hams have been smoked and they are not disposed of rapidly enough, they begin to lose in appearance, and must again be culled and sold with the cheaper grade of Hams. If they are kept in brine longer than is necessary, they must also go into the cheaper quality.

It is, therefore, plain to be seen that what is known as the superior quality is the best Ham that the packer can turn out. As stated, the Hams are superior before they are cured. They are properly kept all through the process of curing, and the moment they are fully cured they are taken out, smoked and sold. It is only by handling Hams in this manner that it is possible to maintain a grade of superior quality. All Hams cannot be handled in this way, owing to the fluctuation of supply and demand, but the packer aims to keep them fully up to superior grade by a frequent and discriminating culling. This should convince anyone in doubt upon this question that they are erroneous in supposing that all hams are alike, and that all hog meat is high grade pork, when, in fact, it has various grades of quality.

HOW TO SMOKE PICKLE-SOAKED MEAT.

It sometimes happens that butchers leave their Hams in brine too long and they become pickle-soaked. Once in this pickle-soaked condition, it is well known that it is a very difficult matter to smoke the Hams, because, even though they are sweet when they go into the Smoke House, they will come out sour. Hams should not be left in brine over ninety days, and at the very outside not more than one hundred days, unless they are put into a freezer and kept at a temperature of 28 degrees, at which they can be kept as long as desired. But it is frequently the case that they are left in pickle five or six months in an ordinary cooler. Hams thus over-pickled cannot fail to cause trouble in the Smoke House, and we would advise that all Hams that have been left in the brine for such a long time should be washed off in warm water after first letting them soak in cold water 2 to 4 hours. They should then be hung up to dry and kept in a well ventilated room where the temperature is not too high. A room in which the circulation of air is good and which can be well ventilated by opening the windows and doors, and which does not rise in temperature above 60 to 70 degrees, would answer the purpose for drying out. It will do no harm to let the Hams hang two or three weeks before smoking. They can then be put in the Smoke House and smoked gently, using as little heat as possible. For the purpose of this light smoking, it is best to use sawdust instead of wood, or mostly sawdust, and a small amount of wood, in order to reduce the heat. The Smoke House should also be constructed in such a way that it can be sufficiently ventilated to let cool air into it and thus make sure of a cool smoke. If Hams are smoked under such conditions, they should come out of the Smoke House without souring.

The souring of pickle-soaked Hams is due to the brine fermenting in the Hams when they are placed in the warm Smoke House. Hence the advisability of drying out the Hams well before placing them in the Smoke House, and of smoking them in a cool smoke. When Meat has been in brine a very long time and has become pickle-soaked, and is afterward soaked in cold water, the greatest of care must be taken not to keep it in cold fresh water too long, otherwise the meat will absorb more moisture. It is also a good plan to soak Meat that has been in brine 60, 70 or 80 days in cold water. When Hams are fully cured, the strength of the brine may be reduced somewhat, after which the Hams may be permitted to remain in the brine about 30 days longer. Hams are fully cured in 70 days, and may be allowed to remain in a weaker brine 30 days longer, but no longer. After 30 days they must be taken out of this reduced brine, and, if it is so desired, they may be kept in a low temperature two or three weeks longer before smoking, but at the end of that time they must be smoked.

CLEANING LARD TIERCES FOR CURING PURPOSES.

(Copyrighted; Reprint Forbidden.)

As is well known, Butchers experience a great deal of trouble when they use second-hand lard tierces for curing meats, owing to the fact that the lard soaks into the pores of the wood, where it becomes tainted and rancid. No amount of washing or scalding will thoroughly cleanse such tierces or make them as good as new. The lard is run into the tierces while it is hot and the  fat naturally soaks very deeply into the wood. After these tierces are emptied and are used for curing purposes, the old lard remains in the pores and becomes rancid and contaminates the brine and also the meat.

It is a fact that many Butchers use old lard tierces for curing purposes and neglect to thoroughly clean them; and even if they have been well cleaned, it is well known that, notwithstanding every precaution taken, there is still left in the tierces a taint which affects the flavor of the meat.

USE ONLY PURE SPICES

We strongly recommend our friends to use only Pure Spices for three very good and sufficient reasons. First, for flavor; second, for uniformity, which will insure your sausage always being the same in flavor; third, for economy, as pure spices are cheapest in the final analysis.

Then again, the Pure Food Laws should not be overlooked. In States where the use of cereal in sausage is forbidden, the one safe-guard against prosecution is to use absolutely Pure Spices and avoid so-called sausage seasonings which contain cereals as an adulterant. In our laboratory we have repeatedly found cases where as much as 50% bread crumbs were mixed into spice to cheapen it. The bread crumbs mixed with the seasoning into the sausage meat would be detected by the chemists and microscopists of the various State Pure Food Departments, making the butcher who used such seasonings liable to prosecution for adding adulterants to his sausage.

If you will bear in mind that spices are of value only to the extent that they contain the flavoring principle of the particular Spice, you will readily understand that buying adulterated Spices is just throwing so much money away. For instance, in the case of White Pepper, there is an Oil of Pepper and certain resins. Presuming that you do pay the legitimate wholesale price for the sausage seasoning which contains only the best Singapore White Pepper and do have to pay a few cents a pound more than for one which is diluted down with 50% bread crumbs, the pure and unadulterated Spice is by far the cheapest in the end. You are also assured of always obtaining a uniform flavor in the finished sausage meat.

There is probably no other material in use by the butcher that is as liable to adulteration as Spice. To the average user the adulteration is very difficult to detect, because the aroma of the Spice is there and the adulterant is so cunningly ground and mixed in with the Pure Spice that, to the naked eye, it looks like the genuine article. But once the chemist or the microscopist secures a sample of these adulterated goods one glance through the microscope and a simple test for starch, which comes from the added cereal present, is sufficient. These adulterations not only occur in the largest used Spice like Pepper, but many of the other higher priced Spices like Cinnamon, Nutmeg, Cloves, Mace, Allspice, Ginger, etc., are equally the subject of adulteration at the hands of unscrupulous manufacturers and jobbers whose only object is to undersell the legitimate importer and grinder of real 100% Spice.

88

A CHEAP TEMPORARY SMOKE HOUSE.

This illustration will give some idea of how a temporary smoke house can be rigged up with very little trouble, which will answer the purpose nicely.

Very often it becomes necessary for a butcher to re-smoke some bologna that has been shipped to him from a packer, and it is sometimes necessary to re-smoke Hams and Bacon. Also, a butcher will often want to cure a small quantity of meat and would like to smoke it.

When butchers who are not equipped with a smoke house have to do this, they may be at a loss to know what to do.

Take a clean sugar barrel and knock out the bottom; then set the barrel on top of a box about four feet long, one or two feet high and as wide as the barrel. If a box of this shape cannot be obtained, a large dry goods box will answer. Bore auger holes through the box under the barrel, to let the smoke through. Get a large piece of tin, galvanized iron or sheet iron, about one foot wide and 2 feet long and bend it into the shape of a pan, or take an old roasting pan. Dig a hole in the ground at the front end of the box, so fire can be put onto this piece of tin, sheet iron or pan and then placed under the box with the fire on it. After the fire is placed under the box, place a board over the hole. All crevices must be banked with dirt around the box, to keep the smoke in.

The meats to be smoked should be hung on sticks with long strings on them, so as to let them down to about the middle of the barrel. Cover the barrel up with a gunny sack, so as to let a draft pass through and still retain the smoke in the barrel.

This makes a first class temporary smoke house with very little trouble and expense.

HOW TO KEEP HAMS, SHOULDERS, BACON, DRIED BEEF, AND ALL KINDS OF PICKLED MEATS IN BRINE FOR A YEAR OR LONGER.

(Copyrighted; Reprint Forbidden.)

All kinds of pickled meat after it is fully cured, if stored in a cooler in which the temperature is kept down to 28 degrees can be kept in this cooler for a year, or even longer, and when removed will come out similar to fresh cured meat. During the time when Hams and other meats are low in price, they can be stored in a freezer, and kept there until such a time as they are in greatest demand and will sell at the highest price. This enables the packer to reap a larger profit. At a temperature of 28 degrees, the meat will not freeze after it is cured, and the brine of course does not freeze, as salt water will not freeze, at that temperature. When meat is taken out of such cold storage to be smoked, it should first be soaked for three to five hours in fresh water, then washed in boiling hot water and smoked the same as regular fresh cured meat.

WASHING CURED MEAT BEFORE SMOKING.

(Copyrighted; Reprint Forbidden.)

Hams, Shoulders, Bacon and all cured meats whether dry salted or cured in brine, should be washed in hot water and scrubbed with a brush before being put into the smoke house. This is very important, as the meat thus scrubbed will come out of the smoke looking much better. The water should be as hot as the men can work with. The hotter the water, the

WASHING MEATS BEFORE SMOKING

better the meat will look after being smoked.

BRINE ABSORBS FOREIGN ODORS

Warm carcasses of meat should never be put into a cooler where meat is being cured in open vats, as the cold pickle will absorb the impure animal heat, and odors which these carcasses give off. Never allow sour pickle of any kind to remain in the curing room, as cold brine or water will absorb all foreign odors. To demonstrate this, take a glass of cold water, set it on a table next to a glass of tainted brine, and cover both with a bucket or pan; allow them to remain over night, and the next morning the cold water will have the same odor as the tainted brine. This will easily prove how meat can be tainted when curing in open tierces or vats, if anything sour or spoiled is in the cooler; therefore, curing rooms must be kept as clean as possible.

HOW LONG BRINE SHOULD BE USED

The length of time that brine should be used depends entirely upon the quantity of brine that you have in the barrel and the amount of meat that you put in each week. When the meat is packed solid it takes about 5 gallons of brine to each 100 pounds of meat. On the other hand if you put 25 gallons of brine in a tierce in which you place but a few pieces of corned beef from time to time as the meat accumulates your brine would be sufficient to cure 500 pounds of meat; if the barrel was nice and clean, the meat in good condition when put in the brine, and generally speaking conditions are favorable it will cure a great deal more than 500 pounds.

The brine may be used until it begins to get thick and show foam on the top; then of course it is advisable to make a new brine, at the same time washing the tierce out thoroughly.

DRY SALT MEATS.

Short Ribs (Regular) are made from the sides of the hog, between the Ham and Shoulder, having the loin and ribs in, and backbone removed.

Extra Short Ribs are made from the sides of the hog, between the Ham and Shoulder, with loin taken out, but belly ribs left in.

Short Ribs (Hard) are made from the sides of the hog, between the Ham and Shoulder, having the loin, ribs and backbone in.

Short Clears are made from the sides of the hog, between the Ham and Shoulder, having the loin in, and ribs and backbone removed.

Extra Short Clears are made from the sides of the hog, between the Ham and Shoulder with loin and all bones taken out.

Long Clears are made from sides, Ham being cut off, but Shoulders left in, back bone and ribs removed, shoulder blade and leg bone taken out, and leg cut off close to the breast.

Extra Long Clears are made from sides, Ham being cut off, back bone, **loin and ribs** removed. Shoulder blade and leg bone taken out and leg cut off close to the breast.

Short Clear Backs are made from the backs of hogs with the loin left in, but ribs and backbone removed; also known as **Lean Backs** and **Loin Backs**.

Short Fat Backs are made from the fat backs of prime hogs, being free from lean and bone, and properly squared on all edges.

Dry Salt Bellies are made from medium size hogs, cut square and well trimmed on all edges, with ribs left in.

Dry Salt Clear Bellies are made from medium size hogs, cut square and well trimmed on all edges, with ribs taken out.

--

HOW TO CURE DRY SALT SIDE MEATS.

(Copyrighted; Reprint Forbidden.)

First—Thoroughly chill the hogs so they are firm and solid. This will require letting them hang in the cooler after they are killed about 48 hours. Should the sides not be perfectly solid and thoroughly chilled, when cut up, spread them on the floor of a dry cooler for 24 hours, which ought to be long enough in a fair cooler to thoroughly chill them.

Second:—Make a tub of brine, using 15 lbs. of salt and 1 lb. of **Freeze-Em-Pickle** to each 5 gallons of brine.

Third:—Take a pickle pump, and pump some of the above brine into the sides along the backbone, being careful to get it all through the thick part.

Fourth:—Dip the sides into the tub of brine, and then lay them on a table or trough and rub thoroughly with dry salt. They must be dipped in brine, so that the **Freeze-Em-Pickle** will get all over the meat, and so the salt will adhere to the meat.

Fifth:—Clean the floor in the cooler or curing room with **Ozo Washing Powder;** sprinkle the floor lightly with salt; and then pile the sides one on top of the other with the meat side always up. Between each side spread a layer of salt, and see that all parts of the meat are covered with the salt. The more salt put on it the better.

Sixth:—Five days after salting the sides, shake off the salt, and pump them again in the same manner as when first salting; dip into the vat of brine, and dry salt again; then stack up the same as in the first instance, putting salt between each layer, and repeating this overhauling every ten days until the sides are cured.

B.HELLER&CO.

HOW LONG TO CURE DRY SALT SIDES.

(Copyrighted; Reprint Forbidden.)

Light sides will fully cure in from 30 to 35 days, and should be resalted three times, which with the first salting received by them, will give them four saltings during the curing period. These saltings are given on the first day, the fifth day, the fifteenth day, and the twenty-fifth day.

HOW LONG TO CURE HEAVY DRY SALT SIDES.

(Copyrighted; Reprint Forbidden.)

Heavy sides will be fully cured in from 50 to 60 days, according to size, and should be resalted five times during the curing, as follows: The first day, the fifth day, and then every ten days. After 45 days, the meat need not be rehandled, and can then remain in the cooler piled up, as long as one wishes to keep it. It should not be taken out of the cooler, however, until it has been in salt 50 to 60 days, according to the season of the year.

TEMPERATURE OF COOLER FOR DRY SALTING.

Full information as to the temperature of the cooler for dry salting will be found on page 46 under the head "Temperature."

DRY SALT CURING BY BUTCHERS WHO HAVE NO ICE MACHINE.

Small butchers, who have no ice machines, and simply use an ice box for a cooler, must use the greatest care to see that the meat is well chilled before salting, and they must also use plenty of salt. For the special benefit of small butchers, we will say that we fully realize the conditions which surround them, and we are well aware that they cannot get the temperature in an ice box as low as with an ice machine; but nevertheless, they can always cure meat with the **Freeze-Em-Pickle** process, and get better results.

CHICAGO U.S.A.

DESCRIPTION OF BARRELED PORK.

Mess Pork is made from the sides of well-fattened hogs, split through the backbone, and cut in strips about six inches wide.

Mess Pork Short Cut is made from the backs of prime hogs, split through the backbone, backbone left in, and bellies taken off; cut into pieces six inches square.

Clear Back Pork is made from the fat part of the backs of prime hogs, being free from lean and bone, even in thickness, and cut into pieces about six inches square.

Family Pork Lean is made from the top of shoulders, when cut into California Hams. It has one-half of the blade bone in, and is about two-thirds fat, and one-third lean.

Clear Bean or Butt Pork is made from the fat cheek or jowl, cut square.

Clear Brisket Pork is made from the Briskets of prime medium weight hogs, ribs removed and pieces cut about five inches wide.

Rib Brisket Pork is made from the Briskets of prime medium hogs, ribs left in, and cut into pieces about five inches wide.

Loin Pork is made from the end of the back next to the Ham, with both lean and fat, and has a portion of the tail bone in.

Pig Pork: Light selected boneless Bellies cut into five inch pieces, trimmed square.

Belly Pork: Selected heavy weight Bellies, cut into five inch pieces, with ribs left in.

Extra Short Clear Pork is made from the sides of hogs, with the loin and backbone removed, and the Belly ribs left in, cut into strips five inches wide, squared at each end.

Lean End Pork is made from selected medium weight Rib Bellies, cut into strips five inches wide.

95

DIRECTIONS FOR CURING BARRELED PORK.

(Copyrighted; Reprint Forbidden.)

Never pack more than 190 lbs. of pork in an ordinary pork barrel.

First:—If it can possibly be obtained, it is always best to use coarse rock salt, or coarse evaporated salt, which is made especially for this purpose; but if coarse salt cannot be obtained, any salt will answer the purpose. In packing it is necessary to use 35 lbs. of salt for each barrel, over and above the salt used in the brine.

Second:—Take a perfectly clean pork barrel, and throw three handfuls of salt on the bottom of the barrel.

Third:—Put in a layer of pork; throw three handfuls of salt over this layer.

Fourth:—Keep packing layer after layer, until the 190 lbs. of pork are packed in the barrel, and while packing put three handfuls of salt over each layer of the pork.

Fifth:—The following are the proper proportions for brine for 190 lbs. of pork: Put 10 gallons of cold water in a keg or tub; dissolve in this water 2 lbs. of **Freeze-Em-Pickle** and 30 lbs. of salt. Stir this well until it is all dissolved, and then pour the brine over the pork which has been packed as above directed.

Sixth:—If the barrels are to be headed up, head up first, and then put in the brine through the bung hole.

TEMPERATURE FOR BARRELED PORK.

(Copyrighted; Reprint Forbidden.)

It is necessary that the greatest care should be exercised not to let the pork freeze while curing. Brine for barreled pork will not freeze at the freezing point of water, but the meat in the brine will freeze, and will not cure if the temperature is lower than the freezing point for any length of time. See instructions as to Temperature to be found on page 46

BARRELED PORK NEED NOT BE OVERHAULED.

Barreled Pork when packed in accordance with these directions with **Freeze-Em-Pickle** and **Salt**, and then stored in a cooler, will not spoil, but will cure with a delicious flavor. It is not necessary that barreled pork should be overhauled; overhauling is required only for dry-salt and sweet-pickled meats. After the pork is fully cured, which will vary according to the size of the pieces, from 40 to 60 days, the pork can be shipped anywhere, into any hot climate and will remain in perfect condition without spoiling.

Extreme care must be exercised to thoroughly chill the pork before it is packed; if animal heat is left in the pork, it will not cure properly, any more than will hams when they are put into brine, with the animal heat left in them. Good results when curing barreled pork, cannot be expected if the meat is not in proper condition when packed.

DRIPPINGS FROM REFRIGERATING PIPES.

Never allow the drippings from refrigerating pipes along the ceiling, or from ice chambers, to drip into open vats containing meats while curing, as they will reduce the strength of the brine and make no end of trouble.

Keep the cooler as dry and as clean as it possibly can be kept. A damp, dirty cooler breeds millions of germs. These germs affect the brine and the curing of the meat.

RECIPE FOR CURING SPARE RIBS.

For each 100 pounds of spare ribs make the brine as follows: 5 pounds of common salt, 1 pound of **Freeze-Em-Pickle**, 2 pounds of best granulated sugar and 5 gallons of cold water.

Cure in this brine from 10 to 12 days. The temperature of the cooler in which the spare ribs are cured can be anywhere from 36 to 43 degrees, but it should not vary from this range of temperature. It is best to leave the spare ribs in the cure from 10 to 12 days, though they will be cured sufficiently in 7 to 8 days.

If the above method is carefully carried out, the result will be a fine, mild, sweet cure and not too salty.

Before placing the spare ribs in the brine they should be handled in the same manner as hams and shoulders. In other words, they should be rubbed in half of the above quantity of salt, **Freeze-Em-Pickle** and sugar, and the mixed **Freeze-Em-Pickle**, sugar and salt that is left after rubbing should be used for making the brine.

HOW TO CURE BEEF TONGUES.

(Copyrighted; Reprint Forbidden.)

First:—Cut the tongues out of the heads as soon as possible, and with warm water scrub off all the slime and dirt, with a stiff brush; hang up in a cooler on a hook at the gullet, to make the tongues thick instead of long and thin.

Second:—Let them hang for at least 24 hours in a cooler.

Third:—When the tongues are thoroughly chilled and firm, cut off the surplus fat and square the tongues at the gullet by trimming off all ragged pieces.

Fourth:—Put them into a strong common salt brine to beach them, and leave them in this brine from 10 to 20 hours.

Fifth:—Take them out of this brine and rub the slime off the tongues and out of the gullet, and also rub the gullet with dry salt.

Sixth:—If only a few tongues are to be cured make a barrel of pickle, as follows, and simply throw the tongues into it: For every 5 gallons of water, add 1 lb. of **Freeze-Em-Pickle**, 2 lbs. of Pure Granulated Sugar, and 7 lbs. of Common Salt.

Seventh:—Where large packers wish to pack tongues in tierces, the tongues should be handled as follows: Weigh out 285 lbs.; then mix together in a box or tub the following:

3 lbs. of **Freeze-Em-Pickle.**

6 lbs. of Best Granulated Sugar.

21 lbs. of Salt.

Eighth:—Rub each tongue with some of this mixture and pack as loosely as possible in the tierce, using about one-half of the mixture of **Freeze-Em-Pickle,** Sugar and Salt for rubbing, and the other half for making the brine. It will require between 14 to 15 gallons of brine to fill the tierces, some tierces vary in size, therefore dissolve the balance of the mixture of **Freeze-Em-Pickle,** Sugar and Salt in about 14 gallons of water, and pour over the tongues, should the tierce hold more simply add enough cold water to cover all the meat as the right amount of salt has already been added.

Ninth:—If the tierces are to be headed up, the heads should be put in, and the brine should be poured into the tierce through the bung hole. The overhauling of tongues is just as important, as is the overhauling of hams and shoulders. They should be overhauled in the same manner, and the same number of times. By reference to directions for curing hams and shoulders, which will be found on previous pages, all the necessary instructions can be followed. To give the tongues a proper flavor, they ought to cure from 50 to 60 days.

GARLIC FLAVORED BEEF TONGUES.

(Copyrighted; Reprint Forbidden.)

Many like Garlic Flavored Tongues, and this desire can be fully satisfied by adding about two tablespoonfuls of Vacuum Brand Garlic Compound to each tierce of tongues; add it to the brine before it is poured over the tongues. This will give them a delicious flavor which will be relished even by people who do not like fresh Garlic.

HOW TO CURE HOG TONGUES.

Hog Tongues should be handled and cured in exactly the same manner as beef tongues. The brine should be made of the same strength and in the same manner, and when so made, it will cure the hog tongues in about 30 days. The directions for curing Beef Tongues can be used for curing Hog Tongues in every particular.

CURING BEEF CHEEKS FOR CANNING.

(Copyrighted; Reprint Forbidden.)

First:—The cheeks should be cut out of the head immediately after the beef is killed, all the fat should be trimmed off, and then the cheeks should be twice cut, lengthwise, through the outside muscles.

Second:—They should be then thrown into ice water to which has been added some salt, and they should be allowed to remain there for an hour or two. This will draw out all the slime and blood.

Third:—The cheeks should then be put on a coarse wire screen, or perforated galvanized iron pan placed in a cooler and spread out as thinly as possible, so as to give them a chance to thoroughly chill. A thorough chilling in a cold cooler will require 24 hours.

Fourth:—The cheeks should then be salted, and packed into tierces; 285 lbs. should be put into each tierce.

Fifth:—Handle the cheeks as follows: For each 285 lbs., mix in a box or tub, 3 lbs. of **Freeze-Em-Pickle,** 6 lbs. of Granulated Sugar and 15 lbs. of Common Salt.

Sixth:—Then put 285 lbs. of cheeks on a table and take half of the mixture of **Freeze-Em-Pickle,** Granulated Sugar and Salt and mix it with the cheeks thoroughly; then shovel into tierces.

Seventh:—If the tierces are to be headed up, put the heads in and take the balance of the mixture of **Freeze-Em-Pickle,** Sugar and Salt and dissolve it in 15 gallons of cold water, which pour into the tierces through the bung hole. Insert the bung, and roll the tierces. This will mix and dissolve the **Freeze-Em-Pickle,** Sugar and Salt. Overhaul in closed up tierces simply by rolling them from one end of the cooler to the other. They ought to be rolled at least 100 feet.

Eighth:—If the tierces are to remain open, take 15 gallons of water in which dissolve the remaining mixture of **Freeze-Em-Pickle,** Sugar and Salt, and pour this brine over the cheeks; put boards over the top to keep the meat from floating or from coming out of the top of the barrel. At the end of five days after salting, the cheeks must be overhauled and rehandled by transferring them to another tierce with a large fork made for such purpose; this should be repeated every five days, viz., on the fifth day, on the tenth day and on the fifteenth day. After each overhauling, the same brine is always used to pour over the meat. If the cheeks are to be kept for any length of time, they should have another overhauling 25 to 30 days from the day they were packed. Cheek meat slime considerably, making it difficult to cure. When the cheeks are overhauled, if the pickle is thick and ropy, new brine of the same strength as the original brine will have to be made and poured over them, instead of the old brine. The cheek meat must be thoroughly washed in cold water before being put into fresh brine.

CURING HOG LIVERS.

(Copyrighted; Reprint Forbidden.)

Cut off plucks and chill livers thoroughly; then pump them in three or four places with a long slender open nozzle, about 3/16 to ¼ inch in diameter, using a pumping pickle made as follows.

1 lb. of **Freeze-Em-Pickle.**
12 lbs. of Common Salt.
5 gal. of Water.

Stick the nozzle of the brine pump into the different veins on the lower side of the livers and pump them until they swell up from the pressure of the brine; then lay them out on a rack for 24 hours in a cooler and allow the blood to ooze out of them.

On the next day after the livers have been pumped, pack them in a 60 deg. common salt brine; nothing else need be added. Those not having a Hydrometer for testing brine can make the brine by dissolving 15 lbs. of salt in 85 lbs. of water, this makes a 60 degree brine. In this way, the livers can be kept for a long time. When pickling livers, it is absolutely necessary that all animal heat should be extracted from them, and that they should be properly chilled and cooled, otherwise, they will not keep.

CURING BEEF LIVERS.

(Copyrighted; Reprint Forbidden.)

Cut off plucks and chill livers thoroughly. Pump the curing brine into them in three of four places by using a long slender open nozzle about 3/16 to ¼ inch in diameter, which insert into the different veins on the lower side of the livers. The brine should be forced into them until the pressure swells them up; after pumping them, lay them out on a rack for 24 hours in a cooler and allow the blood to ooze out of them. The pumping brine for beef livers is made the same as the brine for hog livers as follows:

1 lb. of **Freeze-Em-Pickle.**

12 lbs. of Common Salt.

5 gal. of Water.

The day after the livers have been pumped, they should be packed in a 60 deg. common salt brine, which is made by dissolving 15 lbs. of salt in 85 lbs. of water; nothing else need be added. All animal heat must be thoroughly extracted, and the livers must be properly chilled and cooled.

DIRECTIONS FOR CURING LEAN SHOULDER BUTTS.

(Copyrighted; Reprint Forbidden.)

LIGHT WEIGHT BUTTS.

Use for 100 lbs. Light Weight Butts.
- 5 lbs. of Common Salt,
- 1 lb. of **Freeze-Em-Pickle,**
- 2 lbs. Granulated Sugar,
- 5 gals. of Cold Water.
- Cure in this brine 20 to 30 days.

HEAVY WEIGHT BUTTS.

Use for 100 lbs. Heavy Weight Butts.
- 6 lbs. of Common Salt,
- 1 lb. of **Freeze-Em-Pickle,**
- 2 lbs. of Granulated Sugar,
- 5 gals. of Cold Water.

Cure in this brine from 30 to 40 days according to size.

The sugar used must be **Pure Granulated Sugar;** yellow or brown sugar must not be used.

First:—Sort the Butts, separating the Light Weight Butts and the Heavy Weight Butts.

Second:—Take enough of any one size of the assorted

Butts to fill a tierce which will be 285 lbs.; then thoroughly mix together in a large pail or box the following proportions of **Freeze-Em-Pickle**, the very best and purest Granulated Sugar and Salt.

Use for 285 lbs. of Light Weight Butts, 3 lbs. of **Freeze-Em-Pickle**, 6 lbs. of Granulated Sugar and 15 lbs. of Salt.

For 285 lbs. of Heavy Weight Butts, 3 lbs. of **Freeze-Em-Pickle**, 6 lbs. of Granulated Sugar and 18 lbs. of Salt.

HOW TO CURE BUTTS IN OPEN TIERCES.

(Copyrighted; Reprint Forbidden.)

When the tierces or barrels in which these Butts are cured, are not to be headed up, but are left open, use half of the **Freeze-Em-Pickle**, Sugar and Salt for rubbing as follows:

First:—Rub each Butt well with some of the mixture of **Freeze-Em-Pickle**, Sugar and Salt. Sprinkle a little of the mixture in the bottom of the tierce.

Second:—Pack the Butts in a perfectly clean tierce. The mixed **Freeze-Em-Pickle**, Sugar and Salt that is left after rubbing should be used for making the brine. It will require 14 to 15 gallons of brine for each tierce of Butts. Make the brine by dissolving in cold water all the mixed **Freeze-Em-Pickle**, Sugar and Salt that is left after the Butts are rubbed. Stir well for a minute until it is dissolved, and then pour this brine over the meat. When curing only a small quantity of Butts, cut down the proportions of **Freeze-Em-Pickle**, Sugar and Salt, also the quantity of water, according to the quantity of Butts to be cured.

QUANTITY OF BRINE TO USE FOR CURING 100 LBS. OF BUTTS.

(Copyrighted; Reprint Forbidden.)

Five gallons by measure, or 42 lbs. by weight, is the approximate amount of water to use for every 100 lbs. of meat.

Tierces, after being packed with 285 lbs. of meat, will hold about 15 gallons of water. When curing Butts in vats or open barrels, whether in small or large quantities, always use not less than 5 gallons of brine to 100 lbs. of meat, as this makes the proper strength and a sufficient brine to cover the meat.

105

HOW TO OVERHAUL BUTTS WHEN CUR-ING IN OPEN PACKAGES.

On the fifth day after packing each lot of Butts, it is necessary that they should be overhauled. This must be repeated seven days later; again in ten days, and a final overhauling should be given ten days later. Overhauling Light Butts three times, and Heavy Butts four times while curing, and at the proper time in each instance, is very important, and must never be forgotten, especially when curing with this mild, sweet cure. Overhauling means, to take the Butts out of the brine and to repack them in the same brine. The proper way to overhaul is to take a perfectly clean tierce, set it next to the tierce of Butts to be overhauled, pack the meat into the empty tierce, and then put this same brine over the meat.

HOW TO CURE BUTTS IN CLOSED UP TIERCES.

Large packers who employ coopers, should always cure Butts in closed up tierces, as this is the best method known.

First:—Mix the proper poportions of **Freeze-Em-Pickle**, Sugar and Salt, for the different size Butts to be cured. These proportions are given in the foregoing table, under the heading, ''Light Weight Butts, and Heavy Weight Butts.'' If the tierces are to be headed up, use half of the **Freeze-Em-Pickle**, Sugar and Salt, for rubbing the Butts, and the half that is left over after the Butts are rubbed, should be dissolved in the water which is to be used to fill the tierce. Rub each Butt well before packing; put only 285 lbs. of meat in each tierce, and then head them up.

Second:—Lay the tierces on their sides and fill them through the bung hole, with water in which the half of **Freeze-Em-Pickle**, Sugar and Salt left over after rubbing, has been dissolved.

Third:—Insert the bung and roll the tierces. This will mix and dissolve the **Freeze-Em-Pickle**, Sugar and Salt rubbed on the meat. Where the pieces of meat press tightly against each other, or against the tierce, the **brine** does not act on the meat; but if the pieces of meat are rubbed properly with the mixture of **Freeze-Em-Pickle**, Sugar and Salt before being packed in the tierce, such surfaces will be acted upon by the undissolved mixture, so that the curing will be uniform and no portion of the pieces will be left insufficiently cured, even if the brine does not come in contact with it. For this reason, it is important that each piece of meat should be carefully rubbed with the mixture before being packed in the tierce.

Fourth:—Overhaul five days after packing; again seven days later, again in ten days, and once more ten days thereafter. At each overhauling, examine each tierce for leaks; if any of the Pickle has leaked out, knock the bung in and refill. Remember to overhaul Light Butts three times, and Heavy Butts four times.

Fifth:—Overhaul Butts in closed-up tierces, simply by rolling the tierces from one end of the cooler to the other. They ought to be rolled at least 100 feet.

ROLLED BONELESS BUTTS OR BUTT SAUSAGE.

(Copyrighted; Reprint Forbidden.)

After the Butts are thoroughly cured, they should be stuffed in beef bungs; if they are large only one should be stuffed in each casing; if they are small, two can be stuffed together side by side. The casings should be tied off at each end, and then wound with a heavy string, which should be wrapped as tightly as possible. Perforate the casings with a fork so as to let out any air that may be in them; then smoke them over night in a cool smoke; in the morning boil them. If they are to be sold uncooked, dip them in boiling water for five minutes, and then in cold water so as to shrink the casings. Our new Improved Zanzibar Carbon can be used on the casings to give them an appetizing color. See directions for dipping on page 117.

HOW TO CURE MEAT FOR LUNCH HAM OR NEW ENGLAND STYLE PRESSED HAM
(ALSO CALLED BERLINER STYLE HAM)

(Copyrighted by B. Heller & Co.; Reprint Forbidden.)

The **Freeze-Em-Pickle** Process is especially adapted for curing Ham trimmings which are used for Berliner Style Hams, Lunch Hams, Boneless Hams, New England Style Pressed Hams, etc. It will cure and preserve Ham trimmings perfectly, and will give them a rich, delicate sugar-cured ham flavor. It does not draw the albumen out of the meat, but the natural binding qualities are retained, and the meat has a rich, red, cured-meat color. Trimmings cured with the

Freeze-Em-Pickle Process can be kept in cold storage for a year without getting too salty or becoming short and losing their nice flavor and binding qualities.

The following directions must be carefully followed to get the results desired:

First:—The trimmings should not be larger than an egg, and should be as uniform in size as possible.

Second:—Do not run the trimmings through an Enterprise Grinder to cut them up before packing them, as it has a tendency to heat the meat.

Third:—Trimmings that are to be held for any great length of time must be fresh as possible; if they should be somewhat slimy, they should be washed thoroughly in cold common salt brine and allowed to drain until quite dry. Never mix or salt trimmings that become slimy, with fresh ones; always pack them separately.

Fourth:—It is absolutely necessary that the meat should be thoroughly chilled, and that the packing should be done in the cooler so that the temperature of the meat will not get above the temperature in which it is to be cured.

Fifth:—For each 100 lbs. of trimmings, take 1 lb. of **Freeze-Em-Pickle**, 1 lb. of best Granulated Sugar and 2 lbs. of Common Salt, and mix these thoroughly with the meat. Mixing thoroughly is very important; it should be carefully done so as to insure a uniform cure.

Sixth:—Have the tierces or barrels perfectly clean and sweet; then sprinkle a little salt on the bottom, and fill the barrel or tierce about one-quarter full of salted meat, and pound it down hard with a tamper. Do the same when the barrel is half full and continue in this manner until the barrel is filled. This tamping is done to expel the air between the pieces of meat, and it is an important factor to insure a uniform cure and color. If the trimmings are to be kept any length of time, it will be necessary that the tierces or barrels should be headed up, and they should always be filled with meat as much as possible. When trimmings are to be used as soon as cured, it is not necessary to head them up, simply put a top on them and weight them down, or cover them with a clean cloth and put a layer of salt about one inch thick, over the top of the cloth. This will keep out the air and will give good results. The trimmings will be cured in from two to three weeks, and are then in a perfect condition to be made into New England Style Pressed Hams, etc. They need not be soaked in water, nor need any salt be added as they are ready for instant use just as they are and will have a delicious sugar-cured ham flavor.

See paragraph on Temperature for Curing Meats on page 46.

HOW TO MAKE NEW ENGLAND STYLE PRESSED HAMS

(Copyrighted by B. Heller & Co.; Reprint Forbidden.)

After the meat is cured, it should be stuffed in beef bungs, and should be smoked about three hours, but this depends upon the smoke house and whether wood or sawdust is used. It may be necessary to smoke the Pressed Ham still longer. Boil them in a temperature of 180 degrees Fahrenheit for 1½ hours, then reduce the temperature to 170 degrees Fahrenheit and remove them at the expiration of one hour. After they are boiled for 2½ hours, they should be laid out on a table in the cooler, and then boards should be placed on top of them weighted down with heavy stones, and should remain there over night before being removed.

The casings may be given an appetizing smoke color by momentary dipping in a solution of Zanzibar-Carbon. Brand Casing Brown Mixture (see page 117 for directions)

HOW TO CURE MEAT FOR MAKING FINE BOLOGNA AND FRANKFURT SAUSAGE AND COMPLY WITH PURE FOOD LAWS

In following the old method of making Bologna and Frankfurt Sausage, a large percentage of the albumen is drawn out of the Meat, thus losing much of the richness, flavor and color which should be retained in the Sausage.

B. Heller & Co. have made an important improvement in the process of curing trimmings, and Sausage Makers will find it greatly to their advantage to make an immediate trial of this process. A single batch of Sausage made after this method will convince any Sausage Maker of the mistake of following the old ideas of making Bologna and Frankfurt Sausages.

When Bologna and Frankfurts are made from fresh Meats, they have a gray color and are very difficult to keep in good condition, especially during the warm weather. However, when Bologna and Frankfurts are made by the **Freeze-Em-Pickle** Process, they will have a fine red color and they will comply with the Pure Food Laws, because **Freeze-Em-Pickle** contains no ingredients which have been prohibited by any of the food laws. They will also keep much better than when made in the old way, and will stand shipment during the warm weather with better results.

HOW TO CURE BEEF OR PORK TRIM-MINGS WITH FREEZE-EM-PICKLE

(Copyrighted by B. Heller & Co.; Reprint Forbidden.)

Trimmings that are to be stored away for a few days to two weeks, should be packed with the following proportions of **Freeze-Em-Pickle** and Salt.

To every 100 lbs. of Trimmings use the following:
1 lb. of **Freeze-Em-Pickle**.
1 lb. of Salt.

For Trimmings that are to be stored away for two weeks to three months, the following proportions of **Freeze-Em-Pickle** and Salt should be used:
1¼ lbs. of **Freeze-Em-Pickle** and
1 lb. of Salt to each
100 lbs. of Trimmings.

For Trimmings that are to be stored away for three months to six months, the following proportions of **Freeze-Em-Pickle** and Salt should be used:
1½ lbs. of **Freeze-Em-Pickle** and
1 lb. of Salt to each
100 lbs. of Trimmings.

First:—Weigh the Trimmings and then spread them on a table.

Second:—Weigh out the proper proportions of **Freeze-Em-Pickle** and Salt, mix them together thoroughly, and then sprinkle over the meat.

Third:—Mix the Trimmings well so that the Salt and **Freeze-Em-Pickle** get to all parts of the meat.

Fourth:—Run the Trimmings through the grinder, using what is called the lard plate, a plate that has holes in it from 1 to 1¼ inches in diameter. By first mixing the **Freeze-Em-Pickle** and Salt with the meat and then putting it through the grinder, the **Freeze-Em-Pickle** and Salt become better mixed with the meat.

Another way is to run the Trimmings through the grinder first, using the lard plate with 1 to 1¼ inch holes in it; then put this meat in the mixer and while mixing add the **Freeze-Em-Pickle** and Salt, which have first been thoroughly mixed. Let the mixer run until the **Freeze-Em-Pickle** and Salt are thoroughly mixed with the meat, which only takes a few minutes.

If a plate with large holes in it is not available, cut the Trimmings up small by hand and then mix the **Freeze-Em-Pickle** and Salt with the meat.

HOW TO PACK IN BARRELS OR TIERCES

(Copyrighted by B. Heller & Co.; Reprint Forbidden.)

First:—Take barrels or tierces that are perfectly clean and sweet; this is very important. Then sprinkle a handful of **Freeze-Em-Pickle** and Salt which have first been thoroughly mixed, over the bottom of the tierce.

Second:—Fill tierce about one-quarter full of the meat that has been mixed with **Freeze-Em-Pickle** and Salt, and then with a tamper, tamp it down as tight as can be. The tighter the meat is packed, the better. Then place more of the meat into the tierce and tamp it, and keep on doing this until the tierce is full.

Third:—If the tierce is not to be headed up, don't fill it quite to the top, and after tamping the meat tight, sprinkle a couple of handfuls of the mixture of **Freeze-Em-Pickle** and Salt over the top. Then lay a piece of parchment paper over the meat, and on top of this place a piece of cheese cloth about a yard square.

Fourth:—On top of the cheese cloth put about two or three inches of dry Salt, spread so it reaches to all the edges of the barrel, so as to exclude the air from the meat, and then turn the ends of the cloth over the top, and allow this meat to stay in the cooler until you are ready to make Bologna, Frankfurts, or any similar sausage out of it.

This meat is now ready in four or five days to be made into Bologna, Frankfurts, or any similar sausage, but can also remain in a cooler as long as six months or even longer without being disturbed. This meat will not become too salty no matter how long it stands, and whenever you wish to make Bologna, Frankfurts, or any similar sausage, the meat is ready to be used.

This is known as the **Freeze-Em-Pickle Process**, and by curing the meat in this way no brine or albumen will be found at the bottom of the tierce when the meat is taken out. The meat when taken from the barrel will be found sticky, and to possess good binding quality and a nice cured flavor. It will make delicious Bologna, Frankfurts, or any similar sausage. The meat will have a nice sweet cure and a fine color which will be imparted to the Bologna, Frankfurts or any similar sausage made from it. On account of the meat being cured, the Bologna, Frankfurts and other sausage will not spoil so easily as they would if made from fresh meat.

Beef or pork trimmings should be handled in the same way, and no fresh meat used at all in making the Bologna or Frankfurts.

If the trimmings are to be kept for any length of time, it is advisable to head them up. When tierces are to be headed up, fill them as full as possible, sprinkle two hand-fuls of **Freeze-Em-Pickle** and salt, which have first been thoroughly mixed, over the top and then put on the head.

When making this **Freeze-Em-Pickle** cured meat into smoked sausages, more salt of course must be added, as the meat is not sufficiently salty, so when adding the Sea-soning add sufficient salt to give it the proper taste, and add ½ lb. of sugar to every 100 lbs. of meat in addition to the spice, as it gives the meat a delicious flavor.

PROPER TEMPERATURE FOR STORING TRIMMINGS

(Copyrighted by B. Heller & Co.; Reprint Forbidden.)

If the trimmings are to be used up in two or three weeks, any ordinary cooler that is kept around 40 degrees will be sufficient, but if trimmings are to be kept three to six months, they should be kept in a cooler at a temperature of 35 to 36 degrees to get the best results. Never let the temperature get down below freezing if it can be helped, and do not let it get any higher than 38 degrees, if possible.

HOW TO MAKE BOLOGNA AND FRANK-FURTS FROM FRESH BEEF AND PORK WITH FREEZE-EM-PICKLE WITHOUT FIRST CURING THE MEAT

(Copyrighted by B. Heller & Co.; Reprint Forbidden.)

Run the desired quantity of beef and pork through a grinder, first using a coarse plate, then through a fine one; then finish in a silent chopper. While cutting it in the silent cutter, add to each 100 lbs. of meat 1 lb. of **Freeze-Em-Pickle**, ¾ lb. of "B" Condimentine, 1 to 1½ lbs. of salt and ½ lb. of sugar, according to taste. Chop this up as usual, adding pure artificial ice to keep it cool. First put the beef in the silent cutter and when it is about three-fourths fine add the necessary pork, which has first been run through the ¼ inch plate of a grinder. If a mixer is not used, add the Seasonings and flour to the meat in the silent cutter. When all are thoroughly mixed put into a tub, cover well over with parchment or wax paper to exclude the air and put away until ready to use. The meat can then be taken direct from the tub in 24 to 36 hours, placed into the stuffer, and stuffed into the casings.

The meat should be kept in a temperature of 45 to 46 degrees. This is a fairly high temperature which gives the **Freeze-Em-Pickle** a chance to do its work quicker, and by standing 24 to 36 hours after it is chopped and seasoned, it develops its full binding qualities and saves handling the meat two or three times, which should appeal to every sausage maker.

FORMULA FOR BOLOGNA SAUSAGE

The following formula makes very fine Bologna sausage:

75 lbs. beef trimmings cured by Freeze-Em-Pickle Process.

15 lbs. pork trimmings cured by Freeze-Em-Pickle Process.

10 lbs. pork speck (back fat).

Bull-Meat-Brand Sausage Binder in the percentage amount of cereal allowed by your State Food Law, but not over five pounds to the hundred.

8 to 10 ounces Zanzibar-Brand Bologna Sausage Flavor.

¾ lb. "B" Condimentine

Sufficient cracked ice for cooling.

First:—Salt the pork and beef trimmings according to the directions on foregoing pages.

Second:—When making the Bologna (or Frankfurts), take the beef that has been cured with Freeze-Em-Pickle and run through the grinder, using ¼ or ⅜ inch plate. (Some sausage makers prefer to run this meat through the grinder again, using the smallest plate they have, but this in our opinion takes up unnecessary time and labor. Once running through a ¼ or ⅜ inch plate is sufficient).

Then place this beef in the silent chopper. As soon as this has made one or two revolutions, put in sufficient cracked ice to prevent the beef from becoming heated. Then add about one pound of salt; adding ice if necessary. Then add the pork to the beef, which should have already been run through the grinder, and at the same time add the pork speck.

Third:—Then for seasoning add 8 to 10 ounces Zanzibar-Brand Bologna Flavor, and also about ¾ of a pound of "B" Condimentine. This Condimental preparation is permissible in all Government inspected houses and complies with the Pure Food Laws. "B" Condimentine is used to prevent shrinkage and help keep the sausage, and so the color inside will not fade or turn gray, but retain its bright, rich color for ten days if kept under proper conditions. This is a great advantage, especially to large packers who do shipping. After the Spices and Condimentine are worked in, then add salt to taste. Sausage made with "B" Condimentine does not have to be labeled that a preservative is used.

Fourth:—Then while the meat is being cut in the silent chopper, add the legal amount of Bull-Meat-Brand Sausage Binder to each 100 pounds of meat. Or, if a mixer is used, add the binder in the mixer. When properly mixed and seasoned with spices and "B" Condimentine, and binder has been added, it is already for the stuffer, or if desired, this meat already chopped can be kept in tubs in a cooler of a temperature of 38 to 40 degrees for 24 to 36 hours until required.

Notice:—See our instructions on page 113 for handling beef that has been cured with Freeze-Em-Pickle and stored away from two to six months or longer.

Note:—Since the Pure Food Laws have been enacted, all Antiseptic Preservatives have been ruled out and cannot be used in sausage, so sausage makers must be careful what kind of a Sausage Binder they use in their sausage. Many of the binders on the market start fermentation soon after moisture is added to them. When it is noticed that Bologna does not keep as well as it should, the first thing to be looked to is the binder used, as invariably a binder which is not free from the germs of fermentation will cause trouble, and the losses a butcher has from using such binders will amount to more than the saving in the cost of the binder. Many cheap binders can be bought for less money than Bull-Meat-Brand Sausage Binder, as they cost less to manufacture. We are not trying to see how cheap a binder we can manufacture, but our sole aim in selling Bull-Meat-Brand Sausage Binder is to offer the very Finest Binder that we know how to make, which will help the sausage instead of souring it, and, even if our price is a trifle higher, Bull-Meat-Brand Sausage Binder is much cheaper to use and results are always satisfactory.

Notice:—If a Garlic flavor is desired, add one or two tablespoonfuls of Vacuum-Brand Garlic Compound while the meat is being chopped. Vacuum-Brand Garlic Compound is recommended as it does not sour in the sausage and it does not leave any after-taste nor taint the breath, because it is so finely divided that it is thoroughly incorporated in the meats and is thoroughly digested and absorbed. In States where Cereal is not permitted, use Garlic Condiment instead of Garlic Compound.

Fifth—After the meat is chopped to the proper fineness, stuff it into beef rounds or beef middles. Place the sausage in the smoke house and smoke.

BOILING BOLOGNA.

(Copyrighted; Reprint Forbidden.)

After it is smoked, boil Round Bologna 30 minutes in water 160 degrees Fahrenheit and Long Bologna for 45 to 60 minutes in 160 degrees water, according to thickness.

After they are boiled place them on a table, or hang them up and pour boiling water over them to wash off the grease. Then pour cold water over them to shrink the casings. After that allow them to cool in the open air or a well ventilated room, before placing in the cooler or ice box. This will prevent sweating, which causes mouldy and slimy casings.

BOILING LARGE BOLOGNA.

(Copyrighted; Reprint Forbidden.)

If Large Bologna are desired, stuff the meat into beef bungs and smoke until they are nicely smoked, then boil them from 1¼ to 1½ hours in water 155 degrees Fahrenheit. Vary the time of boiling according to the thickness of the Bologna.

SALTING FAT FOR BOLOGNA.

The Pork Back Fat or Pork Speck will be much better for use in Bologna and Frankforts if it is dry salted with Freeze-Em-Pickle for a few weeks before it is used.

HOW TO COLOR THE CASINGS OF SMOKED SAUSAGE WITH ZANZIBAR-CARBON BRAND CASING BROWN MIXTURE

COLORING BOLOGNA CASINGS

(Copyrighted by B. Heller & Co.; Reprint Forbidden.)

Hang the bologna in the smoke house just long enough to dry the skin well, or hang it in front of a hot fire, or in the sun, any way to get the excess moisture dried out of the casing; then proceed according to the following method:

METHOD OF COLORING THE CASINGS OF SAUSAGE IN GOVERNMENT INSPECTED PACKING HOUSES

In all Packing Houses having U. S. Government inspection, the coloring of casings are allowed only by what is termed "Momentary Dipping". We advise butchers to use this method in preference to any other way whether they have Government inspection or not.

Directions for Momentarily Dipping Smoked Sausage such as Bologna, Frankfurt, etc.

After Sausage has been smoked and cooked, dip it into a solution made up in the proportion of 1 ounce of Zanzibar-Carbon-Brand Casing Brown Mixture to every 20 gallons of water. Always dissolve it first in some hot water (not boiling) in the proportion of one-half gallon water for every ounce used and then pour this solution into the balance of the water to make up the dipping solution.

The water used for dipping should be about the same temperature as that in which the Sausage is cooked. After dipping, the Sausage must be rinsed off with hot water and thereafter with cold water, then hung up in the usual manner to drip off and dry. When Sausage is smoked through and is not cooked, it must be well sprayed with, or dipped into, boiling hot water to remove the grease from the casing before being put into the colored dipping solution.

FRANKFORT SAUSAGE; HOW TO MAKE

(Copyrighted by B. Heller & Co.; Reprint Forbidden.)

Frankfort Sausage is made in most cases in exactly the same manner as Bologna with the exception that it is chopped very fine and Zanzibar-Brand Frankfort Sausage Seasoning is used. To make fine Frankfort Sausage use two parts of Beef and one part of Pork.

If Veal is used in Frankfort Sausage, it improves it considerably, but the price of Veal is so high that it is very seldom used. Stuff in sheep casings and smoke lightly, then dip them in Zanzibar-Carbon Brand Casing Brown Mixture by the method prescribed on the preceding page.

Dipping them in hot water and then in cold takes out all the wrinkles. After they have been dipped, pour a pail of hot water over them to wash off all adhering grease; then dip them for a minute or two in ice water to cool. This will make them contract so rapidly that they will not wrinkle; then put in a cooler to hang up and cool through to the center.

COLORING FRANKFURT SAUSAGE
CASINGS

(Copyrighted by B. Heller & Co.; Reprint Forbidden.)

Follow the directions given on page 117 for momentary dipping.

If a deep color is desired, slightly increase the amount of Zanzibar-Carbon Brand Mixture. You must use your own judgment in producing the right color desired, as the drier the casing the less Zanzibar-Carbon Brand Mixture it takes and the better the color will be.

Always be particular not to smoke with too much heat in the smoke house, so that the grease does not melt in the sausage and come through the casing.

CURING BEEF CHEEKS FOR BOLOGNA
AND FRANKFURTS

(Copyrighted by B. Heller & Co.; Reprint Forbidden.)

First:—The Cheek Meat should be cut out of the heads as soon as possible after the beef is killed, and the gristle should be cut through lengthwise, two or three times. All the fat can also be trimmed off or left on, just as desired; in a large slaughtering establishment, the fat is worth more in the tank than in the sausage.

Second:—The Cheeks should then be thrown into ice water and allowed to remain there for an hour or two. This will draw out all the slime and blood.

Third:—The Cheeks should then be spread out thinly on coarse wire screens, or on perforated galvanized iron pans, in a cooler. They should be spread out as thinly as possible so as to thoroughly drain and chill.

Fourth:—After they are thoroughly chilled, which will take 24 hours, they should be salted as follows:

DIRECTIONS FOR DRY SALTING BEEF AND PORK CHEEK MEAT

Beef and Pork Cheek Meat that is to be stored away for a few days to two weeks, should be packed with the following proportions of **Freeze-Em-Pickle** and salt.

To every 100 lbs. of Beef and Pork Cheek Meat use the following:

1 lb. of **Freeze-Em-Pickle.**
1 lb. of Salt.

For Beef and Pork Cheek Meat that is to be stored away for two weeks to three months, the following proportions of **Freeze-Em-Pickle** and salt should be used:

1¼ lbs. of **Freeze-Em-Pickle** and
1 lb. of Salt to each
100 lbs. of Beef and Pork Cheek Meat.

For Beef and Pork Cheek Meat that is to be stored away for three months to six months, the following proportions of **Freeze-Em-Pickle** and salt should be used:

1½ lbs. of **Freeze-Em-Pickle** and
1 lb. of Salt to each
100 lbs. of Beef and Pork Cheek Meat.

First:—Weigh the Beef and Pork Cheek Meat and then spread it on a table.

Second:—Weigh out the proper proportions of **Freeze-Em-Pickle** and salt, mix them together thoroughly, and then sprinkle over the meat.

Third:—Mix the Beef and Pork Cheek Meat well so that the salt and **Freeze-Em-Pickle** get to all parts of the meat.

Fourth:—Run the Beef and Pork Cheek Meat through the grinder, using what is called the lard plate, a plate that has holes in it from 1 to 1¼ inches in diameter. By first mixing the **Freeze-Em-Pickle** and salt with the meat and then putting it through the grinder, the **Freeze-Em-Pickle** and salt become better mixed with the meat.

Another way is to run the Beef and Pork Cheek Meat through the grinder first, using the lard plate with 1 to 1¼ inch holes in it; then put this meat in the mixer and while mixing add the **Freeze-Em-Pickle** and salt, which have first been thoroughly mixed. Let the mixer run until the **Freeze-Em-Pickle** and salt become thoroughly mixed with the meat, which only takes a few minutes.

If a plate with large holes in it is not available, cut the Beef and Pork Cheek Meat up small by hand and then mix the **Freeze-Em-Pickle** and salt with the meat.

Fifth:—If the tierces are to remain open, they can be covered with a clean cloth and a layer about two or three inches thick of dry salt should be put over the top of the cloth. This will exclude the air and keep the top meat from getting dry and dark.

Sixth:—Cheek Meat that has been properly chilled and packed in this manner can be kept for any length of time and need not be overhauled. It can be kept for a year or longer and whenever it is taken out of the barrel and used, it will make fine Bologna and Frankforts with a fine color and a delicious flavor. Dry salted Cheek Meat makes much better Bologna than the pickled Cheek Meat. Sometimes Cheeks are very low in price, and they can be packed and stored as above directed and kept until the market advances; by this method quite a sum of money can be made each year.

Seventh:—See paragraph on Temperature for Curing Meats on page 46.

CURING BEEF AND PORK HEARTS FOR BOLOGNA AND OTHER SAUSAGE.

(Copyrighted; Reprint Forbidden.)

First:—As soon as the beef or hog is slaughtered, the hearts should be cut open; the pork hearts should be cut into four squares, and the beef hearts into six or eight pieces, being sure to cut them so that all the crevices are open and exposed. They should then be placed in ice water in which they should be allowed to remain for two to three hours.

Second:—Spread the hearts on trays or racks in a cooler as thinly as possible, and allow them to drain and chill for 24 hours; they must be thoroughly chilled so that all animal heat leaves them.

Use for 100 lbs. of Beef or Pork Hearts. { 1¼ lbs. Freeze-Em-Pickle. 1 lb. of Common Salt.

Third:—Run hearts through an Enterprise grinder, using a lard plate with 1½-inch holes; then place in a mixer and gradually add the mixture of Freeze-Em-Pickle and salt. Be sure it is evenly divided and thoroughly mixed.

121

Fourth:—Take a perfectly clean tierce, and sprinkle a handful of salt, and a little Freeze - Em - Pickle on the bottom; put the salted hearts into the tierce and tamp them down with a tamper as hard as possible.

The object in tamping with a tamper is to get all the air out and to close up all the cavities in the barrel. The less air cells in the barrel, the better the hearts will cure and keep.

Fifth:—If the tierces are to be headed up, sprinkle a handful of salt on top of the tierces, cover nicely with a piece of parchment paper and put in the heads, being careful that the tierces are as full as they possibly can be before the heads are put in, and also that the tierces are perfectly sweet before packing.

Sixth:—If the tierces are to remain open, they can be covered with a cloth and about two or three inches of dry salt should be put over the top of the cloth. This will exclude the air, and will keep the top meat from getting dry and dark.

Seventh:—Hearts that have been properly chilled and packed in this manner can be kept for any length of time and need not be overhauled. They can be kept for a year or longer, and whenever taken out of the tierces to use, they will make fine bologna and such sausage as hearts can be used for. Quite a quantity of properly cured hearts can be used in the manufacture of sausage with very good results. They will have a fine color and a delicious flavor. Hearts should never be pickled for Bologna, but should always be dry salted as above directed. It is very often the case that hearts can be bought at a small cost when the market is low, and if so purchased and packed and stored as herein directed until the market advances and meat is high, they can be made into bologna with a very handsome profit.

Eighth:—See paragraph on Temperature for Curing Meats on page 46.

GERMAN STYLE HAM SAUSAGE

(Copyrighted by B. Heller & Co.; Reprint Forbidden.)

German Style Ham Sausage is made very much like Bologna, except that the meat should be chopped finer. For every 100 lbs. of Ham Sausage, take the following:

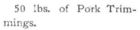

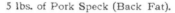

50 lbs. of Pork Trimmings.

40 lbs. of Beef Trimmings.

5 lbs. of Pork Speck (Back Fat).

Bull-Meat-Brand Sausage Binder in the percentage proportion of cereal allowed by your State Food Law.

¾ lb. "B" Condimentine.

2 lbs. of Salt.

6 to 8 ounces Zanzibar-Brand Frankfort Flavor.

First:—Salt the Pork and Beef Trimmings four or five days ahead, using to each 100 lbs. of meat 1 lb. of **Freeze-Em-Pickle**, as directed on page 111. No salt or anything in addition to the **Freeze-Em-Pickle** should be added when the meat is put down to cure. The salt is added when the Sausage is made.

Second:—When making Ham Sausage, use the Pork and Beef in the proportions as stated above and when about half chopped add the Speck or Back Fat.

Third:—After adding the Fat, add sufficient salt so as to have 2 lbs. to each 100 lbs. of finished Ham Sausage. Also add 6 to 8 ounces Frankfort Flavor.

Fourth:—Now proceed to chop or grind the meat according to directions given on page 114, using cracked ice to keep the meat cool.

123

Fifth:—When the meat is chopped, stuff it into Beef Bung Casings. After the Sausage is stuffed, it is well to wrap string around it tight, so the Sausage will be firm when cooked and will not drop in the smoke house.

Sixth:—Smoke this sausage carefully over a medium warm fire.

Seventh:—Cook the Sausage from $1\frac{1}{4}$ to $1\frac{1}{2}$ hours, in water 155 degrees hot. Vary the time according to the thickness of the Sausage. See directions on page 117 for coloring Bologna casings and color the casings of this Sausage the same way.

Eighth:—After Sausage of any kind has been cooked, it should be handled as follows: Pour boiling water over it to wash off the surplus grease that adheres to the casings and then pour cold water over it to shrink and close the pores of the casings. This is very important and it should be closely observed by all packers and sausage makers who wish to have their Sausage look nice and fresh in appearance.

HOW TO PREPARE CASINGS BEFORE STUFFING.

(Copyrighted; Reprint Forbidden.)

Before casings are stuffed, they should always be soaked in warm water, so as to make them pliable, so they will stretch to their utmost limit when being stuffed. If they are properly soaked, they will stretch considerably and will not burst as easy as they will if they are not properly soaked. The casings should be soaked in water about 90 degrees temperature Fahrenheit, from one to two hours, depending upon how old and dry they are. If the casings are very old and dry, they will have to be soaked until they are perfectly soft and pliable. When casings are soaked in water that is too hot, the casings are scalded and become tender and will burst when being stuffed, and the heavy Sausage will tear loose in the smoke house.

CHICAGO, U.S.A.

HOW TO PREVENT BURSTING AND SHRINKING OF SAUSAGE.

(Copyrighted; Reprint Forbidden.)

Many undergo a great deal of trouble from the bursting and shrinking of Sausage and it is a trouble which can be easily avoided, as it is entirely owing to the manner of boiling the Sausage. Ordinary round or long Bologna should be kept in water at 160 to 170 degrees Fahrenheit for about 30 minutes, and thick large Bologna should be kept in water from 155 to 160 degrees Fahrenheit from three-quarters of an hour to one hour, according to the size. If the Sausage is very large, it will take from one and one-quarter to one and one-half hours to cook them thoroughly. When Sausage is boiled in water that is too hot the particles of meat will crumble and separate. The Sausage will taste dry, although water will be in the crevices between the small pieces of meat. The Sausage will look rough on the outside and will also lose more weight than when boiled as above directed. Many of them will burst when the water is too hot. After Sausage of any kind has been cooked, it should be handled as follows: Pour boiling water over it to wash off all the surplus grease that adheres to the casing and then pour cold water over it to shrink and close the pores of the casing. This is very important and should be closely observed by all packers and sausage makers who wish to have their Sausage look nice and keep its fresh appearance.

B. HELLER & CO.

HAMBURGER STEAK

HOW TO SEASON HAMBURGER SO AS TO MAKE IT MORE PALATABLE AND PLEASING.

(Copyrighted; Reprint Forbidden.)

A very successful way of increasing trade on Hamburger is to season it with one ounce of Zanzibar-Brand Hamburger Seasoning to every 25 pounds of meat. This gives the meat a Delicious Flavor, makes it more Palatable and Pleasing to the Taste and much more Appetizing and Satisfactory to the Customer. Sometimes Hamburger when made without Seasoning has a peculiar flavor and meat odor which many customers object to.

All this trouble is overcome by Seasoning all Hamburger with our Zanzibar Brand Hamburger Seasoning, as it gives the meat a Delicious Flavor and Aroma.

This is something that will increase the sale on Hamburger wherever it is used.

HAMBURGER SAUSAGE

Below we give the recipe for a New Sausage that is well liked wherever it is being tried, and we advise every butcher to make use of it. This Sausage is a success, takes well with the trade when made up right and is very easy to make. It is a nice eating Sausage and customers are always pleased to get hold of something new for a change. Making Hamburger Sausage gives the butcher an opportunity for selling all the small pieces of beef and a large percentage of beef fat at a good profit, which is very often not easily sold otherwise.

DIRECTIONS FOR MAKING HAMBURGER SAUSAGE.

(Copyrighted; Reprint Forbidden.)

Take—

70 lbs. Beef Trimmings.

20 lbs. Beef Fat.

Bull-Meat-Brand Sausage Binder in the percentage proportion of cereal allowed by your State Food Law.

20 lbs. Water.

6 to 8 ozs. Zanzibar Brand Hamburger Seasoning.

1 lb. **Freeze-Em-Pickle.**

2 or 3 large size Onions.

2 lbs. Salt.

First:—Take the 70 lbs. of Beef Trimmings and trim out all the sinew and cut them into small pieces.

Second:—Spread the meat on a table and sprinkle over it 1 lb. of **Freeze-Em-Pickle** to 70 lbs. meat. Mix it thoroughly so that the **Freeze-Em-Pickle** gets to all parts of the meat and then run the meat through a sausage grinder, through a medium fine plate, so as to cut the meat into small pieces, so that the **Freeze-Em-Pickle** is thoroughly mixed with the meat. Then place it in the cooler in tubs or boxes not deeper than six inches and allow it to remain there from one to two days to cure. It is better to allow the meat to cure for two days or longer.

Third:—After the Beef is cured take 20 lbs. of Suet or Beef Fat, from the Brisket is the best, cut it up with 2 or 3 large Onions and run the Beef Fat and Onions through the meat grinder and grind it very fine, then mix the ground Beef Fat with the 70 lbs. of Cured Beef.

Fourth:—Put Legal amount of Bull-Meat-Brand Sausage Binder, 6 to 8 ozs. Zanzibar-Brand Hamburger Seasoning and 2 lbs. of Salt in a pail and add 20 lbs. of cold water. After mixing, add this to the ground Beef and Suet.

Fifth: — Mix the Beef, Suet, Bull-Meat-Brand Sausage Binder, Seasoning, Salt and water together as well as possible and then run it through the meat grinder again.

Notice:—Hamburger Sausage can also be made without curing the meat in advance, if one prefers.

Simply mix the Beef, Fat, Bull-Meat-Brand Sausage Binder, Hamburger Seasoning, Finely Cut-Up Onions, **Freeze-Em-Pickle** and Salt all together, run it through a Grinder and add the water while grinding and mixing, and when ground it is ready for sale. This sausage will, however, have a different flavor than when made of cured meat as above.

Sixth:—After the Sausage is ground, spread it out on a platter, decorate it nicely with parsley, a few pieces of sliced lemon or orange, which adds to its attractiveness.

With each can of Hamburger Seasoning we furnish some of these cards free. Take a beef skewer, split the end of it so the card can be put into the slit and then stick this skewer into the platter of Hamburger Sausage. This little card will help the sale and you will be surprised at the many compliments you will receive on this new Sausage. We will gladly furnish as many as are desired of these cards free of charge to any butcher who is using our Hamburger Seasoning.

DIRECTIONS FOR MAKING
FRESH PORK SAUSAGE

(Copyrighted by B. Heller & Co.; Reprint Forbidden.)

Take 100 lbs. of Fresh Pork Trimmings and while chopping add

Bull-Meat-Brand Sausage Binder in the percentage proportion of cereal allowed by your State Pure Food Law.

¾ to 1 lb. "A" Condimentine.

1 lb. Salt.

8 to 10 ounces Zanzibar-Brand Pork Flavor.

Use sufficient cracked ice to keep the mixture cold. This will make a most delicious pork sausage.

When this is properly mixed it is ready for the stuffer. Pork Sausage should be stuffed into hog casings, or it may be simply put up in bulk.

Note:—By using the above quantity of "A" Condimentine to each 100 lbs. of trimmings, it will prevent fresh pork sausage from turning sour or gray for several days, if kept under proper conditions and at a low temperature. It keeps the pork sausage in a firm, fresh condition. "A" Condimentine does not alter or affect the color of the sausage meat, but simply enables the meat to retain its own natural color. The use of this harmless condimental preparation is a great advantage to all packers and sausage manufacturers, especially when the sausage is shipped distances or is delivered from wagons to the small retailers. "A" Condimentine is guaranteed to comply with the Pure Food Laws and the Federal Meat Inspection Law. Its use is permitted in all U. S. Government Inspected Packing Houses. Sausage does not have to be labeled to show the presence of a preservative when "A" Condimentine is used.

There are many kinds of Flours and Binders on the market, but the Sausage Maker will find Bull-Meat-Brand Sausage Binder to be thoroughly reliable, especially for Pork Sausage, as it does not so easily sour or ferment and it makes an emulsion of the fat and water, and when the Sausage is fried the grease and meat juices will not fry out of it readily, but will remain in the Sausage. Pork Sausage made with Bull-Meat-Brand Sausage Binder is much more easily digested than when made without it, because the fat goes into the stomach in the form of an emulsion when it is eaten, and in this way is more easily digested and absorbed. In using a Binder for Sausage, if it is the Butcher's desire to turn out a Fine-Flavored Sausage and one that is juicy when eaten, it is very important that he be very careful what kind of a Binder he uses. There are many Binders on the market, sold simply for the purpose of making money, which are *utterly worthless*. They make the Sausage dry and instead of improving the quality of the Sausage, they are a great detriment to it. If the Butcher takes a pride in his goods and wants to make Sausage that his trade will like, he should not buy these Binders, as he is simply throwing his money away and spoiling his goods by using them. Therefore, it is always advisable when buying from jobbers to insist upon getting the *Genuine B. Heller & Co.'s Bull-Meat-Brand Flour*, as you will then know exactly what you are getting, as our guaranty is on every package.

SMOKED PORK SAUSAGE

(Copyrighted; Reprint Forbidden.)

Pork Sausage not sold the day it is made may be smoked the following day and sold for Smoked Pork Sausage. Pork Sausage smoked the day after it is made will keep much better than when they are smoked as soon as made, because Sausage that have been kept in a cooler for 24 hours after being made are thoroughly cured, so they will stand the heat of the smoke house, and will have an entirely different flavor than if they are subjected to the heat when the meat is fresh and is not fully cured.

HOW TO CURE MEAT FOR HEAD CHEESE.

(Copyrighted; Reprint Forbidden.)

The proper way to make Head Cheese is to make it from Cured Meat only, and all the Heads and Meat used for it should be cured for 10 to 14 days in a brine made as follows:

1 lb. **Freeze-Em-Pickle.**
7 lbs. of Salt.
5 gals. Water.

Head Cheese made from Meat cured by this process will have a fine red color and will keep well under proper conditions in warm weather. Always add Bull-Meat-Brand Sausage Binder to Head Cheese, as it makes it firm and combines with the fats and juices of the meat, so as to keep the Head Cheese from drying out and thereby losing its flavor.

DIRECTIONS FOR MAKING HEAD CHEESE.

(Copyrighted; Reprint Forbidden.)

The proper meat to use for making Head Cheese is that which has been cured by the **Freeze-Em-Pickle** Process, as above described, but it can also be made from fresh meat if desired. It will, however, be much better and will keep for a longer time if made from meat cured by the **Freeze-Em-Pickle** Process.

First:—Boil the Heads slowly, and long enough so that the meat can be easily stripped from the bone.

131

Second:—Boil the Hog Rinds and the Hog Fat in nets at the same time as when boiling the heads. When the Rinds are almost cooked through, remove them from the kettle and chop or grind them fine. The Fat when cooked, should be cut up into 1¼ to 1½ inch square blocks.

Third:—Also boil about 15 lbs. of Cured Hog Tongues, and when they are cooked, cut them in strips.

Fourth:—The proper proportions for making good Head Cheese are as follows, but, the quantity of the different kinds of meat can be varied according to the stock on hand:

10 lbs. of Fresh Hog Back Fat.

15 lbs. of Cured Hog Tongues.

25 lbs. of Hog Rinds.

60 lbs. Cured Hog Head Meat (after removal from bone). Bull-Meat-Brand Sausage Binder in proportion as allowed of cereal by your State Pure Food Law, but not over 5 pounds.

1 lb. of "A" Condimentine.

1 lb. of White Berliner Brand Konservirung Salt.

If any salt is needed add sufficient to suit the taste. If the meat is fully cured, no salt need be added.

Fifth:—The 60 lbs. of Head Meat must be cut into small pieces ½ to ¾ inch in size, either by hand or by machine.

Sixth:—The Rinds must be cut fine; the finer the better.

Seventh:—The Tongues must be cut into strips. The more Tongues used, the better will be the Head Cheese.

Eighth:—Mix thoroughly together the Tongues, Rinds, Head Meat, Bull-Meat-Brand Sausage Binder, the Prepared Head Cheese Seasoning and 1 lb. "A" Condimentine. At the same time mix into the Meat as much of the Water in which the meat was boiled as the Meat will absorb while being mixed. This water, in which the Heads have been cooked, contains Gelatine which has been drawn out of the meat while boiling, and this water congeals like Jelly when it becomes cold. The more of this water put into Head Cheese the better it will be, therefore add all of it that the meat will absorb. Bull-Meat-Brand Sausage Binder, in the proportion given in the above formula, will make a very different Head Cheese from what can be made with some of the other Binders on the market. It will pay sausage makers to use B. Heller & Co.'s Genuine Bull-Meat-Brand Sausage Binder instead of any of the imitations now on the market. None of the other Binders that we have tested in our laboratory will prove as satisfactory as Bull-Meat-Brand Sausage Binder. If the Butcher uses the best of ingredients and follows the proper methods, he is bound to make the best products; but the most careful sausage maker cannot make fine products unless he uses **good material.**

Ninth:—After the Head Cheese Meat, Bull-Meat-Brand Sausage Binder and water in which the Heads have been boiled are mixed as above directed, stuff in Beef Bungs or Hog Stomachs and boil in water 155 degrees hot until they are cooked through. This will require from one to one and one-half hours, depending upon the thickness.

Tenth:—When cooked, remove from the kettle and place in cold water until they are partly cooled; then lay them on boards and press them down by putting boards over the Head Cheese with weights on them. Head Cheese is sometimes smoked after it is pressed.

Eleventh:—If they are not smoked, rub them with White Berliner Brand Konservirung Salt in order to prevent them from getting slimy.

133

CURING MEATS FOR LIVER SAUSAGE.

Good Liver Sausage should always contain a certain amount of Meat and Fat in addition to the Liver. This Fat and Meat should be cured for a week or two, before making the Sausage, in a brine made as follows:

1 lb. Freeze-Em-Pickle.
7 Ibs. Salt.
5 gals. of Water.

Liver Sausage made from Meat which has been cured in this manner will keep much better after it is made. Where it is necessary to ship Liver Sausage any great distance, or to keep it on hand any length of time after it has been made, the Livers should also be cured in the above brine for two weeks before making the Sausage. The best way to cure the Livers for this purpose is to cut them into strips after they have been chilled for 24 hours and then put them into the brine to cure. Packers who must ship Liver Sausage during the summer months will find the above directions in making Liver Sausage very valuable.

DIRECTIONS FOR MAKING LIVER SAUSAGE.

Take 70 lbs. of Hog Livers, 25 lbs. of Pork Necks; the entire Boned Head can be used instead of the Necks, or the trimmings which are cut from Bellies will work into Liver Sausage very nicely.

First:—Scald the Livers by pouring boiling hot water over them or dip them into boiling water until they are scalded through to the center. Then throw them into the ice water or put them into a tub of cold water and allow the water to run into the tub until the Livers are cooled through to the center, otherwise, they might sour in a short time.

Second:—Cook the Hog Necks, Heads or Bellies and remove all the meat from the bone.

Third:—Chop the meat as fine as possible. When an Enterprise Grinder is used, grind the meat as fine as it can be ground through a fine plate; then add the Livers, which have also been ground as fine as it is possible to get them. The finer and better the Livers and Fat are ground, the finer and better will be the Liver Sausage.

Fourth:—When grinding, add to 100 lbs. of Sausage: 3 large size Onions.

Bull-Meat-Brand Sausage Binder in percentage proportion of cereal as allowed by your State Pure Food Law.

6 to 8 ozs. of Zanzibar-Brand Liver Sausage Seasoning.

1 lb. "A" Condimentine

All of these should then be well mixed, and as much of the Water in which the Meat was boiled should be added to the mixture as the Meat will absorb.

Fifth:—Stuff very loosely into Hog Bungs or Beef Casings, and boil very slowly, otherwise, they will burst; never have the water hotter than 155 degrees. The length of time to boil is ½ to 1 hour, which will depend entirely upon the thickness of the Sausage.

Sixth:—After they are boiled, place in ice water, in which they should be kept until they have been chilled through to the center; then remove them from the water and place in the cooler. After the Sausages are chilled rub the casings with some White Berliner Brand Konservirung Salt, to prevent the Sausage from getting slimy.

DIRECTIONS FOR MAKING BRAUN-SCHWEIGER LIVER SAUSAGE.

(Copyrighted; Reprint Forbidden.)

Braunschweiger Liver Sausage is made of neck pieces from Lean Hogs, Hog Livers, Gut Fat, Trimmings from Bellies and Back Fat, all of which must be steamed before being chopped. For 150 lbs., or less amounts in the same proportion, take:

10 lbs. Gut Fat.
30 lbs. of Belly Trimmings.
20 lbs. of Back Fat.
40 lbs. of Neck Pieces.
50 lbs. of Hog Livers.

First:—Take the above quantities, put them into a kettle and steam them at about 180 degrees or 190 degrees until the meat is tender. Care must be taken

135

that the water does not boil. It should not be hotter than 190 degrees or just enough heated to make it simmer.

Second:—Separate the Livers from the other Meat that has been steamed and chop it or grind it fine.

Third:—Take all of the other Meat out of the kettle, strip it from the bones and rinds, put it in a chopper or grinder, and chop, rock or grind fine. The finer the better. While chopping add:

5 large size Onions.

The Bull-Meat-Brand Flour

10 to 12 ozs. Zanzibar Brand Liver Sausage Seasoning.

1 lb. "A" Condimentine, and as much of the Soup in which the Meat was steamed as the Meat will absorb.

Fourth:—Then put all of the chopped Meat, including the Livers, into a trough and mix all the Meat thoroughly, adding as much more of the Soup while mixing, as the mixture will absorb.

Fifth:—Stuff loosely into Hog Middles or Hog Bungs, and boil very slowly, otherwise, they will burst; boil them until they are filled and swell out. Never have the water hotter than 155 degrees. The length of time to boil is ½ to 1½ hours, which will depend entirely upon the thickness of the Sausage.

Sixth:—After they are boiled, place in cold water—ice water is the best—in which they should be kept until they have been chilled through to the center, but while chilling the Sausages must be turned frequently to keep the grease from congealing to one side; then remove from the water, and place in a cooler. After the Sausages are chilled, rub the casings with some White Berliner Brand Konservirung Salt, to prevent the Sausage from getting slimy.

Seventh:—If it is desired to smoke the Braunschweiger Liver Sausage it can be smoked the following day.

SMOKED COLORED LIVER SAUSAGE

Color the casings in a solution of our Zanzibar-Carbon Brand Casing Yellow Mixture by momentary dipping before watering, cutting and tying them. This will give Liver Sausage the desired smoke shade color.

BLOOD SAUSAGE.

Blood Sausage is always made from partially Cured Meat. This Meat should be cured for 10 to 14 days in a brine made as follows:

1 lb. **Freeze-Em-Pickle.**

7 lbs. Salt.

5 gals. Water.

Blood Sausage made from Meat which has been cured by the **Freeze-Em-Pickle Process** will have a delicious flavor and will keep well in any climate.

Use **Bull-Meat-Brand** Sausage Binder, in percentage proportion of cereal allowed by your State Food Law, in making Blood Sausage, as it tends to absorb fat and meat juices, preventing the Sausage from drying out so readily and becoming unpalatable.

TONGUE BLOOD SAUSAGE

Tongue Blood Sausage is made the same as either Formula No. 1 or Formula No. 2, with the exception that Cured Hog Tongues are added to it. The more Tongues used, the better will be the sausage. Always use Tongues that have been thoroughly cured by the **Freeze-Em-Pickle Process** as they will have a nice red appearance in the Sausage. Boil the Tongues until they are done and then cut into strips and mix into the sausage at the same time as the blood is added.

137

DIRECTIONS FOR MAKING BLOOD SAUSAGE.

(Copyrighted; Reprint Forbidden.)

To make 100 lbs. of Blood Sausage, use the following proportions which we will call **Formula No. 1:**

20 lbs. of Cheek Meat, either fresh or salted.

15 lbs. of Hearts, either fresh or salted.

15 lbs. of Pork Rinds, either fresh or salted.

20 lbs. of Pork Speck (back fat), either fresh or salted.

25 lbs. (3 gallons) of Hog or Beef Blood.

Bull-Meat-Brand Sausage Binder in percentage proportion of cereal as allowed by your State Pure Food Law.

6 to 8 ozs. Zanzibar-Brand Blood Sausage Flavor.

½ lb. "B" Condimentine

2 lbs. of Salt, to suit taste.

½ lb. **Freeze-Em-Pickle.**

Salted Meat is preferable in making Blood Sausage but fresh Meat can be used if desired.

First:—Take 25 lbs. of Fresh Hog or Beef Blood, and stir until the blood remains thin and will not congeal.

Second:—Put the Pork Rinds in a pudding net and boil until about three-quarters done. Care must be taken not to boil them too long, otherwise they will become too pulpy when boiled the second time in the Sausage.

Third:—Boil the Cheek Meat and Hearts until done. The Cheek Meat and Hearts should be boiled as slowly as possible. The slower the boiling the better will be the Sausage.

Fourth:—After they are cooked, put the Pork Rinds in a chopper or meat grinder and cut them as fine as possible. The finer the better. After the Cheek Meat and Hearts have been cooked, they should be cut up coarse by hand, or chopped coarse in a chopper.

Fifth:—The Pork Back Fat must be scalded by pouring boiling water over it for a few minutes. It should then be cut into small squares or cubes by hand or with a pork back fat cutting machine.

Sixth:—After the Meat and Fat are all cut, add to it:

25 lbs. of Beef Blood
The legal amount of Bull-Meat-Brand Sausage Binder.
6 to 8 ozs. Zanzibar Brand Blood Sausage Seasoning.
Salt to suit taste.

Seventh:—Mix these thoroughly and stuff into Beef Bungs, Beef Middles or Rounds. Fill the casings only three-quarters full.

Eighth:—Blood Sausage should be boiled very slowly, the water should not be hotter than 155 degrees. The length of time for boiling depends entirely upon the thickness of the Sausage. When done, the Sausage will float on top of the water and will be firm and plump. It will be necessary to prick the Casings when boiling to let out the air.

Ninth:—When the Sausage is cooked through, remove it from the kettle and place it in cold water; ice water is the best. Allow it to remain in this cold water until it is thoroughly cooled. Then, place on a board in a cooler and allow it to remain there 24 hours before cutting.

Tenth:—It is always advisable to use pickled or dry-salt cured Cheek Meat and Hearts for Blood Sausage instead of fresh ones. To cure them especially for Blood Sausage, they should be cured in brine made with **Freeze-Em-Pickle** according to directions in first paragraph of this article, for two weeks before being made into Sausage. Some prefer to grind the Hearts fine, and leave the Cheeks coarse, and if this is preferred, the Hearts can be ground with the Pork Rinds.

Formula No. 2, for making 100 lbs. of Blood Sausage:

30 lbs. of Pork Speck (back fat).
35 lbs. of Pork Snouts or Ears.
30 lbs. of Hog or Beef Blood.
Bull-Meat-Brand Sausage Binder in the percentage proportion of cereal as allowed by your State Pure Food Law.
6 to 8 ozs. Zanzibar-Brand Blood Sausage Flavor
½ lb. "B" Condimentine.
¼ lb. of **Freeze-Em-Pickle.**
2 lbs. Salt.
Cook and handle Formula No. 2 the same as Formula No. 1, with the exception of leaving out the Hearts and Cheek Meat.

DIRECTIONS FOR MAKING SUMMER
SAUSAGE (CERVELAT)

(Copyrighted by B. Heller & Co.; Reprint Forbidden.)

Use 70 lbs. of Pork Trimmings, 20 lbs. of Lean Beef, 10 lbs. of Pork Back Fat.

First:—Before being made into Sausage, the Back Fat must first be dry salted for two weeks in order to get it properly cured and firm.

Second:—After the Pork Back Fat has been dry salt cured, it should be cut up into small pieces of about one-half inch square.

Third:—The Beef should be first finely chopped; then the Pork Trimmings should be added and then the Pork Back Fat. The meat should be chopped until fine and while it is being chopped add:

2 lbs. of Salt.

½ lb. "B" Condimentine.

8 ozs. Best Granulated Sugar.

10 to 12 ozs. Zanzibar-Brand Summer Sausage Seasoning.

Bull-Meat-Brand Sausage Binder in percentage proportion of cereal as allowed by your State Pure Food Law.

Fourth:—When the Meat is chopped, it should be packed tightly in pans or boxes which should be placed in a cooler having a temperature of about 40 degrees; these pans or boxes should hold about 50 lbs. and should be shallow, not over six to eight inches deep, so that the Meat can be thoroughly chilled through. The Meat in these pans or boxes should remain in the cooler from four to six days before it will be ready to stuff into the Casings.

Fifth:—Stuff the Sausage into Hog Bung Casings or Beef Middle Casings and hang them in a dry room in a temperature of about 45 to 50 degrees for two or three weeks.

Sixth:—They can then be smoked and are ready for the market.

DIRECTIONS FOR MAKING ITALIAN STYLE SALAMI SAUSAGE

(Copyrighted by B. Heller & Co.; Reprint Forbidden.)

Take 60 lbs. of Pork Trimmings.

20 lbs. Lean Beef.

20 lbs. Pork Back Fat.

Bull - Meat - Brand Sausage Binder in percentage proportion of cereal allowed by your State Pure Food Law.

1 lb. of **Freeze-Em-Pickle.**   8 ozs. of Granulated Sugar.
¾ lb. of "B" Condimentine.   2 lbs. of Salt.
10 to 12 ozs. of Zanzibar-Brand Summer Sausage Flavor.
2 to 3 ozs. of Vacuum-Brand Garlic Compound or Garlic Condiment.

First:—Before being made into sausage, the Back Fat must first be dry salted for two weeks to get it properly cured and firm.

Second:—Chop Pork Trimmings and Beef quite coarse, coarser than for Summer Sausage. While chopping add the Bull-Meat-Brand Sausage Binder, **Freeze-Em-Pickle,** Salt, Sugar, Seasoning, "B" Condimentine and Garlic Compound or Garlic Condiment, and when it is partly chopped add the Back Fat which has previously been cut in cubes about one-half inch square. By adding the Back Fat last it will still be in quite large pieces when the Meat is sufficiently chopped. The Fat should show quite prominently in Salami, as it must be fatter than Summer Sausage. Two or three ounces of Vacuum-Brand Garlic Compound or Garlic Condiment should be added while being chopped to give it a delicious Garlic flavor. See pages 260 and 261. The quantity may be varied according to the demands of the trade.

Third:—When the Meat is chopped, it should be packed tightly in pans or boxes, which should be placed in a cooler having a temperature of about 40 degrees. These pans or boxes should hold about 50 lbs. and should be shallow, not over six to eight inches deep, so that the Meat can be thoroughly chilled through. The Meat in these pans should remain in the cooler from four to six days before it will be ready to stuff into Casings.

Fourth:—Stuff the Sausage into Hog Bung Casings or Beef Middle Casings and hang them in a dry room in a temperature of about 45 to 50 degrees for two or three days, then wrap twine around them nicely as shown in cut and again hang up to dry for two to three weeks.

Fifth:—They can then be smoked with cool smoke made with hardwood sawdust only. Wood makes too much heat. Then they are ready for the market.

DIRECTIONS FOR MAKING HOLSTEIN STYLE SAUSAGE

(Copyrighted; Reprint Forbidden.)

Take 50 lbs. of Pork Trimmings.

40 lbs. of Beef Trimmings.

10 lbs. of Pork Back Fat.

First:—Before being made into Sausage, the Back Fat must first be dry-salted for two weeks in order to get it properly cured and firm.

Second:—Put the Beef into the chopping machine and while chopping it add:

2 lbs. of Salt.

¾ lb. "B" Condimentine

1 lb. of **Freeze-Em-Pickle.**

8 oz. of Best Granulated Sugar.

Bull-Meat-Brand Sausage Binder in percentage proportion of cereal as allowed by your State Pure Food Law.

1 small teaspoonful of Vacuum-Brand Garlic Compound or Garlic Condiment.

Let the Beef chop until about one-half done before adding the Pork; then chop the Pork and Beef some before adding the square cut pieces of Pork Back Fat.

Third:—After the Meat is chopped and spiced put it in shallow boxes or pans not over eight inches thick, and put it in a good cooler. Keep the Meat in a cooler for from 4 to 6 days so it is thoroughly cured before it is stuffed.

Fourth:—Stuff in Beef Round Casings and let the Sausage hang in a dry room at 45 to 50 degrees of temperature for a week.

Fifth:—Then give them a good smoke and they are ready for the market. Cool smoke is produced with hickory, hard maple or oak saw dust only. Wood gives off too much heat.

HOW TO COLOR THE CASINGS FOR HOLSTEIN STYLE SAUSAGE

(Copyrighted by B. Heller & Co.; Reprint Forbidden.)

See directions for momentary dipping on page 117. This method can be used equally well on the empty casings. After the casings have a light orange color take them out of the solution and wash them well in hot water, cut and tie them, then stuff the casings and hang the sausage up to dry.

After the sausage has hung a week or two and is dry, hang it in the smoke house for a few days to give it a smoke flavor and it is ready for shipment. This will save a large shrinkage and the sausage will have a better appearance. Sausage that has had the casing colored before being stuffed need not become rancid, as it is not exposed to the heat in a smoke house, which heat always causes the stearin and oil in the fat to separate, and as soon as this change takes place the sausage begins to become rancid.

SWEDISH STYLE SAUSAGE

(Copyrighted by B. Heller & Co.; Reprint Forbidden.)

Take 60 lbs. of Beef. (Boneless Chucks, Briskets and Shank Meat can be used.)

30 lbs. of Pork Ham Trimmings.

10 lbs. of Back Fat.

First:—Before being made into Sausage, the Back Fat must first be dry-salted for two weeks in order to get it properly cured and firm.

Second:—Cut up the Pork Back Fat into square half-inch cubes by hand or with a Pork Back Fat Cutting Machine.

Third:—Put the Beef and Pork on the block

143

and when partly or coarsely chopped add the cubes of Back Fat, and when the Beef and Pork are cut fine, the Pork Back Fat should show prominently through the meat.

While it is being chopped add:

2 lbs. of Salt.

¾ lb. "B" Condimentine.

Bull-Meat-Brand Sausage Binder in percentage proportion of cereal as allowed by your State Pure Food Law.

1 lb. **Freeze-Em-Pickle.**

8 ozs. Best Granulated Sugar.

10 to 12 ozs. Zanzibar-Brand Swedish Style Sausage Seasoning.

Fourth:—After chopping fine, put the Meat in a trough and knead it with the Bull-Meat-Brand Sausage Binder until it is tight and hard.

Fifth:—Pack the Meat tightly in 50 lb. pans or boxes which place in a cooler having a temperature of about 40 degrees; these pans or boxes should be shallow, not over 6 to 8 inches deep, so that the Meat can be thoroughly chilled through. The Meat in these pans or boxes should remain in the cooler 4 to 6 days before it will be ready to stuff into the Casings.

Sixth:—Stuff the Sausage into Beef Middles and hang them in a dry room in a temperature of about 45 to 50 degrees for two or three weeks.

Seventh:—They can then be smoked with cool smoke made with sawdust and are ready for the market.

HOW TO COLOR THE CASINGS FOR SWEDISH STYLE METWURST

(Copyrighted by B. Heller & Co.; Reprint Forbidden.)

See directions for momentary dipping on page 117. This method can be used equally well on the empty casings. After the casings have a light orange color take them out of the solution and wash them well in hot water, cut and tie them.

After the Sausage has hung a week or two and is dry, hang it in the smoke house for a few days to give it a smoke flavor and it is ready for shipment. This will save a large shrinkage and the Sausage will have a better appearance.

Sausage that has had the casing colored before being stuffed need not become rancid, as it is not exposed to the heat in a smoke house, which heat often causes the stearin and oil in the fat to separate, and as soon as this change takes place the sausage begins to become rancid.

DIRECTIONS FOR MAKING POLISH STYLE SAUSAGE

(Copyrighted; Reprint Forbidden.)

Take: 50 lbs of Pork Trimmings.
40 lbs. of Beef Trimmings.
10 lbs. of Pork Back Fat.

Before being used in the Sausage, the Pork Back Fat should be dry-salt cured for at least two weeks or it can be cut from dry salt sides.

First:—Cut up the Pork Back Fat into square half inch cubes by hand or with a Pork Back Fat Cutting Machine.

Second:—Chop the Pork Trimmings, Beef Trimmings and Pork Back Fat quite coarse, and while being chopped add:

2 lbs. Salt.
¾ lbs. "B" Condimentine.
1 lb. of Freeze-Em-Pickle.
10 to 12 ozs. Zanzibar-Brand Polish Style Sausage Seasoning
8 ozs. of Granulated Sugar.
2 to 3 ozs. Vacuum Garlic Compound or Garlic Condiment.

Bull-Meat-Brand Sausage Binder in percentage proportion of cereal as allowed by your State Pure Food Law.

Third:—After the Pork Trimmings and Pork Back Fat have been chopped and mixed with the Salt, "B" Condimentine, Bull-Meat-Brand Sausage Binder, **Freeze-Em-Pickle** and Vacuum Brand Garlic, stuff into beef round casings.

Fourth:—After the sausage has been stuffed into casings place them in the smoke house and thoroughly smoke with wood. This Polish Style Sausage should not be boiled when made. It is boiled when eaten.

HOW TO COLOR THE CASINGS FOR POLISH STYLE SAUSAGE

(Copyrighted by B. Heller & Co.; Reprint Forbidden.)

See directions for momentary dipping on page 117. This method will work equally well on the empty casings. After the casings have a light orange color take them out of the solution and wash them well in hot water, cut and tie them.

After the Polish Style Sausage is stuffed, hang it in the smoke house for a few hours, using wood so as to have a hot smoke. This drys it and gives it a smoke flavor. Then it is ready for shipment. This will save a large shrinkage and the sausage will have a better appearance. Polish Style Sausage that has had the casing colored before being stuffed need not become rancid, as it is not exposed to so much heat in a smoke house, which heat always causes the stearin and oil in the fat to separate, and as soon as this change takes place the sausage begins to become rancid.

THERE IS NO HIGHER ART THAN THAT WHICH TENDS TOWARDS THE IMPROVEMENT OF HUMAN FOOD

HENRY WARD BEECHER

HOW TO MAKE FINE QUALITY BOCKWURST

(Copyrighted by B. Heller & Co.; Reprint Forbidden.)

First:—Take 45 pounds Beef, 20 pounds Veal, 20 pounds Lean Pork, 5 pounds Pork Back Fat (Speck).

Second:—The Meat should all be chopped very fine except the Speck, which should first be cut into small cubes and then added to the rest of the Meat when it is partly chopped so that small cubes of fat will show in the Sausage.

Third:—While chopping, add the following:

Bull-Meat-Brand Sausage Binder in percentage proportion of cereal as allowed by your State Pure Food Law.

½ lb. of **Freeze-Em-Pickle.**

¾ lb. "B" Condimentine.

1½ to 2 lbs. of Salt.

8 to 10 ozs. of Zanzibar-Brand Frankfurt Sausage Seasoning.

3 tablespoonfuls of very finely cut Chives.

6 heaping tablespoonfuls of finely chopped Parsley.

Sufficient artificial ice to keep the meat cool while grinding, added a little at a time.

Fourth:—When the meat is all cut up fine and properly mixed with the spice, it should be stuffed in Narrow Sheep Casings and turned off in links about 2½ inches long.

Fifth:—As a rule Bockwurst is sold without smoking, but it can be given a light smoke if desired.

Sixth:—To prepare Bockwurst for the table, it should be steamed five or six minutes in hot water.

KEEPING SAUSAGE IN WARM WEATHER

Pork Sausage, Bologna, Frankforts, Head Cheese, Liver Sausage, etc., can be kept in a good condition, by simply putting them, every night, in a solution of 1 lb. of Cold-Storine dissolved in three gallons of water. This solution should be kept in the Cooler. In the morning remove the Sausage from the solution, hang it up and expose it for sale, and what remains unsold in the evening, simply put back in the brine for the night.

In this way Sausage can be kept fresh and nice appearing for some time, and it will not **shrink** and **dry up**. This enables the dealer to keep a large, attractive display on hand in his shop without any danger of the goods spoiling.

By keeping the Sausage in this way, it does not dry out, nor become slimy or moldy as it would if hung up in the cooler. Sausage can also be shipped a reasonable distance in a Cold-Storine solution to better advantage than if shipped in any other way.

On arrival it should be removed from the solution, hung up and allowed to drain and dry. In the evening it should be replaced in the same solution for keeping over night.

Never put Smoked Sausage and Fresh Sausage in the same solution. Each kind of Sausage should be kept in a separate solution.

FRESH TRIPE AND PIGS FEET.

Fresh Tripe and Fresh Pig's Feet turn dark and spoil very easily, but by placing them every evening in a Cold-Storine solution made of one pound of Cold-Storine dissolved in three gallons of water, they can be kept in a good condition for a number of days. Every morning they may be taken out of the solution, and those not sold during the day should be put back into the Cold-Storine solution overnight. The solution for Tripe and Pig's Feet should not be used for storing anything else in it.

SWEET BREADS AND BRAINS.

Sweet Breads and Brains can also be kept in the same way as Tripe and Pig's Feet.

First:—Clean the Feet as carefully as possible and then cure them in brine made as follows:

> 6 lbs. of Salt.
> 1 lb. of **Freeze-Em-Pickle**.
> 5 gals. of Water.

The Feet should be cured in this brine from four to five days. This brine can be used over and over again for curing Pickled Pigs Feet, until it becomes thick from the substances drawn out of the Feet.

Second:—After the Feet have been cured for four or five days, cook them as follows: Heat a kettle of water boiling hot; then throw the Pigs Feet into it and keep the heat on until the water begins to boil; then check the fire or steam, and simply let the water simmer just as slowly as possible until the Feet are nicely cooked. The slower they cook, the better, and they ought to remain in the hot water for about four hours, when cooked at a low temperature.

Third:—When they are cooked through, turn on cold water and let the water overflow until all the heat is out of them, and nothing but cold water overflows, and then let the Feet cool well.

Fourth:—Split the Feet through the center and pack them. If they are to be packed in tierces and kept on hand for any length of time, the vinegar that is put over them should be 60 grains strong, but when they are packed in small packages for immediate use 40 grains is strong enough.

Fifth:—When packing the Feet add to every 100 lbs. 8 to 10 ounces of Zanzibar Brand Pickled Tongue Seasoning.

STORING PICKLED PIGS FEET.

(Copyrighted; Reprint Forbidden.)

There are certain seasons of the year when Pickled Pigs Feet are in great demand, while there are other seasons when they are a slow sale. We, therefore, give here a formula for keeping Pickled Pigs Feet in vinegar so they can be kept for one year if necessary in a perfect condition. Salt, cure and boil the Pigs Feet the same as above, but instead of boiling them all done, boil them only about half done; then split them and put them in tierces and fill the tierces with 60-grain vinegar and store in cold storage. The 60-grain vinegar has a tendency to soften the meat. After they have been in this strength of vinegar for some length of time, they will become soft just as if they were thoroughly cooked, but if it is necessary to use them before they are soft, roll them into the engine room or in a place where it is very warm, and turn the tierces on their end. Keep the top of the barrel covered with water—we mean on the top of the head—so that the head will not dry. The bottom of the barrel will not shrink and dry because the vinegar on the inside keeps it moistened, but if the top is not kept wet the barrel will shrink and begin to leak. By allowing the Pigs Feet, which are packed in strong vinegar, to remain in a very warm place for a week or so, they will become nice and tender; they are then to be repacked with 40-grain vinegar in small packages for the market.

PICKLING TRIPE.

(Copyrighted; Reprint Forbidden.)

Select Tripe that is fresh and has not been lying around long enough to attract the bacteria ever present in the air.

Tripe should be prepared by thoroughly cleaning and washing the paunch in at least three or four changes of water. After that, a tub of cold water should be prepared and a lump of unslaked lime, the size of an English Walnut, should be added to about 50 gallons of water. Allow the lime to dissolve and then stir the water to thoroughly mix it. In this solution place the washed Tripe and allow it to soak for five or six hours. The water should be kept cold. A small piece of ice may be put in the water if necessary. Before the Tripe is put into the last soaking water, the inside should be scraped with a hog-scraper so as to remove the inside skin. The outside film or skin should also be scraped off. The boiling vessel should be thoroughly washed before the Tripe is placed in it for cooking. If there is any foreign substance whatever in the kettle, it will discolor the Tripe. On the other hand, it may be turned out perfectly white if the boiling vessel is in proper condition. Two ounces of B. Heller & Co.'s Lard Purifier mixed in 50 gallons of boiling water will assist to keep the Tripe White.

Scald the Tripe thoroughly and scrape both sides well with a hog-scraper. The Tripe is then ready to be cooked.

In cooking, allow the water to come to the boiling point. It should then be reduced to a simmer until the Tripe is thoroughly cooked. When cooked, cold water should be turned on and allowed to overflow until the Tripe has thoroughly cooled. After it is thoroughly cooled, pack in tierces with vinegar that is 60 degrees strong. Always use White Wine Vinegar. If it is desired to ship Tripe after it has been vinegar-cured, it should be repacked in vinegar 40 degrees strong.

To give the Tripe a nice flavor, add to every 100 lbs. of Tripe 8 to 10 ounces of Zanzibar Brand Pickled Tongue Seasoning.

Many have trouble through their inability to cook Tripe tender. This, in most cases, is owing to the fact that the Tripe is boiled too much in water that is too hot. Water in which Tripe is being cooked should be allowed to come to a boil, after that, it should be put on a slow fire where it will cook the Tripe by simmering. A simmer is water that is hot, but not boiling, or 155 to 160 degrees. Boiling water will always shrink and toughen Tripe. It will take longer to cook some Tripe than others, depending upon the age of the animal from which it is taken. Tripe should be allowed to simmer until it is cooked tender.

MINCE MEAT.

(Copyrighted; Reprint Forbidden.)

The following directions will make a delicious Mince Meat:

Take 4 lbs. of lean Beef, boil it until it is fairly well cooked and then chop or grind it very fine.

Add 8 lbs. of Hard Green Apples, cut into small cubes.

1 lb. of very finely chopped suet.

3 lbs. of seeded Raisins.

2 lbs. of Picked Currants, carefully washed and dried.

2 to 5 lbs. of Citron, cut up into small pieces.

1 lb. of Brown Sugar.

1 pint Cooking Molasses (pure New Orleans Molasses is the best, and it must be free from Glucose).

1 quart of Sweet Cider.

1 Tablespoonful of Salt.

1 Teaspoonful of Ground Black Pepper.

1 Teaspoonful of Mace.

1 Teaspoonful of Allspice.

½ Teaspoonful of Cinnamon.

A little grated Nutmeg.

A pinch of Cloves.

Mix the above thoroughly, then heat slowly on the stove and boil for half an hour.

If the Mince Meat is to be put in jars and sealed up tight, the hot Mince Meat should be put into pint and quart jars, the jars should be filled up to the brim and the tops screwed down tight immediately.

If the Mince Meat is to be kept in bulk and not sealed up in jars, add ½ pint of good Brandy after the Mince Meat has been cooked and allowed to become nearly cold, stirring the Brandy into the Mince Meat thoroughly and then pack into stone crocks, cover tightly and keep in a very cool place where the Mince Meat will not freeze. This Mince Meat will keep all winter.

The above quantities can be increased or decreased proportionately, according to the total amount of Mince Meat desired at one time.

Dry or concentrated Mince Meat is made same as above, except that dried apples are used instead of fresh apples, and no liquids are added. Wet Mince Meat is better than the dry and will give better satisfaction.

DIRECTIONS FOR MAKING SOUSE.

(Copyrighted; Reprint Forbidden.)

First:—Take nicely cleaned Pigs Feet, Pigs Snouts, Hocks, Tails or Ears, and put them in a kettle on a stove, or fire or in a steam jacket kettle.

Second:—Add just enough cold water to entirely cover them.

Third:—Boil until the Meat can be removed **from** the bones.

Fourth:—Remove the Meat from the bones, **and** put it back into the water in which it was boiled; then add to this water enough White Wine Vinegar to give it a nice sour taste. The quantity of vinegar will depend upon its strength.

Fifth:—Add the following proportions of spice, which can be changed to suit the amount of Souse you are making. For 100 lbs. Souse use:

2 lbs. of Granulated Sugar.

8 to 10 oz. Zanzibar-Brand Pickled Tongue Seasoning.

Sixth:—Mix the spice with the Meat, and boil about 15 minutes; then remove from the fire. Put the Souse into square tin pans, and allow it to set 24 hours before removal. If desired, a lemon and 2 or 3 good sized Onions may be cut into small pieces, and mixed in the Souse before it is boiled; some like this, and some prefer it without Onion or Lemon. Do not use **too** much Lemon as it will make the Souse taste bitter.

VINEGAR PICKLED PIGS TONGUES.

(Copyrighted; Reprint Forbidden.)

Take salted Pigs Tongues that have been cured for 30 days and scald them in hot water; then remove the skin and gullet. Boil slowly for three hours, the same as boiling Pigs  Feet; the slower they are boiled the better; then cool the Tongues, in the same manner as directed for cooling Pigs Feet.

Another way is to take them out of the Brine and cook them, and then take off the skin and gullet after they are cooked. When handling large quantities, this latter method will not work as well as the first method, because after the Tongues are boiled, they must be cooled in the same vat, and after they are cooled, the skin does not remove so easily. That is why it is better to scald them in boiling water first and then remove the skin and gullet, then boil them.

Split the tongues through the center and pack in Vinegar the same as Pigs Feet and add to every 100 lbs. of Tongues 8 to 10 ounces Zanzibar-Brand Pickled Tongue Seasoning.

HORSERADISH.

(Copyrighted; Reprint Forbidden.)

Home-made horseradish is a relish that every household demands. It is impracticable to put grated horseradish upon the market except when bottled, as exposure to the air discolors it and dries it out. An excellent bottled article which will prove a good keeper as well as a good seller can be made as follows: To ten parts of grated horseradish add one part of granulated sugar and one part of pure vinegar. In preparing horseradish none but white wine vinegar should be used. One of the best means of getting new trade is for a Butcher to sell home-made grated horseradish.

SAUER KRAUT.

(Copyrighted; Reprint Forbidden.)

Select sound cabbages and peel off the first or damaged leaves, then slice or shave with a cabbage cutter as fine as possible. The object desired in making first-class Sauer Kraut is to obtain a perfect fermentation under pressure with the aid of salt alone. The brine, therefore, results from the water contained in the salt and cabbage, no water being added. First secure a good strong cask, which should be

well scalded and cleaned. Sprinkle on the bottom of this cask a small quantity of salt, then put in a layer of cabbage and while adding the cabbage sprinkle some salt through it, so that the salt is as much divided as possible and then tamp well with a wooden tamper, so as to pack it as tight and solid as possible. Continue putting in layer of cabbage and tamping this way until the barrel is full. The salt to be used should always be of the best grade and one pound of salt to one hundred pounds of cabbage should be used but may be varied according to the taste. Some prefer it saltier than others. After the cask is filled or as full as desired, the cabbage should be covered with a clean cloth on which should be laid hardwood boards. Use the boards taken out of the head of a whiskey barrel or tierce as this makes the best cover, as they fit in the barrel and are made of hardwood and will not give the cabbage a taste. Carefully weight the boards down with heavy stones, always remembering that the fermentation should be accomplished under pressure. Once a week take off the stone, board and cloth from the cabbage and wash them clean and replace the cloth and boards and stones on top of the barrel after they have been washed. By repeating the washing of the boards and cloth and stones every week, the top of the cabbage will be kept perfectly sweet and the foam which comes to the top is removed, so that the top of the Sauer Kraut will be as good as that in the bottom of the barrel. The Kraut should be left to ripen for about four weeks in a warm temperature. It is always best not to offer it for sale until it has sufficiently ripened and is tender and juicy and that it has the proper flavor. This can only occur after perfect fermentation has taken place.

PICCALILLI.

(Copyrighted; Reprint Forbidden.)

This sauce is easily prepared and is in considerable demand by some trades. Select good, firm, green tomatoes, wash them thoroughly and cut away all defective portions of the tomatoes. They should then be sliced or quartered and placed in a salt brine made with one pound of salt to each gallon of water with a supply of green peppers. Let them cure in this brine for two weeks. They may then be taken out and chopped very fine, about $\frac{1}{8}$ to $\frac{1}{4}$ inch in diameter. They are then ready for the vinegar, which should be pure in quality, the white wine vinegar being preferred. The vinegar should be first prepared or sweetened and spiced with pure granulated cane sugar, cloves, cinnamon, mustard seed and a small quantity of celery seed. This can be poured over the chopped tomatoes and peppers, either hot or cold. Piccalilli should be sold nearly or quite strained of its vinegar.

CHOW CHOW.

(Copyrighted; Reprint Forbidden.)

Chow Chow is a popular sauce that can be readily prepared. It is strictly a Chinese innovation which was introduced to the American palate during the first immigration of Chinamen. It is merely the cucumber pickle cut up into small pieces with the addition of cauliflower, onions, etc., over which is poured a preparation of mustard, vinegar and various condiments which taste may demand. Chow Chow is a good keeper and a good seller, but in order to retain its flavor and color, it should be carefully covered and kept from exposure to the air.

DILL PICKLES.

(Copyrighted; Reprint Forbidden.)

All butchers should put up home made pickles of all kinds and such relishes as horseradish and sauer kraut. Dill pickles are very popular and they are always salable in the butcher shop. They may be made as follows: Select large pickles of as near an even size as possible and soak in water over night; then wash them thoroughly. Next,

HOME-MADE DILL PICKLES

take a barrel and put a layer of dill about one inch thick on the bottom of it, upon which place the pickles three layers deep. Over these pickles place another layer of dill and repeat the layer of pickles as in the first instance. Continue this operation of the layer of dill and then pickles until the barrel is as full as desired, leaving sufficient space for the brine. The brine should be made of the best quality of salt, using ½ lb. to each gallon of water. Brine thus made will make the natural soft home-cured dill pickles. After the brine has been placed over the pickles, place them in a cooler and let them ripen for about four weeks. The ripening process may be quickened about two weeks by leaving the pickles in a room of moderate temperature. Some prefer dill pickles hard and for such taste it is necessary to put a little alum in the brine. Pickles treated with alum must be labeled to show this. A piece about as big as an egg for a full barrel of pickles is the proper amount. Dissolve this in the brine. This will keep the pickles firm and hard. It will be found, however, that most tastes prefer the natural brine without the alum, as the soft pickle seems to have a more appetizing flavor. There is no appetizer more appreciated than the dill pickle and it comes nearer appealing to the general trade than most any relish that can be offered.

HOW TO DRESS POULTRY.

The Butcher who will make a specialty of dressed poultry will make a hit with his customers and good profit on sales if he will be careful to get his Chickens dressed decently, and to educate his customers to pay prices that will be commensurate with the quality of the meat offered. Very often it is almost an impossibility for the consumer to secure sweet, untainted Poultry Meat. Much of this trouble is owing to the fact that large shippers kill the Chickens, dry pick them or scald them, and the food that remains in the intestines ferments and taints the meat, with the result that the Chicken, when cooked, has an abominable taste.

When a Butcher is so situated that he can dress his own Chickens, and he would be fully justified in making all preparations in that direction, he ought to open, draw and wash out thoroughly every chicken as fast as it is killed, just as he would wash out Hogs, Calves or Sheep. Chickens that have been nicely drawn and washed immediately upon killing are always sweet in flavor, and the Butcher who will take the pains to offer such goods and to acquaint his customers of their quality can not only establish a large trade and a great reputation, but he can offer the public an article that is pure and sweet, and difficult to obtain. No doubt he could command the Chicken trade of any neighborhood by this means, down all competition, and obtain good prices for his Meat, as people would be willing to pay for the original weight of the chicken before drawing, and at the same time would be much better satisfied with what they get. If desired, the Butcher could weigh the chickens after they are dressed, tag and draw them, and then could say to his customers: "This Chicken weighed so much before it was drawn, but in order to retain the sweetness of the meat, we draw it as it ought to be drawn, wash it out, and sell it to you for just what it is worth." A Butcher's statement upon these points would not be doubted. Furthermore, the Butcher would not lose anything by this method, as Chickens shrink after they are dressed and kept two or three days before sold. The loss from this shrinkage is considerable. Therefore, the trouble and expense of drawing Chickens and handling them in the manner described would be fully repaid.

STICKY FLY PAPER.

Every Butcher can make his own Sticky Fly Paper with very little trouble. It is made as follows:

1 lb. Rosin.

3½ oz. Molasses.

3½ oz. Boiled Linseed Oil.

Boil the three together until they get thick enough and then spread on heavy Manilla paper. The proper and quickest way is to take a sheet of heavy Manilla paper and spread the mixture on half of the surface of it, then double the paper over; the mixture put on the half will be quite sufficient to coat the face of the other half that is doubled over on it. The cost of making this sticky fly paper is very small and in an hour any Butcher can make enough Sticky Fly Paper to last the entire summer.

B. HELLER & CO.

RENDERING LARD

One of the things much neglected in many butcher shops is the making of Lard. Butchers who do not cut up enough hogs to have fat for making Lard each day, allow the fat to accumulate until they have sufficient so as to make it worth their while to render it. Many butchers do not keep this fat in the ice box, but let it stand anywhere, because they imagine that it does not spoil; then, when they make Lard out of it, they wonder why the Lard is not better.

Lard should always be made as soon as possible, and the fat trimmings should be kept in the cooler and not allowed to remain standing around in a warm place. To make high grade Kettle-Rendered Lard, always cut the rinds off of the fat. The rinds can be put into pickle and stored until a quantity has accumulated and then they can be cooked and utilized in Liver Sausage, Head Cheese or Blood Sausage. When the rind is cooked with the lard, it always causes more or less detriment to the lard.

Before rendering, if one has the machinery, the fat should be run through a regular fat hasher or a **Meat Grinder, and** it should be ground up into small pieces. The smaller it is ground the better, for if the fatty tissues are thoroughly mangled and disintegrated, the oil will separate more readily when the heat is applied. Those butchers not having a machine in which they can cut up the fat should cut it into small pieces by hand.

For making Kettle-Rendered Lard a steam jacket kettle is the best, but if one does not have steam, a common caldron will answer, but great care must be taken not to scorch the lard or allow it to become too hot when a caldron is used.

RENDERING LARD IN JACKET KETTLE OR CALDRON.

Before putting the fat into the kettle, put in a gallon of water for every 100 lbs. of fat, as the water prevents the lard from scorching. Then put in all the fat to be rendered and start the fire or slowly turn on the steam, as the case may be.

In rendering Lard the heat should be brought up gradually, so that quite a little of the fat is melted before the full heat is applied. If the heat is brought up too rapidly, it will cause the Lard to be darker in color than when it is gradually heated.

Lard should be boiled about 1½ hours after the entire mass is boiling.

Those butchers who wish to render their Lard scientifically, with the aid of a thermometer, can do so by hanging a thermometer in the Lard and bringing the temperature gradually up to 255 to 260 degrees Fahrenheit, and then turn off the steam or check the fire, as the case may be, and allow the Lard to cook slowly until it is finished.

A butcher can always tell when the Lard has cooked sufficiently by the way the cracklings press out.

After the Lard has all been tried out, skim out all the cracklings, put them into a press and press out all the Lard, adding what is pressed out to that in the kettle.

Now the Lard is ready to be strained through a piece of cheese cloth.

LARD PRESS

IF ONE HAS A LARD SETTLING TANK, AS HERE ILLUSTRATED, HANDLE THE LARD AS FOLLOWS:

(Copyrighted; Reprint Forbidden.)

SETTLING TANK

After treating the Lard as directed, with Lard Purifier and water, and after the Lard has been treated enough to make it foam, and the foam has been skimmed off, dip the Lard and water out of the kettle, run it through a piece of cheese cloth into the settling tank. A settling tank is simply a galvanized iron tank with a large faucet at the bottom. The bottom can be made to taper to the center and the faucet placed in the center, so all the water can be drained off, or the bottom can be made flat with the faucet close to the bottom, and the tank can be set slanting, so the water or Lard will all drain out.

After the Lard is in the settling tank, let it settle for one or two hours, according to the size of the tank and quantity of Lard in it. Then drain off all the water and the impurities which have settled to the bottom. After these are drawn off, the Lard is ready to be run into buckets, which should be placed in the ice box to cool.

A better way is to let the Lard settle in the settling tank and, after the water is drawn off, stir the Lard with a large paddle until it is thick and creamy, and then it should be put into buckets. By letting it cool in the settling tank and stirring it until it is thick and creamy, Lard will have a much better appearance when cold than Lard that is run into buckets hot.

162

HOW TO PURIFY LARD WITH ONLY A COMMON RENDERING KETTLE.

(Copyrighted; Reprint Forbidden.)

After the Lard has been rendered as above, treat as follows: The kettle must not be too full of Lard; it should not be more than three-fourths full when being treated with the Purifier.

Put a thermometer into the Lard to test the temperature. If the temperature of the Lard is below 200 degrees Fahrenheit, add to every 100 lbs. of Lard 3 ounces of B. Heller & Co.'s Lard Purifier, dissolved in one quart of water. For example, if the kettle contains 400 lbs. of rendered Lard, add 12 ounces of Lard Purifier dissolved in one gallon of water.

Should the temperature of the Lard be over 200 degrees F., do not add the Lard Purifier and water, but let the Lard stand for half an hour or so, until the temperature comes below 200 degrees.

If the Lard Purifier and water are added to the Lard when it is as high as 212 degrees F., the water will at once be converted into steam as soon as it gets into the Lard, because water is converted into steam at that temperature. When the Lard Purifier and water are added to Lard that is too hot, the Lard will foam up and boil over; but, when the Lard is below 200 degrees F. and the Lard Purifier and water are added, it will not boil up.

After adding the Lard Purifier and water, take a paddle and stir the Lard thoroughly, so the Lard Purifier is mixed thoroughly with every part of the Lard; then turn on the steam or build up the fire slowly, as the case may be, and heat the Lard up to 212 degrees F. The minute 212 degrees is reached the Lard will begin to foam. When the Lard gets to this point, it should not be left for a moment, because if it gets too hot it will boil over the top of the kettle; but if one stays right with it when it begins to foam, and checks the fire, it will not boil over but will foam a little and most of the impurities will rise to the top of the Lard. Now stop the fire and skim off all the impurities on the top of the Lard and allow the Lard to settle for about two hours, when all the water and the smaller impurities that did not rise to the top will have separated from the Lard and will be at the bottom, and one will be

- - -

surprised at the amount of impurities that will thus be separated from the Lard.

If the kettle has a faucet at the bottom, draw off the water and the impurities which have settled and then run off the Lard. Should the kettle not have an opening at the bottom, dip out the Lard from the top, being careful not to dip out any of the water which will be at the bottom. When most of the Lard has been taken out, that remaining, which is near the water, can be dipped out together with the water, and put in a bucket or tub and allowed to harden.

The lard will float on the top and when hard can easily be taken off from the top of the water, and should be kept until the next Lard is rendered, when it should be re-melted with the next batch of Lard.

Before running the Lard into buckets, it is always well to run it through a piece of cheese cloth, so as to remove any small pieces of detached cracklings. It is advisable to put the Lard into the ice box as soon as it is run into buckets, so as to set it, which will prevent the separation of the oil from the Stearin.

IF ONE HAS NO SETTLING TANK, BUT SIMPLY HAS A RENDERING KETTLE AND AN AGITATOR, HANDLE LARD AS FOLLOWS:

(Copyrighted; Reprint Forbidden.)

First:—Render the Lard in the Rendering Kettle, and treat it with B. Heller & Co.'s Lard Purifier, the same as directed in the foregoing. After it is treated, run the Lard through two or three thicknesses of cheese cloth, into the Agitator. Allow it to settle in the Agitator for two hours, then run off all the water from the bottom, and start the Agitator. The Lard should be agitated until it is thick like cream, then it is ready to run off. We, however, recommend that Lard should be taken from the Rendering Kettle and put into the Settling Tank and allowed to settle, and then the Lard should be run from the Settling Tank through the faucet about an inch above the bottom, into the Lard Cooler, and while in the Cooler it should be agitated until it becomes thick. There are always small particles of charred tissue which will settle to the bottom of the Settling Tank, which cannot be gotten out in any other way, and the Lard will be whiter and purer if allowed to settle in the Settling Tank and then drawn off into the Cooler.

IF ONE HAS A LARD SETTLING TANK AND AN AGITATOR, HANDLE THE LARD AS FOLLOWS:

A Packer or Butcher who makes any quantity at all of Kettle Rendered Lard, should have a Rendering Kettle in which the Lard is rendered, a Settling Tank in which the Lard is settled, and a Lard Cooler with an Agitator in it. The Lard Cooler and Agitator should be double-jacketed, so that cold water can be run into the jacket to cool the Lard.

When equipping a plant with a Settling Tank and Cooler, we advise that the Settling

COOLER AND AGITATOR

Tank have two faucets in it; one at the extreme bottom and the other about one inch from the bottom. Then, when the water is drawn off of the Settling Tank, it should be drawn off from the lowest faucet, and when the Lard is drawn off into the Agitator, it should be run off through the faucet which is an inch from the bottom. In this way, small particles which may be in the Lard will remain in the bottom of the Settling Tank, in the one inch layer of Lard which remains in the bottom of the Settling Tank. After all the Lard is run off through the upper faucet, what remains between the upper faucet and the bottom of the Settling Tank should be drawn off through the lower faucet and should be kept until the next time Lard is rendered, and then should be re-rendered with the next batch.

After the Lard has been rendered and has been treated in the Rendering Kettle, with the Lard Purifier, strain it through a cheese cloth into the Settling Tank, allow it to settle for two hours, then draw off all the water from the bottom faucet. After the water has been drawn off, draw off the Lard from the top faucet and again run it through cheese cloth, into the

Cooler and Agitator. Start the Agitator and allow it to run until the Lard is thick and white, like cream, and then run it off into buckets or tubs.

A good way to set up the Settling Tank and the Cooler and Agitator, is to have the Settling Tank high enough up, on a bench above the Agitator, so that the Lard can be run out of the Settling Tank into the Agitator. The Cooler and Agitator should also be high enough from the floor so the Lard can be run from it into buckets or tubs.

It costs very little to properly equip oneself with the proper apparatus, and if properly rigged up it is a pleasure to make the Lard and requires very little work.

HOW TO PURIFY RENDERED LARD.

(Copyrighted; Reprint Forbidden.)

First:—Put 100 lbs. of water into the lard kettle and add to it one-quarter to one-half pound of B. Heller & Co.'s Lard Purifier; then on top of the water put 100 lbs. of the rendered Lard.

Second:—If a steam kettle is used, turn on the steam; and if the kettle is heated by fire, start the fire; the heat should be applied slowly and must be closely watched, so that the Lard does not get too hot and boil over. In no case should more Lard and water be put into the kettle than to fill it one-half full. By thus having the kettle only half full it leaves plenty of room for the Lard to boil and foam and prevents it from boiling over the top of the kettle.

Third:—While the Lard is being heated stay right with it at the kettle to watch it and continually stir it.

Fourth:—When the Lard begins to boil check the fire and let it simmer from 10 to 15 minutes, then put out the fire or turn off the steam and let the Lard settle for about three hours; all the impurities that come to the top skim off carefully.

Fifth:—After the Lard has settled for three hours all the water will be at the bottom. If the kettle is provided with a faucet at the bottom so the water can be let off, let the water run out slowly until it is all drained out; if the kettle has no opening in the bottom, skim the Lard off from the top of the water and place the Lard in a Lard Cooler. If you have a

Lard Cooler with an Agitator, start the Agitator and keep it running until the Lard gets thick like cream; it is then ready to run off into buckets. If you have no regular Agitator, it is necessary to stir the Lard by hand occasionally until it gets thick and creamy; stir it as much as possible until it gets thick, and then run it into buckets.

LARD NOT PURIFIED.

If Lard is made without taking out the impurities with water and our Lard Purifier, the Lard will become rancid if it is to be kept during the hot weather, and it will not be so sweet in flavor nor as clean and white as it is when treated with our Purifier according to the preceding directions. Our Lard Purifier neutralizes the free fatty acids in the Lard, thus to a considerable extent preventing rancidity and helps keep the Lard Sweet and Pure.

Lard made with our Lard Purifier according to the foregoing directions will comply with the regulations under the various Pure Food Laws.

COMPOUND LARD.

(Copyrighted; Reprint Forbidden.)

In the Southern States, where the climate is warm, it is necessary to add either Tallow or Tallow Stearin or Lard Stearin to Lard, so as to stiffen it in order that it can be handled at all.

To make Compound Lard, first render the Lard and press out the cracklings as directed; then add from 10 to 20 per cent of either Tallow, Tallow Stearin or Lard Stearin and stir until it is all melted and thoroughly mixed with the Lard. The quantity of Tallow or Stearin to add depends upon the climate and season of the year, and also the price of the different materials.

After adding the above, purify the mixture, the same as directed for handling Pure Lard. However, Compound Lard must always be agitated until it is thick and cream-like before it is run into buckets. If one has no Lard Agitator, it must be stirred by hand until it is stiff and cool.

It is perfectly legal to add Tallow, Tallow Stearin or Lard Stearin to Lard for this purpose, but such

167

Lard must be sold as Compound Lard. It cannot be sold as "Pure Lard" when these ingredients are added to it.

COTTON SEED OIL-LARD COMPOUNDS.

(Copyrighted; Reprint Forbidden.)

For certain purposes Cotton Seed Oil added to Lard is preferred to straight Lard, and the Cotton Seed Oil is added after the Lard has been purified and is ready to put in the Agitator.

To make a really good Compound Lard, a Cooler with an Agitator is absolutely necessary, but if one hasn't a cooler with Agitator, it can be done by stirring by hand continuously, so the Lard and Oil do not separate while cooling.

When Cotton Seed Oil is used, it must be Refined Cotton Seed Oil, and the more it is refined the better the compound will be. Lard should always be run through cheese cloth before putting it in the Lard Cooler, so as to take out any small particles of detached cracklings which may remain in the Lard.

The formula for making Compound Lard with Cotton Seed Oil varies according to the relative values of the ingredients and the quality of Compound desired. The usual Compounds found on the market, as sold at the present time under trade names, and which contain no Lard at all, are made of 80 per cent Cotton Seed Oil and 20 per cent Tallow Stearin . (Tallow Stearin is Tallow with the oil pressed out of it.) A small butcher can make this Compound by using 80 per cent Cotton Seed Oil and 20 per cent Rendered Tallow, which has previously been purified with B. Heller & Co.'s Lard Purifier.

If it is desired to make a better quality of Compound, use less Cotton Seed Oil and add sufficient Lard to bring the cost and quality to the desired degree.

All such Compounds must be sold as "Compound Lard" when Lard is added; but when no Lard is added, they must be sold as "Lard Substitutes." These preparations are perfectly legal, and comply with the Pure Food Laws provided they are labeled and sold for what they are, but no one should make a Lard Compound or Imitation Lard and sell it for Pure Lard.

REFINING LARD WITH FULLER'S EARTH.

THE METHOD USED FOR REFINING LARD IN LARGE PACKING HOUSES.

The large packers all refine Lard and Tallow with the Fuller's Earth process, and for the benefit of the small packers, who would like to know how it is done, we will give the full directions, although a small packing house can hardly afford to put in a plant for the process, as it requires a man who is experienced to refine Lard and Tallow in this manner. If a packing house does not make enough Lard and Tallow to afford to keep a man especially for this purpose, it will not pay to put in a refinery, which consists of the following machinery: A Receiving Kettle, which is a large open tank with steam coils in it to dry the Lard or a large Jacket Kettle will do. A Clay Kettle, which is a tank with steam coils in it for heating the Lard and an air pipe at the bottom of it connected to an air compressor. A Lard Cooler with Agitator to cool and stir the Lard while it sets so as to have it thoroughly mixed. A Pump, Air Compressor and Filter Press. An ordinary size outfit will cost from $2,000 to $3,000.

First, the Lard, Tallow or Cotton Seed Oil, which is termed stock, is placed in the Clay Kettle. The Clay Kettle is simply an iron jacket with a coil in the bottom of it through which air is pumped. In this kettle, the Fuller's Earth is added. To each and every 100 lbs. of stock, there is added from one to two lbs. of Fuller's Earth; the quantity depending upon the grade of stock. Before the stock is treated a small test is made as follows. A small quantity is heated; in a part of it one per cent of clay is put, in another part 1½ per cent, and in another two per cent. Mix each lot thoroughly, put them into a funnel over filter paper and allow them to filter. By examining these samples, one can tell how much earth to use to the stock in the kettle. This must be done when the stock varies. Of course, when the Lard, Tallow, or Oil are running uniform, it is not necessary to make the test, but where the stock changes, it is always advisable to test before treating, for the reason that too much Fuller's Earth put into the stock will give the Lard an objectionable flavor. Before stock of any kind can be treated with Fuller's Earth, all the moisture must be out of it; Lard usually contains two to three per cent of moisture, and very often considerably more, so it must be heated in a Jacket Kettle until all the water is evaporated. If there is any water in the Lard, the Fuller's Earth attacks the water first, and the Lard is not affected, because wet Fuller's Earth has absolutely no effect upon Lard. When the Fuller's Earth is added to Lard, it must be 155 degrees hot; Tallow must be 185 degrees hot, and Cotton Seed Oil 140 degrees hot. After the desired heat is obtained, regulate the steam so the temperature will remain stationary, turn on the air, and when it is blowing hard, put in the Fuller's Earth and blow for about 20 minutes; then start the force pump and pump the stock through the Filter Press. If the stock is of fine quality and only a small percentage of Fuller's Earth is used, it can be pumped directly into the Receiving Kettle, but if a large percentage of Fuller's Earth is used, it is advisable to let the Lard run back into the Clay Kettle, and keep on letting it run through the filter and pumping it round until it is thoroughly clarified; then allow it to run into the Receiving Kettle.

If inferior stock is used, sometimes as much as four and five per cent of Fuller's Earth is used to refine it, but it is not advisable to use that large amount as the clay gives off an odor which the stock sometimes absorbs. Always use the least amount of clay that good judgment indicates will do the work, and after pumping through the filter, if it is not as it should be add more clay and refilter it.

To make Compound Lard, treat the different stocks separately, run them in different tanks, and then mix them. After they have been put into the receiving tank or the mixing tank, it is advisable to mix them by blowing air into the bottom of the kettle in which are

Lard, Tallow and Oil; this will mix even better than any process or method that we know of. The amount or kind of stock to be used depends upon the season of the year, and the kind and quantity of goods you wish to make. Equal parts of Tallow, Lard and Oil make a very good Compound. All the cloths for the Filter Press should be washed every day after using them as they must be kept perfectly clean; the cleaner the better.

After the Compound Lard has been thoroughly mixed it must be put into an Agitator and agitated until it is thick like cream before it is run off into buckets.

HOW TO RENDER TALLOW WHITE, ODORLESS, FLAKY AND SOFT, LIKE LARD IN TEXTURE

(Copyrighted; Reprint Forbidden.)

It is an easy matter to render Tallow so it will have a very light color, in fact, will be almost white and at the same time flaky and soft like Lard, if the instructions which follow are carried out. When so rendered, the Tallow will sell at a good price, as it will be entirely free from a tallowy odor, and is an excellent thing for baking purposes. Tallow rendered according to these instructions can be mixed with Lard and it will even improve the Lard. But it must be sold for what it is.

Take Beef Suet and all the Beef Fat trimmed from steaks and other cuts, and run it through a Chopper, chopping it very fine. It will thus become soft and sticky so it can be rolled in small balls about one and one-half to two inches in diameter. While this is being done, fill Rendering Kettle half full of water, dissolving in the water about two ounces of Lard Purifier to every 100 lbs. of Tallow to be rendered, and start it to boil. While the water is boiling the small balls of Tallow should be placed on top of the water until a sufficient number of balls have been thus put into the water to make a layer three or four inches deep, but not deeper. After the Tallow is rendered out of the balls, the heat should be turned off and the Tallow should be permitted to cool. Just as soon as the boiling has ceased, all the cracklings that are on the surface should be skimmed off, put into a press **and**

171

pressed out. The Tallow that is on the surface should be skimmed off and put into buckets. Care should be taken that no water is taken out with the hot Tallow. The tallow which remains on the water can be left there until it is hard, when it can be taken off and melted if desired, and then run into buckets. The advantage in rendering Tallow in this manner is to prevent the Tallow from becoming too hot, and thus to keep it from turning dark; besides, the water and Lard Purifier purifies the Tallow and also draws out the tallowy odor.

Any butcher can build up a large trade on home-rendered tallow when it is prepared in this manner. In fact, his trade will like the Tallow so well that he will not be able to supply the demand. As a rule, the butcher sells his Tallow unrendered at a low price, but if he will render it himself and follow the above instructions carefully, he can sell the Tallow for at least 10 to 12 cents per pound, owing to the fact that Tallow rendered in this manner produces a very fine fat for cooking purposes. We believe it is much better than Lard.

NEAT'S FOOT OIL.

(Copyrighted; Reprint Forbidden.)

Neat's Foot Oil is made by simply boiling the feet of cattle in a water bath, in an open kettle. The oil will come out of the feet and float on the top of the water. After the oil has been cooked out of the feet, they should be skimmed out of the kettle. The oil should then be treated with our Lard Purifier, the same way as directed for treating Lard. Simply let the water and fat cool down to 200 degrees Fahrenheit or below, and to every 100 lbs. of oil add about four ounces of our Lard Purifier dissolved in a quart of water. Stir the water, Lard Purifier and Neat's Foot Oil thoroughly, and then start up the fire and bring it to a boil. Skim off any foam and impurities that may come to the surface and then stop the fire and allow it to settle about two hours; then skim the oil off of the top of the water and you will have genuine, sweet and refined Neat's Foot Oil.

KILLING ON THE FARM.

Very often butchers in the smaller towns find it convenient to slaughter live stock in the country where it is purchased. In order to meet such cases we submit the following directions for slaughtering cattle, hogs and sheep, and no doubt they will be found useful and suggestive.

It is absolutely necessary that only healthy animals shall be slaughtered for food. It is not so important that stock should be fat, although no one can expect the best results from lean animals, but as there is a demand for all grades of meat, condition is not so exacting as health.

In the case of injured animals, crushed ribs, broken limbs, etc., the flesh is not good for food unless the stock has been slaughtered immediately upon receiving the injuries.

AGE FOR KILLING.

It is a well known fact that the meat of old animals is tougher than that of young ones. The flesh of young animals frequently lacks flavor and is not solid. An old animal in proper condition and good health is preferable as food to a younger one in poorer condition.

Cattle if properly fed are fit for beef at 12 to 24 months, although the meat from these animals often lacks flavor, especially if they have not been well fed. The best meat is from aged steers 30 to 40 months old. A calf should not be slaughtered under four weeks and is not at its best until about eight weeks of age. There is a law in many States confiscating veal offered on the market under six weeks of age.

Pigs may be used after six weeks but the most profitable age at which to slaughter hogs is between eight months and one year.

Sheep may be used at from 3 to 4 months of age; but are at their best from eight to twelve months.

PREPARING FOR SLAUGHTER.

Experience dictates that an animal intended for slaughter should be kept from eating for twenty-four to thirty-six hours before killing. If kept on full feed the system is gorged and the blood, loaded with assimilated nutrients, is pumped to the extremities of the capillaries. It is impossible to thoroughly drain the blood from the veins when the animal is bled, and the result will be a reddish-colored, unattractive carcass. Again, food in the stomach decomposes very rapidly after the animal is slaughtered. Where the dressing is slow, as it must be on the farm, the gases generated from the stomach often flavor the meat. It is well to give water freely up to the time of slaughter as it aids in keeping the temperature normal and helps in cleaning out the system, resulting in a nicer colored carcass.

It is but natural that the condition of animals prior to slaughter should have a positive effect on the keeping qualities of the meat. There should be no excitement sufficient to raise the temperature of the body. Excitement creates fever, prevents proper drainage of the blood vessels, and, if intense, will cause souring of the meat very soon after dressing. No animal should be killed after a long drive or rapid run about the pasture. It is always better in such cases to permit the animal to rest over night rather than to risk spoiling the meat. The flesh of an animal that has been overheated and then killed is usually of a dark color and frequently develops a sour odor within a few hours after dressing. Bruises cause blood to settle in the affected portions of the body, often causing loss of a considerable part of the carcass. A 24-hour fast, ample water, careful handling and rest are necessary in order that the meat may be in the best condition for immediate use or curing.

KILLING AND DRESSING CATTLE.

The first step in killing is to secure the animal so that, in no emergency, it can escape. Use a rope one inch in diameter. Put a slip noose in one end with a knot just far enough from the noose to prevent choking when drawn tight, but it should at the same time allow the noose to draw tight enough so that there is no danger of escape, in the event of the rope becoming slack. If the animal has horns, pass the noose over the head, back of the ear and horn on the right side, but in front of the horn on the left side of the head. This operation leaves the full face of the animal bare and does not tighten on the throat. When a dehorned or polled animal is to be slaughtered it

will of course be necessary to put the noose around the neck. Attach an ordinary pulley to a post or tree close to the ground, to the barn floor or sill, pass the rope through it and draw the animal's head down as close to the pulley as possible.

Administer a heavy blow in the center of the forehead at a point where lines from the base of the horns to the eyes would cross. Shoot-

Fig. 2—Beef: Illustrating method of securing to stun. Intersection of dotted lines show place to strike.

ing has the same effect as stunning and may be resorted to. Frequently where an animal can not be brought to the pulley it is necessary to shoot. In shooting use only a rifle of good caliber.

Bleed the animal immediately by sticking just in front of the breast bone as shown in Fig. 3. Stand in front of the animal with back toward the body after the manner of a horseshoer. Reaching down between the front feet, lay open the skin from breast-bone toward the chin for a distance of 10 to 12 inches, using the ordinary skinning knife. Insert the knife

175

with the back against the breastbone and the tip pointing to the spinal column at the top of the shoulders, cutting just under the windpipe and about 5 to 6 inches in depth at the junction of the jugular vein near the collar bone; at this point if the vein is severed the blood will run out rapidly. If stuck too deep, the pleura will be punctured and blood will flow in the chest cavity, causing a bloody carcass. It requires practice to become expert in the sticking of beef. Not so much skill is required to simply cut the animal's throat back of the jaws but the time required for bleeding is very much longer and the bleeding less thorough.

SKINNING AND CUTTING.

Begin skinning at once while the carcass is lying on its side by splitting the skin through the face from the head to the nose as shown in Fig. 4. Skin the face back over the eyes on both sides and down over the cheeks, cutting around the base of the horns so as to leave the ears on the hide. Split the skin down the throat to meet the cut made in bleed-

ing. Start the skin in slightly on the sides of the neck and down to the jaws. Now remove the head by cutting just back of the jaws toward the depression back of the head as shown in Fig. 5. The atlas joint will be found at this point and may be easily unjointed with the knife.

Fig. 3—Beef: Place to stick and manner of sticking.

At this point the carcass should be rolled on its back and held in position by a small, strong stick, say 18 inches long, with a sharp spike in both ends. Insert one end in the brisket and the other in the floor or ground. This will hold the carcass in position. Then split the skin over the back of the four legs from between the dew-claws to a point three or four inches above the knees. Skin around the shin and knee, unjointing the knee at the lowest joint as seen in Fig. 6 and skin clear down to the hoof.

The brisket and fore-arms should not be skinned until after the carcass is hung up. Now cut across the cord over the hind shin, splitting the skin from the dew-claws to the hock up over the rear part of the thigh to a point from four to six inches back

Fig. 4—Beef: Skinning the face, illustrating manner of starting.

of the cod or udder. Skin the hock and shin, removing the leg as shown in Fig. 7. In splitting the skin over the thigh turn the knife down flat with the edge upward to avoid the cutting of flesh. While the hind leg is stretched ahead it is skinned down over the rear of the lower thigh but do not skin the outside of the thigh until the hind-quarters are raised. After the legs are skinned split the skin of the carcass over the midline from the breast to the rectum.

Fig. 5—Beef: Removing the head.

Now begin at the flanks and skin along the midline until the side is nicely started. With a sharp knife held flat against the surface have the hide stretched tightly and remove the skin down over the sides with steady down-strokes of the knife, as shown in Fig. 8. But it is necessary that the hide should be stretched tightly and without wrinkles. Care should be taken to leave a covering of muscles over the abdomen of the carcass as it keeps it better. In siding the

Fig. 6—Beef: Showing manner of unjoining fore leg and skinning shank.

beef, it is usual to go down nearly to the back bone,

177

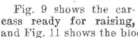

leaving the skin attached at thighs and shoulders; skin over the buttock and as far down on the rump as possible, always avoiding cutting the flesh or tearing the membrane over it. A coarse cloth and a pail of hot water should be at hand while skinning and blood

spots wiped quickly from the surface, but the cloth should be nearly dry, as the less water used the better. Open the carcass at the belly and pull the small intestines out at one side. Use a saw or sharp ax in opening the brisket and pelvis. After raising the windpipe and belly and cutting loose the pleura and diaphragm along the lower part of the cavity, the carcass will be ready to raise.

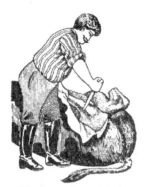

Fig. 7—Beef: Unjointing the hind leg.

Fig. 9 shows the carcass ready for raising, and Fig. 11 shows the block and tackle rigging attached to the carcass about to be raised.

When the carcass is raised to a convenient height, skin the hide over the thigh, rump and hips. While in this position, it is well to loosen the rectum and small intestines and allow them to drop down over the

Fig. 8—Beef: "Siding down;" knife held flat against the tightly stretched skin.

paunch. The fat lining, the pelvis and the kidney fat should not be disturbed nor mutilated. The intestines may be separated from the liver to which they are attached by the use of a knife. The paunch is attached to the back at the left side and may be torn loose. Let it roll on the ground and cut off or draw off the

178

gullet. The carcass at this point is shown in Fig. 11. Now raise the carcass a little higher and take out the liver, having first removed the gall bladder. Now remove the diaphragm, lungs, the heart, and finish skinning over the shoulders, forearms and neck, as shown in Fig. 12. Sponge all the dirt and blood off with a cloth, split the carcass in halves, using a saw, c l e a v e r or sharp ax, wash out the inside of the chest cavity and wipe it dry.

Fig. 9—Beef: Ready to raise: Breast, forearms and neck, left covered to protect the meat until the carcass is raised.

Trim off all bloody veins and s c r a g g y pieces of the neck and leave the beef to cool before quartering.

Fig. 11—Beef: Removing paunch and intestines.

Fig. 12—Beef: Skinning
shoulders and forearms.

13.—Beef raised out of the
way of animals to cool.

Fig. 13 shows the finished carcass hanging high up
and cooling.

180

KILLING AND DRESSING MUTTON.

If the sheep is an old one, it should be stunned. If a young one, dislocating the neck after cutting the throat serves the same purpose. This is accomplished by placing one hand on top of the head, the other under the chin, and twisting sharply upward. Lay the sheep on its side on a platform, with its head hanging over the end. Grasp the chin in the left hand and stick the knife through the neck back of the jaw, turning the cutting edge of the knife toward the spinal column and cut the flesh to the bone. By so doing it is impossible to cut the windpipe. (See Fig. 14.)

Fig. 14—Manner of Sticking a Sheep.

Split the skin over the back of the front leg from the dewclaws a little above the knee. (See Fig. 15.) Open the skin over the windpipe from breast to chin, starting in slightly on the sides of the neck. Split the skin over the back of the hind leg through the middle line and skin the buttock. Raise the skin over the udder or cod and flanks. Skin around the hocks and down to the hoofs, cutting off the feet at the toe joints. Run the knife between the cord and bone on back of the chin and tie the legs together just above the pastern joint. Do not skin the legs above the hock until the carcass is hung up.

Fig 15.—"Legging out" a sheep.

Hang the sheep up by the hind legs, split the skin over the middle line; start at the brisket and "fist off" the skin. This is done by grasping the edge of the pelt firmly in one hand, pulling it up tight and working the other with the fist closed between the pelt and the body, over the fore-quarters downward and upward and backward over the hind-quarters and legs. It is unwise to work down on the skin over the hind legs, as it would rupture the membrane. The wool should always be held away from the flesh as a matter of cleanliness, and the skin on the legs should be pulled away from the carcass rather than toward it. When the pelt has been loosened over sides and back, it should be stripped down over the neck and cut off close to the ears.

Fig. 16—Fisting off the Pelt.

Remove the head without skinning by cutting through the atlas joint.

GUTTING.

Remove the entrails by cutting around the rectum and allowing it to drop down inside, but do not split the pelvis. Open down the belly line from cod or udder to breast bone; take out the paunch and intestines, leaving the liver attached to the diaphragm. It is not best to split the breast. Reach up in the pelvis and pull out the bladder. Wipe all blood and dirt from the carcass with a coarse cloth wrung dry from hot water. Double up the front legs and slip the little cord found by cutting into the fleshy part of the forearms into the ankle joints.

Fig 17.—Removing the intestines of sheep.

KILLING AND DRESSING HOGS.

A good sticking knife, hog hook, scrapers, a barrel or a trough for scalding, and a convenient place for working are the important necessities. Set the barrel at the proper slant with the open end against a table or platform of the proper height, with the bottom securely fastened; a strong tackle built for the purpose is desirable, but not necessary. Hogs should not be excited or heated, and in catching and throwing them bruising must be avoided. However, it is not necessary to stun hogs before sticking them. At slaughter houses they are usually hung up by one hind leg. If

Fig. 18.—Manner of holding and sticking a hog.

there is no hoisting appliances, lay the hog on its back and hold it there until stuck. Two men can handle a hog if they will but work with intelligence. By reaching under the animal, one at the fore leg and the other at the hind leg, they can turn a heavy hog on its back easily. One man, standing astride the body, with his feet close against the side and holding its front feet, can control it while the other does the sticking.

Fig 19.—Scalding a hog. Note arrangement.

The knife should be eight inches long, straight bladed and narrow, and stuck into the hog's throat just in front of the breast bone, the point directed toward the root of the tail and held in line with the back bone. This is necessary to prevent cutting between the ribs and the shoulders, which would cause the blood to settle there with waste in trimming of the shoulder. When the knife has been stuck in six or eight inches, according to the size of the hog, turn the knife quickly to one side and withdraw it. The arteries that are to be cut run close together just inside of the breast bone and both are cut when the knife is turned, providing the edges are sharp at the point.

The water for scalding when heated in the house should be boiling when removed from the stove. If put into a cold barrel it will be about the right temperature when the hog is ready for scalding. During the scalding process the water should be about 185 to 195 degrees, if the scalding tub holds only enough water to scald one hog. Water at 150 degrees will scald a hog, but, of course, more time is required. In large packing houses where a large tub is used and steam is continually blowing into the water, the water is kept at 150 degrees. Too hot water is likely to cause more trouble than too cold, and for this reason it is always best to have a thermometer at hand. Of course, the temperature may be reduced by putting in a little cold water. A hog should not be scalded before it is dead or the blood in the small blood vessels near the surface of the skin will cook and give a reddish tinge to the carcass.

To make the hair easy to remove and to cleanse the skin of the hog and free it from all the greasy filth which forms a scurf on the skin of all hogs, our Hog-Scald should always be used. Hogs scalded with the aid of Hog-Scald do not require so much heat to loosen the hair, it requires much less labor to clean them, and the dressed hogs will look much nicer and the rinds will cure and smoke nicer than when it is not used. No Farmer or Butcher will dress his hogs without Hog-Scald after giving it a trial. For description and price list on Hog-Scald, see page 278.

While being scalded the carcass should be kept moving constantly to avoid cooking the skin. While scalding, the hog should occasionally be drawn out of the water for air, when the hair may be tried. When both hair and scurf slip easily from the skin, scalding is completed. Remove the carcass from the water and begin scraping. The head and feet should be cleaned first, as they do not clean easily when cold. Use a "candlestick" scraper on the head. Use the hands and a knife if you haven't this tool. The feet and legs are easily cleaned by grasping them firmly with the

Fig. 20.—A convenient way of hanging up a hog.

hands and twisting them around and back; pull the little bristles of the body by hand and remove the scurf and fine hair with the scraper, long corn knife or other tool. Wash the entire carcass with hot water and shave it with a sharp knife. Insert a stick under the gambrel cords and hang up the hog.

Wash down with hot water, shave patches and rinse with cold water. Occasionally the hog is too large to scald in a barrel. Cover it thickly with blankets or sacks containing a little bran, pour hot water over it and the hair will be readily loosened.

GUTTING HOGS.

Split the hog between the hind legs, separating the bones with a knife. Run the knife down over the belly line, guiding it with the right hand and shielding the point with the fingers of the left hand and thus avoid the danger of cutting the intestines. Split the breast-bone with a knife or an ax and cut down through the sticking place to the chin. Cut around the rectum and pull down until the kidneys are reached, using a knife whenever necessary to sever the cords attached to the back. Do not disturb the kidneys or the fat covering them, excepting in warm weather, when the leaf may be removed to allow quicker and more thorough cooling. Remove the paunch and the intestines. The gall bladder lies in plain sight on the liver, and it lies attached to the diaphragm and hypatic vein. It should be stripped off after starting the upper end with a knife. Avoid spilling the contents on the meat. Insert the fingers under the liver and strip it out. Cut across the artery, running down the backbone, and cut around the diaphragm, removing them with the pluck, that is, heart, lungs, liver and gullet. Open the jaw and insert

Gutting the Hog

a small block to allow free drainage. Wash out all blood with cold water, and dry with a coarse cloth. In hot weather the backbone should be split to facilitate cooling. The fat should be removed from the intestines before they get cold. It is strong in flavor and should not be mixed with the leaf lard in rendering.

CLEANING CASINGS.

Those who undertake to clean casings have great trouble in getting them white and many resort to lime and other methods for both bleaching them and freeing them of fat. Notwithstanding all such efforts, the casings remain dark and unattractive. The reason for much of this difficulty lies in the fact that the casings are not properly washed and cleaned in the first operation. Casings should be washed thoroughly in three different changes of water. The fat should then be scraped off from the outside. Water must also be run through the casings and they should be turned inside out so that they may become thoroughly washed and cleaned. After casings have been perfectly washed and scraped in this manner, they should be dry-salted by packing them in a liberal quantity of salt. Casings thus cured will remain sweet and white.

HANDLING HIDES.

The proper handling of the hides of slaughtered animals, so as to obtain the best possible prices for them and avoiding excessive shrinkage before they are marketed, is a very important matter and should have the Butcher's careful attention.

In the first place, it should be borne in mind that it is an easy matter to badly damage the hide of an animal before killing by prodding it with a pole. This of course should always be avoided.

The killing floor should be kept as clean as possible. If there is blood on the floor and this gets on the hair and remains there, when the hides are stacked up this blood comes in contact with the fleshy side of the hide next to it and will make a spot which gives the hide a very bad appearance. By keeping the hides entirely free from blood, they make a better appearance and bring a better price.

The greatest care should be given to the removal of the hide, so they are not scored, as this greatly reduces the value of the hides to the tanner. A good, careful skinner is worth several dollars a week more to the Butcher who kills many animals than a skinner who is careless in his work. (The hide should be so nicely removed from the animal that when it comes to the tanner it should look like it had been planed from the animal, it should be so so free from cuts or scores.)

PROPER STORAGE OF HIDES.

(Copyrighted; Reprint Forbidden.)

This is a point of very great importance. If many hides are kept on hand for any length of time before shipment, the difference in shrinkage between hides which are properly kept and those which are not so stored is very great. The careful storing and handling of hides will always repay the time and trouble necessary, not only in the weight of the hides, but in the condition in which they are marketed.

Hides should be kept in as cool a room as possible and all windows and doors should be kept closed, so as to have no circulation of air.

SALT TO USE IN SALTING HIDES.

(Copyrighted; Reprint Forbidden.)

The best salt to use for this purpose is Crushed Rock Salt. Large lumps of salt are objectionable, on account of leaving indentations in the hides where they are pressed together, which injures their appearance in the eyes of the buyer.

One part of Fine Salt to three parts of Crushed Rock Salt makes a fine mixture for salting hides, as the fine salt quickly dissolves and makes a moisture on the hide, which the hide absorbs.

When re-using old salt for salting hides, always add about one-third of new salt to it, as this gives much better results. About one-third of the salt used is consumed in salting hides, so by adding one-third additional of fresh salt each time, the supply of salt is kept the same. Always keep the salt as clean as possible. If there is much dirt or manure in it these will discolor the hides and they will not make as good a showing to the buyer.

QUANTITY OF SALT TO USE ON HIDES.

(Copyrighted; Reprint Forbidden.)

In large Packing Houses about 35 lbs. of salt is used for each hide. The Packers find that by using this quantity they get better results than if a smaller quantity is used. Very few Butchers in the country use as much salt as this on their hides, but they would find it greatly to their advantage to use about 100 lbs. of salt to every three hides, and if the proper quantity of salt is used, as described in the foregoing, it can be used over and over again with a loss of about one-third for each time used. It is much better for the Butcher to invest more money in salt and give the hides a proper amount, as he will thus save on the excessive shrinkage of the hides, which would amount to more than the cost of the salt.

HOW TO STACK HIDES WHEN SALTING.

(Copyrighted; Reprint Forbidden.)

One of the most important features in salting hides is the way they are stacked when salted. The hides must be so piled that they are perfectly level and the salt must be distributed over every part of the hide. The flesh side should be up, and the salt should be rubbed over them evenly. The hides can be piled about two feet high. The legs of the hide should be kept straight and flat, so the salt gets into all crevices. The edges of the stack of hides should be kept a trifle higher all around than the center of the stack, so the natural moisture that comes out of the hide and the dry salt will remain on them. If the hides are salted on a slanting floor, or if the hides are piled up carelessly so the hides lie slanting, the brine composed of moisture of the green hide and the salt will run off and then the percentage of loss from shrinkage will be large.

HOW LONG TO CURE HIDES.

Hides should lie in the pack and salt for 25 to 30 days, so as to be fully cured and ready for shipment.

TRIMMING OF GREEN HIDES.

(Copyrighted; Reprint Forbidden.)

Before the hides are salted the switches should be cut off of the tail and all loose ends of the hide should be cut off. The butt of the ears should also be split; if the hides go into the pack without attention to this point, it makes the pack very uneven on account of the thickness of the ear, and the salt does not have a chance to properly penetrate the ears, and they are liable to spoil. Loose pieces of meat that are carelessly left on the hides and all excessive fat should be trimmed off. Hides must not be salted until five hours or longer after the animal is killed, and they must not be piled closely, as this would prevent the animal heat from escaping. If hides are salted with the animal heat in them, very often the hair will slip, which will make No. 2 hides.

SALTING SWITCHES.

Switches should be spread out on the floor so they will thoroughly cool off. After they are thoroughly cool, they can be piled into a heap and salt applied so they are entirely covered. The more salt put over them the better, as they spoil very easily.

TANNING SKINS.

(Copyrighted; Reprint Forbidden.)

Butchers can easily tan the skins of Sheep, Goats, Cattle and Calves with Tanaline, and they can often pick up fine skins of wild animals, which can also be easily tanned. By tanning the fancy skins that the Butcher frequently can get, he can sell them for three or four times as much as he would realize when sold to the Hide Buyer.

DIRECTIONS FOR TANNING SKINS.

First:—After weighing the skins, soak them in plain cold water; fresh or salted skins for 24 hours, and air dried skins for at least 48 hours. Then scrape off all the fat with a dull instrument, such as a putty knife or sharp piece of hard wood. Then wash thoroughly, with cold water, both sides of the skin.

Second:—Use, for every 30 pounds of skins, a 2-pound package of Tanaline and 4 pounds of salt. Dissolve 2 pounds of Tanaline and 4 pounds of salt in 5 to 6 gallons of cold water, and when thoroughly dissolved, place the skins into it. Have sufficient water so that all the skins are entirely covered. Tan small, thin skins in this solution for 24 hours. Goat, sheep, calf and dog skins should be allowed to tan from two to three days, according to their thickness. Cattle or horse skins, or skins of a similar nature, require one week in this solution to properly tan them. During the tanning process remove the skins and replace them in the same solution twice a day, so that the solution gets over all parts of the skins uniformly. After tanning, drain off all the solution that can easily be drained off, and spread the skins out with the flesh side up, away from the sun.

Third:—Make a heavy flour paste; thin enough to spread easily. Now cover the entire flesh side of the skin with a thin layer (about one-eighth inch) of this paste. Let the skins and flour paste dry for two to four days, according to the weather. The paste will absorb the moisture out of the skins and soften them.

Fourth:—When the skins become dry, work them so that the paste is shaken off. If the skins have been allowed to dry too long, they will be too hard to work, and they should be softened by sprinkling some dampened sawdust over the skins and leaving it on them over night. The skins should next be softened and worked by pulling them over the edge of a table or box, until soft and pliable.

POLISHING HORNS.

(Copyrighted; Reprint Forbidden.)

If the horns are rough, first take a file and file through the rough horn, down to the solid horn, and file the horn into proper shape, smoothing the tip and shaping the large end to suit the fancy. After they have been filed, take sand paper and rub the horn with the sand paper until it is nice and smooth, then finish the rubbing with very fine sand paper, so as to take out all the scratches. After it has been sand papered, take a piece of glass and scrape it until very smooth. Polish by rubbing with powdered rotten stone and machine oil. The polishing must

be done with the palm of the hand, and the horn should be rubbed until beautifully polished.

WHY DRIED BEEF DOES NOT THOROUGHLY DRY.

Query.—R. B. writes: "We are having trouble with our Dried Beef. It doesn't seem to dry out. We have it hanging in the cooler."

Ans.—Your beef doesn't dry out because you keep it in the cooler. In order to dry beef, it is necessary to hang it in a dry room. You can hang it right out in the market for that matter and there it will dry rapidly, in fact, it will dry too quickly so that it will become hard. Dried Beef will dry some in the smoke house, but not sufficiently. We send you a copy of our book, "Secrets of Meat Curing and Sausage Making," which will give you full particulars in reference to this entire subject.

BULL-MEAT PREFERABLE FOR SAUSAGE.

Query.—Z. & R. write: There is a prevailing notion among local butchers that bull meat possesses qualities which make it superior to first-class steer or cow meat for making bologna and weiners. Is this not an erroneous idea? How can bologna and weiners be prevented from turning dark and shrinking within a few days after making if exposed to the air?

Ans:—The opinion of your local butcher is correct as far as it concerns bull meat as the best meat for bologna and wienerwurst. The reason for this is that bull meat contains a great deal of gelatine in various forms and far more than even the meat of either steer or cow. If you take the bull meat and chop it up, you will find that it is sticky and binds together, while if you take meat from an aged cow and chop it up it will not bind together, is mushy and soft to the touch, and when cooked frequently crumbles and falls apart.

In answering your next question, we can say that the probable cause in most cases why sausage dries up, shrivels up, shrinks or turns dark within a short time after being made is because it was not properly handled. It is also possible that these effects of which you complain were due to causes produced by the way you salted your meat or what you salted it with. If you will follow our instructions on Bologna making given in our book "Secrets of Meat Curing and Sausage Making," you should have no further trouble. The book is sent free.

HOW TO MAKE A PAPER BAROMETER

Question.—J. K. writes: Can you tell me how a Barometer can be made with paper that tells what the weather is going to be?

Answer.—Paper barometers are made by impregnating white blotting paper in the following liquid, and then hanging up to dry:

Cobalt Chloride	1 oz.
Sodium Chloride	½ oz.
Acacia	¼ oz.
Calcium Chloride	75 gr.
Water	3 fl. oz.

The amount of moisture in the atmosphere is indicated by the following colors:

Rose Red	Rain
Pale Red	Very Moist
Bluish Red	Moist
Lavender Blue	Nearly Dry
Blue	Very Dry

B. HELLER & CO.

SOUR SAUSAGE

Question.—B. & W. write: We have been using your Bull-Meat-Brand-Flour through all of last winter, and found it satisfactory in every way. We have been using also your Freeze-Em Pickle. Since hot weather began our sausage has soured. We have lost over 100 lbs. of sausage through its souring. Can you tell us what is the probable cause of our sausage becoming sour?

Answer.—We will say that the cause of your sausage souring may be due to several things. Either your grinder has become dull, causing the meat you run through it to heat in the grinding, or it may be due to the fact that the meat was not cold enough to prevent it from heating while being ground.

Another cause for trouble of this kind is in the mixing machine. In mixing meat too much, a considerable quantity of air is forced into the meat, which will often cause it to sour during the warm seasons of the year. During hot weather it is advisable to grind a small quantity of ice with the meat to keep it cold.

We also advise the use of our "A" Condimentine preparation. This is a very useful product for keeping in condition all fresh sausage. It is entirely harmless, containing no substances injurious to health. Complies with all pure food laws.

We are quite positive that you are souring your meat in the grinding, or in the mixing. Please let us know if you have a mixing machine, or whether you mix your meat by hand. If you have no mixing machine you are souring your meat while grinding it. You should mix ice with your meat before grinding it. Grind the meat and the ice together, and use "A" Condimentine. Your troubles will then disappear.

194

SPICED BEEF

Question.—W. C. K. writes: I was very much interested in your magazine "Success With Meat," and wish you would send me a formula for the making and curing of Spiced Rounds of Fresh Beef. In our city we have a great demand for spiced beef and I want the very best formula obtainable, which I know you can furnish me. I have used Freeze-Em-Pickle for a good many years and always get splendid results from its use.

Answer.—We are very glad that you like "Success With Meat," and are pleased to learn you have obtained such uniformly good results with Freeze-Em-Pickle.

To make rolled spiced beef take 100 lbs. of boneless beef plates and cure them in brine made as follows:

5 gallons of cold water.
5 lbs. of common salt.
1 lb. Freeze-Em-Pickle.
2 lbs. of granulated cane sugar.
6 to 8 ounces Zanzibar Brand Corned Beef Seasoning.

Cure the plates in this brine 10 to 20 days in a cooler. The temperature should not be higher than 42 to 44 degrees Fahr., but a temperature of 38 to 40 degrees is better for curing purposes.

The Zanzibar Brand Corned Beef Seasoning gives a delightful flavor to the brine. After the meat has been fully cured in accordance with the above formula sprinkle some Corned Beef Seasoning on the meat; then roll the meat and tie it tight with a heavy string. Some people also like a garlic flavor and if desired a small quantity of Vacuum Brand Garlic may be added to the brine or sprinkled over the meat before it is rolled. Where you want to cure rumps or rounds of beef that weigh from 12 to 25 lbs. each, we advise that you pump them just the same as a ham would be pumped with a pumping brine made as follows:

½ lb. of Freeze-Em-Pickle.
1 lb. of pure granulated sugar.
2 lbs. of salt.
1 gallon of water.

By following the above suggestions carefully you should have no trouble in turning out delicious corned beef.

SOUR HAMS—HOW TO PREVENT.

Query.—F. B. writes: "Have you any chemical compounds that will help us to take care of some sour hams? We have some hams that are just a little sour and thought perhaps you would help us in the matter."

Ans.—We do not prepare anything which would help you in the least. The trouble arises from imperfect curing and the only time that we could have been of help to you would have been when you commenced to put the hams in the pickle; we could have then given you full instructions for pickling the hams in such a way that they could not have soured. In nearly all cases the souring is around the bone. In your case it is best to cut out the bone and trim away the sour meat. After being thus carefully trimmed, they can be rolled, tied and sold for boned hams. You can always avoid the danger of sour hams by exercising extreme care in properly chilling the meat before curing. Most all souring arises from the fact that the meat is not chilled through to the bone. If all the animal heat is thoroughly removed before curing, the hams will come out of the pickle cured all the way through.

If you will follow closely the directions contained in our book, "Secrets of Meat Curing and Sausage Making," you will never have trouble with your hams. We take great pleasure in sending you a copy of this book free of charge.

FREEZE-EM-PICKLE LEGAL EVERY-WHERE.

Query.—S. G. Co.: You will please send us a 500-lb. barrel of Freeze-Em Pickle, if you can guarantee it to comply with the Pure Food Laws.

Ans.—Shipment of 500 lbs. Freeze-Em-Pickle, which you ordered by mail, went forward today. We beg to inform you that this product complies with requirements of all Pure Food Laws and is perfectly legal to use everywhere. We know that you will be highly pleased with Freeze-Em-Pickle. The Freeze-Em-Pickle process of curing meat gives it a uniform bright red color and a sweet sugar cured flavor and enables it to retain all of its albumen. It also prevents the meat from drying up and hardening when fried or cooked, or from crumbling when sliced up after being cooked. It may be used in the brine, or it can be sprinkled dry over the meat before it is packed for storage. See our directions for using it.

MAKING SOAP FROM RENDERED FAT

Question.—C. J. B. writes: Can you give me a formula for making soap? I have a surplus stock of rendered fat that I would like to convert into soap.

(Copyrighted by B. Heller & Co.; Reprint Forbidden.)

Answer.—We will give a very good formula for making soft soap and hard soap.

To 20 pounds of clear grease or tallow take 17 pounds of pure white potash. Buy the potash in as fine lumps as it can be procured and place it in the bottom of the soap barrel, which must be watertight and strongly hooped. Boil the grease and pour it boiling hot upon the potash then add two large pailfuls of boiling hot water; dissolve 1 pound of borax in 2 quarts of boiling hot water and stir all together thoroughly. Next morning add 2 pailfuls of cold water and stir for half an hour; continue this process until a barrel containing 36 gallons is filled. In a week, or even in less time, it will be ready for use. The borax, and also one pound of rosin, can be turned into the grease while the grease is boiling.

Soap made in this manner is a first-rate article, and has a good body. The grease must be tried out, free from scraps, ham rinds, bones, or any other similar kind of matter; then the soap will be as thick as jelly, and almost as clear. To make soft soap hard put into a kettle four pailfuls of soft soap, and stir in it by degrees about one quart of common salt. Boil until all the water is separated from the curd, remove the kettle from the fire and draw off the water with a siphon (a yard or so of rubber hose will answer); then pour the soap into a wooden form in which muslin has been placed. For this purpose a wooden box sufficiently large and tight, may be employed. When the soap is firm turn out to dry, cut into bars with a brass wire and let it harden. A little powdered rosin will assist the soap to harden and give it a yellow color. This must be added in the kettle when the soap is boiled. If the soft soap is very thin, more salt should be added.

WHY BOLOGNA DRAWS WATER WHEN IT IS BOILED

Question.—J. B. writes: I again write you for information. When I boiled my bologna the meat drew water. I added the water the second time I ground the meat. Why did the meat draw water while the sausage was being boiled?

I am glad to say that your advice in reply to my last letter enabled me to completely overcome the trouble I had with my corned beef. I am now using the galvanized iron tank as you recommended, and have discarded my old corned beef barrel. I will further say that since I began using your products, that I am selling three times as much sausage as I formerly did. I am greatly pleased with all the goods that I have bought from you.

Answer.—There are three principal reasons for meat drawing water while the bologna is being boiled. The first is that you probably "killed" the meat in the grinding of it, by your knife not being sharp enough, or that your meat soured in the grinding of it by the meat not being cold enough. If you desire to work in some water while grinding the meat, use chipped ice instead of water. The ice will keep the meat cool and stiff, and the meat will not quash, or mash down. The use of ice will prevent the meat from getting warm.

Another cause for bologna drawing water while being boiled is that you have heated the bologna too hot while it was in the smokehouse, or you are boiling bologna at too high a temperature. Boiling bologna at 160 degrees Fahrenheit would hardly spoil it, but we recommend boiling bologna at 155 degrees Fahrenheit.

Possibly you boil the bologna too long. When you take your bologna out of the cooking water do you pour cold water over them? This also has a bearing on the case. Watch carefully all of the above points and you will not have any more trouble. Refer to our book.

OLD BARRELS INFECTED WITH GERMS
WILL CAUSE ROPY BRINE

Question.—W. & Sons write: Can you advise us about our corned beef pickle? We made it according to directions given in your book, "Secrets of Meat Curing and Sausage Making." But our brine gets "ropy" as you call it. We use pure cane sugar. We keep our cooler at 38 to 40 degrees Fahr., and are at a loss to know what is the cause of our trouble. Please advise us in this matter.

(Copyrighted by B. Heller & Co.; Reprint Forbidden.)

Answer.—Ropy brine can come about even when pure cane sugar is used in curing. This condition is caused by germs which develop in the brine and cause the brine to thicken. You will find that the barrels which contain your brine are infected with germs. The best way to get rid of these germs is to first empty the barrels; then put the barrels into a vat and boil them. Also scrub the barrels inside and outside. For this purpose they should be rinsed with boiling water to which has been added Freeze-Em, 4 ounces to each gallon, and afterwards a last rinsing with our Ozo washing powder, or soda, in the water that you use for washing the barrels. After the barrels are thoroughly washed and rinsed with cold water, they should then be put out of doors where the sun can shine upon them and in them for several days before they are again used and placed in the cooler.

Barrels in which corned beef is cured should be made of hardwood. If you are using a syrup barrel or a molasses barrel, you will find that the pores of the wood have become filled with syrup or molasses, which causes the brine to become thick. We think this is the cause of your trouble.

The best barrels to use are tierces that are made of oak, such as lard is shipped in by the packers. The wood of these tierces becomes saturated or filled with lard, and the lard prevents the brine from penetrating or soaking into the wood. Be sure that whatever barrels you use are made of hardwood, and not of white wood or other soft wood, of which many kinds of barrels are made.

HOW TO MAKE FERTILIZER FROM BEEF BLOOD

Question.—J. E. P. writes: Please tell me how to utilize and handle beef blood so as to make fertilizer out of it. I am killing from ten to fifteen head of cattle each week, and thus have quite a quantity of blood.

Answer.—Blood in a packing house is handled as follows: It is first drained from the killing floor into vats and when the vats are filled, live steam is turned on and the blood is boiled until congealed. It is then put in large powerful presses and all the water pressed out, the congealed blood remaining in the press cloth. From the presses it is put through a fertilizer dryer and then is known as dried blood.

Where you only kill 10 to 15 head of cattle a week, it would not pay you to dry the blood in this way. A very fine fertilizer, however, can be made from the blood either for your own use or to sell by boiling the blood in a kettle over a fire or else putting it into a tank and blowing live steam in it; then separate from the water as best you can and mix with black earth, spreading it out thin in the sun to dry. The boiled blood should be mixed with about its own weight in black earth. This makes a wonderful fertilizer and ought to bring you many extra dollars.

ICE VS. ICE MACHINE IN SMALL PLANTS

Query.—F. S. writes: "I would like to know if an ice machine can be had small enough for a retail meat market and would it be profitable to take the place of an ice box? If you can do so, please give me this information and where I can get the ice machine. Ice here for a summer's use will cost about $75."

Ans.—You state that the cost of ice for the summer season in your market would be about $75.00; therefore, it will not pay you to put in an ice machine, as the cost of operating such a machine for an ice-box would be a great deal more than $75.00 for the season. For instance, if you could obtain electric power or a gas engine for operating the ice machine, you could figure on using at least $7.50 to $10.00 a month for power alone. In addition to this, you would have the expense of repairs and the wear and tear on the machinery, also the cost of ammonia and the interest on your investment. For a small plant, it is always cheaper to use ice for an ice-box, when it is possible to secure the ice at a reasonable figure.

WHAT IS THE DIFFERENCE BETWEEN POTATO FLOUR AND BULL-MEAT BRAND SAUSAGE BINDER?

QUERY.—J. G. Co. writes: Will you kindly state the difference between your Bull-Meat-Brand Sausage Binder and Potato Flour, as we have received several circulars from you on Bull-Meat-Brand Sausage Binder and have always been using potato flour heretofore, and if you will explain to us the difference, and if your Bull-Meat Sausage Binder is better for us, we will be glad to use it.

Answer.—The difference between Bull-Meat-Brand Sausage Binder and Potato Flour is this, potato flour is made from potatoes and the absorbing properties of a pound of potato flour or potato starch are much less than you would imagine. If you will take a gallon of water and put into this water one pound of potato flour and let it stand for one hour, all the Potato Flour will have settled to the bottom and you can pour off the gallon of water and then weigh the pound of potato flour and you will be surprised that it will weigh less than two pounds, it will have taken up less than one pound of water. Also make a test by putting one pound of Bull-Meat-Brand Sausage Binder in a gallon of water and you will find that the pound of Bull-Meat-Brand Sausage Binder will have absorbed almost the entire gallon of water. You can easily see by making this test the difference in the action of the flours when used in different kinds of sausage. When Bull-Meat-Brand Sausage Binder is used it helps to hold the fat and then when the sausage is fried it looks different and tastes different than sausage made with potato flour. Bull-Meat-Brand Sausage Binder absorbs fat and juice in the meat and tends to hold it in the meat and it does not fry out so readily. If you will try the Bull-Meat-Brand Sausage Binder and make a test, you will prefer it to potato flour.

CAUSE OF BOLOGNA DRAWING WATER AND BEING SHORT GRAINED.

Query.—J. L. B. writes: "Will you kindly answer the following questions: First, What is the cause of bologna drawing water while being cooked? Second, What is the cause of short grain bologna?"

Ans.—We do not exactly understand your first question and cannot tell whether you mean that moisture draws out of the Bologna or whether water draws into the Bologna. As a rule, when the Bologna is cooked, especially in water that is too hot, it will shrink very much, become dry and crumble and break up. This effectually answers your second question also. The trouble you are experiencing is due to your method of making Bologna, which is not exactly right. In the first place good Bologna cannot be made without the use of a binder like our Bull-Meat-Brand Sausage Binder. A binder and absorbent of this kind causes the meat to hold together. It also makes the juices of the meat remain in the Bologna. When Bologna does not properly bind, it shrinks up and gets watery inside.

This is owing to the fact that the meat does not hold together properly and the water, instead of being absorbed right into the meat as it should be, gets between the small particles of meat and separates them. If you use our **Bull-Meat-Brand Sausage Binder** and follow the methods set forth in our book, "Secrets of Meat Curing and Sausage Making," you will never have any trouble from your Bologna breaking up or getting crumbly or watery, as you call it.

CAUSE OF LARD FOAMING WHEN USING LARD PURIFIER.

Query.—W. & Son write: "Will you kindly tell us what, in your opinion, accounts for our lard foaming after treating it with your B. Heller & Co.'s Lard Purifier when placed in the frying pan? Our customers are complaining about this feature, although the lard is nice and satisfies them in every other respect."

Ans.—The complaint which your customers make concerning the foaming and spluttering of the lard is in all probability due to the fact that all the water was not separated from the lard after treating the lard.

CHICAGO. U.S.A.

Whenever lard is treated with our Lard Purifier, it must be heated hot enough and allowed to stand long enough so that all the water separates and settles out to the bottom. If this is always done, the lard will not splutter when used in the frying pan.

IMITATION BULL-MEAT-BRAND SAUSAGE BINDER.

QUERY.—G. W. writes: "I find that I have been imposed upon by a salesman with a binder which is claimed to be Bull-Meat Binder. Owing to the fact that I have not been able to get satisfactory results from the use of it, I have examined the package closely, and find that the labels are not the same as yours. I enclose a rough drawing of what this label is like and would like to know if the goods are of your manufacture. It doesn't act like your Bull-Meat Binder and I have had very poor success with it; in fact, so very poor that I have sent it back to the jobbers and told them that I could not use it."

Answer.—You most certainly received an imitation of Bull-Meat-Brand Sausage Binder. The very fact that the preparation you received failed to give satisfaction was, in itself, sufficient to convince you that you had been imposed upon, as Bull-Meat-Brand Sausage Binder always produces excellent results. Your idea of examining the label is the proper one. Bull-Meat-Brand Sausage Binder is not only a Binder but also an Absorbent. It has its Flavoring Qualities as well as its tendency to Bind and Blend the Juices of the Meat, thus absorbing those constituents that enables Bull-Meat-Brand Sausage Binder to give sausage such a Delicious and Superior Flavor. When purchasing our goods in the future, we would ask you to kindly examine them closely upon their receipt to see that you are receiving the Genuine and nothing but the Genuine. In this way it will not be necessary for you to spoil a lot of Sausage in order to find out that you have been imposed upon by irresponsible imitators who try to pirate our goods. Never use any goods shipped you until you have examined them closely to see that the name of B. Heller & Co. and no other is upon the label.

203

HOW TO CONSTRUCT A MODERN SMOKE HOUSE.

Query.—The S. P. Co. asks: "Would you kindly tell us, and we will gladly pay you for the information, how to construct a modern, up-to-date smokehouse?"

Ans.—We will be very glad indeed to tell you all about this subject without charging you any fee. We are always glad to tell customers or prospective customers how they can profitably conduct their business and make money. As you are located in California, where the weather is always warm, the building of a smoke house becomes simple, because the smoke house will not sweat like it does in a climate where the weather gets cold in winter. Here in the Middle West, or farther East, it is more difficult to get a good color on meats smoked in a smoke house in winter. One of the principal points to be considered in laying out your plans is to get the proper height, and the higher you build your house and the less floor space it occupies, the better will be your results. An 8x10 or an 8x12 foot house gives the best results. In this you could put an arch about nine or ten feet from the ground, and under the arch smoke your fresh sausage and above it smoke the meat. In this way the heat and smoke used for the sausage would also be utilized for smoking the bacon and hams and none would be wasted. If you build the way we have indicated be sure and put ventilators right above the arch so that cold air can be let into the smoke house during the real hot weather. If your fire gets too hot, you can feed cold air to the interior chamber, and if your smoke house is tall you can create a good draught and will soon get up a circulation which will cool the air so that the meat will not shrink too much. A smoke house built for simply two tiers of meat, that is, two rows, is better than one built wider. The walls of your smoke house can be built either of brick or wood, whichever you prefer, brick being the safer of the two. If you do not intend to smoke fresh sausage but only bacon and hams, it is unnecessary to put in an arch. In that case simply construct some iron bars about eight feet above the fire and on top of these put a heavy iron screen, so in case any hams should fall that they do not fall into the fire. Of course, you know that many smoke houses catch on fire and burn up, due to not having an iron screen above the fire and by meat falling directly into the fire.

PREVENTING PORK SAUSAGE FROM SOURING IN WARM WEATHER

QUESTION.—W. G. F. writes: "I make my own sausage, using your Bull-Meat-Brand Sausage Binder and your Sausage Seasoning. My sausage is good when it is fresh-made, but it soon becomes sour in warm weather. What can I do to prevent this trouble?

Answer.—The best and easiest way to overcome the difficulty you report about your fresh pork sausage souring in warm weather is to use our "A" Condimentine. In making your sausage, for each 100 pounds of meat add ¾ to 1 pound of Heller's "A" Condimentine. This will prevent fresh pork sausage from turning gray and souring for from eight to ten days, according to the temperature in which the sausage is kept.

"A" Condimentine will keep pork sausage in condition, so that it may be shipped, if necessary, for a considerable distance and still retain its own natural color. Your sausage maker will find this method of keeping fresh pork sausage from souring for a reasonable length of time in warm weather of great advantage and save you from severe losses. "A" Condimentine is legal to be used under the National and all State Pure Food Laws. The sausage does not have to be labeled to show the presence of "A" Condimentine. We will be pleased to have you try out our recommendation for retarding fresh pork sausage from souring and report to us your success at an early date.

IS FREEZE-EM PICKLE LEGAL
TO USE?

Query.—W. K. I am a butcher and sausage maker, and also cure a great many hams and bacon. I have used a good bit of your Freeze-Em Pickle and am well pleased with it, and I wish to ask if it can be used with safety under the new pure food laws. That is, the new state food law. The man I have been getting Freeze-Em Pickle from says "Yes" and the State's Attorney says "No," so I write you and would like to have you explain the situation and oblige.

Ans.—Replying to your recent favor it affords us pleasure to advise you that **Freeze-Em-Pickle** does comply with the requirements of your new state food law, and that you need have no fears in continuing its use. In fact, **Freeze-Em-Pickle** complies with the requirements of all the state food laws, as well as with the regulations under the National Pure Food Law, and it is being used all over the U. S. It is evident that the State's Attorney confuses **Freeze-Em-Pickle** with the preservatives which are prohibited under your new state law. All antiseptic preservatives, for the purpose of keeping fresh meat fresh and meat food products in a fresh condition, are positively prohibited under your new state food law. **Freeze-Em-Pickle** does not come in this class. The ingredients of which **Freeze-Em-Pickle** is composed have not been ruled against by any of the pure food laws. We are pleased to hear your praise of **Freeze-Em-Pickle**, although this is the universal report we get when it is properly used. We enclose a circular concerning its use, which you may not have seen, and this will give you further information concerning the manufacture of Bologna and Frankfort Sausage, Corned Beef, etc. We also enclose circular concerning our Bull-Meat-Brand Sausage Binder, which is unquestionably the best Binder on the market. This also complies with the pure food law. So does our Vacuum Brand Garlic Compound and our Prepared Sausage Seasoning, and Red and White Konservirungs-Salt. We will be pleased to hear from you whenever we can be of further service to you.

ADVICE TO A PACKER WHO WAS DECEIVED.

N. & W. complain that a firm to whom they gave an order for 25 pounds of Freeze-Em Pickle and a barrel of Bull-Meat Sausage Binder, sent them 25 pounds of an inferior substitute and a barrel of flour which was an imitation of Bull-Meat Sausage Binder The firm states that they did not know very much about how the label of Freeze-Em Pickle looked and, therefore, did not notice the fraud until after they had used some of the imitation. They ask what they should do about it.

Ans.—Return the goods to your jobber, even though you have used half of them, inform him that you will not pay for the goods on the ground that you did not order them, but had ordered B. Heller & Co.'s goods, and that you will in future buy your goods from such firms as will send you what you want and order. This is a simple remedy for the trouble which you have.

ADVANTAGES OF STEAM-JACKET KETTLE IN RENDERING LARD.

Query.—C. W. F. asks: Is there any advantage in rendering lard in a steam-jacket kettle?

Ans.—There is. Both a caldron and a steam-jacket kettle work well. The best lard is made in one or the other. A steam tank in which the fat is put, and the steam turned right into it, will not produce as good lard as either the caldron or the steam-jacket kettle. The steam mixes right with the lard and the latter therefore contains a large amount of moisture and the lard does not keep well. Another disadvantage is that water used in the boiler is not always pure. If the boiler is not cleaned once a week the water will have a bad smell. Steam made from this water and turned into lard can not be expected to improve its flavor, even though it should not actually harm it. Those who kill large numbers of hogs usually have a steam tank for making steam rendered lard and a steam-jacket kettle for making their finer brands of kettle rendered lard.

207

SEASONING FOR SAUSAGES.

Query.—T. U.: Will you please send me a copy of your book, "Secrets of Meat Curing and Sausage Making." I have always used the following seasonings in my sausage: Pepper, summer savory and sage, and would like to know if you can recommend anything to me which will give the sausage a better flavor than these spices will. Any information you can give me in the seasoning of sausage will be very much appreciated.

Ans.—The Seasonings which you have been using are being used by a good many Sausage Makers, but a real fine flavored Sausage cannot be made with them. If you wish to increase your Sausage trade right along, and want to make Sausage that your trade will relish and enjoy, you must use the very finest Seasonings obtainable, as the Seasoning really is the life of the Sausage. We are manufacturing the Zanzibar Brand Sausage Seasonings, which we make for all kinds of Sausage. These Seasonings are made after secret formulas which have been in our family for a good many years. The flavor that these Seasonings impart to the Sausage is something very fine; it must be tasted to be appreciated, as we cannot describe in a letter what the flavor really is. It is a peculiar combination which everyone likes and it is something that will soon increase your Sausage trade. Zanzibar Brand Sausage Seasonings are manufactured from only high grade Spices and we guarantee them to be absolutely free from any adulteration. We are sending you our circular and price list and would be pleased to receive your order for any quantity that you may desire, and we will say in advance that when you once use them you will never again want to make Sausage without these Seasonings.

SOLE MANUFACTURERS OF ZANZIBAR CARBON.

Query.—C. & K. write: "Are you the sole manufacturers of Zanzibar Carbon?"

Ans.—Yes, and we were the first to put a preparation of this kind upon the market.

QUICKEST WAY TO CURE MEATS.

Query.—W. & B. write: Our capacity for curing meats is limited for the want of room. Can you give us a formula or a recipe that will give a good cure in the shortest possible time? We would like something that is reliable.

Ans.—Our Book, "Secrets of Meat Curing and Sausage Making," will give you all the information in reference to curing meats which you may desire. The curing period can be greatly shortened by pumping the meat. It will also give you a better article. Our book, which is mailed to anyone requesting it, free of charge, will give you full directions for pumping, and also the formula for making the pumping brine. By following the instructions which this book contains, you will be able to turn out the finest kind of mild cured and sweet pickled meats, which will have a delicious flavor and a fine color. It will be necessary, however, for you to fully carry out our directions in reference to chilling meats and overhauling them, also the temperature to be maintained during the curing period.

DIFFERENCE BETWEEN FREEZE-EM AND FREEZE-EM-PICKLE.

Query.—L. B.: We have been using some of your goods and notice that you speak of Freeze-Em-Pickle for curing meats. Is this product the same as Freeze-Em? We have been getting our goods from our jobbers, and in their catalogue they also speak of Freeze-Em-Pickle. We would like one of your books on the secrets of meat curing and methods of smoking and curing, as we are young in the curing of meats yet and would like all the information possible.

Ans.—Your letter received and we are pleased to note that you have been using some of our goods and find them very satisfactory. You say you have read of our Freeze-Em and also our Freeze-Em-Pickle, and you would like to know whether they are both the same. They are not the same. Before the various pure food laws went into effect, we sold **Freeze-Em** as a preservative, also as a cleansing agent. As so many of the pure food laws objected to the use of preservatives, we discontinued selling **Freeze-Em** as a preservative, and now sell and recommend it as a cleansing agent only.

Freeze-Em-Pickle is an entirely different preparation. This was placed on the market with a special view to supply the butcher with a preparation that will comply with all food regulations under all food laws. **Freeze-Em-Pickle** is to be used for curing all kinds of meat, such as hams, bacon, corned beef, bologna trimmings, pork sausage trimmings, and meats of all kinds, and it is also excellent for use in chopped beef, to keep it in a fresh condition. **Freeze-Em-Pickle is not a Chemical Preservative.**

DIFFICULTIES WITH CURING BRINE AND HOW TO OVERCOME THEM.

Query.—W. S. & Co.: We are so situated that we have to boil all the water that we use in our brine. After boiling it we run it into a cooling tank and let it cool. We have made some experiments with your Freeze-Em Pickle and like it to cure very well, and have decided to adopt its use in the curing of all of our meats. Now, what we want to know is, can we dissolve the Freeze-Em Pickle in the boiling hot water and then cool it and run it through coils the same as we do now with the water? Would the heat affect the Freeze-Em Pickle? Our vats when full hold 6,900 lbs. of medium sized hams. According to the size of the kettle and the amount of water to boil at one time, it would require 58 pounds of Freeze-Em Pickle. What we want to do is this: we do not want to weigh the Freeze-Em Pickle for each vat, but simply want to make a large quantity of brine and then run the prepared brine on to our hams. We have been using saltpetre and molasses for our brine and we are having trouble with it getting ropy and stringy. Will syrup answer the same as molasses or sugar, and is New Orleans molasses the best, or should granulated sugar be used entirely? Kindly let us know what you consider the best for hams.

Ans.—First of all, we advise that after the water is boiled, that it is allowed to settle and precipitate so that all the solids will settle to the bottom of the settling tank. It should settle at least 24 hours before the solids will have separated and gone to the bottom. Then the water should be drawn off, but not from the bottom of the tank, but at least a foot from the bottom. The water that will come off from above will be nice and clear. This water should then be run into another tank, called the mixing tank, in which the sugar, salt and **Freeze-Em-Pickle** should be dissolved;

this will make the stock brine which can be run down into the cellar over cooling pipes, so as to chill it properly before it is put on the meat. The reason the brine that you are making becomes ropy is that you are using the wrong sugar. If you will use absolutely pure granulated sugar or absolutely pure syrup made from granulated sugar you will have no trouble from ropy brine. We strongly advise the use of nothing but absolutely pure granulated sugar. We find that it gives the best results. It costs a little more than the unrefined product but you get less vegetable substance in your brine, and the brine will therefore keep much longer. The brine in which hams have been cured can be used a second time for curing breakfast bacon, and the breakfast bacon will be even better than if put into fresh brine. As your vats are large, the meat will pack very tight on the bottom, and we wish to caution you to be sure and overhaul your meat promptly five days after it is packed and continue overhauling as per directions in our book on curing meats and making sausage. If you follow these directions you will not have any ropy brine or any spoiled meat, but all your meat will come out uniform and will have the proper flavor.

TOUGH AND SALTY CORNED BEEF.

Query.—E. W. G. writes: I have had complaints from several large institutions I serve that my corned beef is tough and too salty. I would like to know about what proportions of salt and saltpetre to use. It is only recently that I have had these complaints, in fact, I have been in the retail business for about ten years and have been very successful with my corned beef.

Ans.—If you will use the following in curing plates, rumps, briskets, etc., for corned beef, you will have no trouble. Use for 100 lbs. of meat:

Five pounds of common salt, 1 lb. of **Freeze-Em-Pickle**, 2 lbs. of best granulated sugar, 5 gallons of cold water.

Cure the meat in this brine fifteen to thirty days, according to weight and thickness of the pieces. If you are taking pieces out of the brine from day to day and adding others, you should keep up the strength of the pickle to sixty degrees by adding a small quantity of **Freeze-Em-Pickle** and salt from time to time as you withdraw and replace the meat. One of the first essentials to producing first-class corned beef is to be careful about the temperature during the curing period. An even temperature of 38 degrees Fahrenheit is always the best for coolers and for curing meat. If maintained at this degree, there will be no trouble from taking on too much salt, provided, of course, the meat has been properly chilled through before placing it in the brine for curing. In order to produce a good cure, all the animal heat must be extracted from the meat before it is packed, otherwise it will become soft and spongy in the brine, and pickle-soaked.

KEEPING HAMS AND BACON SIX MONTHS.

Query.—A. J. M. writes: I would like to know how to keep hams and bacon in first class shape for the next six months without their getting mouldy and with the least possible shrinkage.

Ans.—There is no practical method for keeping hams and bacon for so long a time after they are smoked without their getting mouldy. There is a method for keeping them in sweet pickle for any length of time, provided you have cold storage facilities. All kinds of pickled meat if stored in a cooler in which the temperature is kept down to 28 degrees can be kept in this cooler for a year or even longer, and when removed will come out like fresh cured meat. Hams and other meats are often purchased when the market is low and stored in a freezer and kept here until such a time that they are in greatest demand and will sell at the highest price. At a temperature of 28 degrees the meat will not freeze after it is cured, and the brine, of course, does not freeze at that temperature. When meat is taken out of such cold storage to be smoked, it should be first soaked from three to five hours in fresh water, and then washed and smoked the same as regular fresh cured meat. Farmers often bury their smoked meats in their oat bins, and are enabled to keep them in good condition for some time, but this is a method which, perhaps, does not suit your purpose. It is best to keep the meat in sweet pickle until you are ready to smoke it, as this will insure a much better article.

USES FOR DRIED BEEF ENDS.

Query.—C. E. C. writes: "Can you inform me the best and most profitable way for disposing of my Dried Beef ends? I am in the sliced Dried Beef business and have no way of using up my ends. Thanking you in advance."

Ans.—There are three ways for disposing of beef ends to advantage and profit. They may be ground up in an Enterprise Chopper and sold to hotels and restaurants for use as Minced Dried Beef to be prepared and served in cream. They can also be sold to concerns engaged in the baked bean business, where the ends can be cut up and baked with pork in the beans. Restaurants can also use dried beef ends to excellent advantage by putting them in soup. They will give a delicious flavor to all kinds of soups, if boiled at the same time with other soup meats.

HOW TO PREVENT HAMS FROM SOURING IN THE HOCK.

Query.—C. F. G. Co. write: "We have a lot of hams that we put down in dry salt to cure about six or seven weeks ago, and we have discovered that they have become tainted in the hock, while the balance of the piece of meat is all right. Can you tell us any way to rehandle or overhaul these hams to save them? The front or butt end of the ham is sound and all right and sweet; the bad part is in and around the hock end or leg end. Could this taint and odor be removed and the meat made sweet by putting these hams down now in a strong salt brine and punching holes in the hock end of the pieces so that the brine could quickly get into the tainted part? Would salt brine save them now? We will thank you for any advice or plan of action that will help to save us from loss."

Ans.—It is more difficult to cure hams by the dry salt process than it is by the brine process. If these hams had been pumped before packing them in the salt, there would not have been so much danger of shank sour. Hams being very thick, it takes a long time for the salt to draw through them; therefore, if they are first pumped and packed in dry salt, you can readily see that the salt draws through quicker and thus gives them a chance to cure from the inside as quickly as they would cure from the outside. Only under one condition can you pump these hams, make them sweet and save them. For instance, if the hams are taken from the salt and upon trying them with a ham trier they are found to be sweet but turn sour when they are placed in the smoke house, then you can save them. Such a condition would show that the hams are not fully cured around the bone and around the shank joints. In that event, they can be pumped with pickle and fully cured around the bone so that they will not sour when placed in the smoke house. It is necessary to explain that meat is frequently perfectly sweet when it comes out of cure, but it is not fully cured. In such a condition when it is placed in a warm smoke house, it will sour in the smoke house. This, of course, can be avoided by fully curing the hams. If, on the other hand, the hams are already sour and tainted when they come out of the cure, whether it be dry salt or sweet pickle, then nothing can be done with them to make them sweet. Meat once spoiled, remains spoiled. If the hams are sour when they come out of the cure, but sour only in the shank, then the proper thing to do is to cut off the shank; in other words, cut off all the sour or tainted meat and use the butt ends for boiled hams. You can boil and slice them and sell them in your store. You must be careful to cut off all the tainted parts because any of the tainted meat which is left will taint all the rest of the meat when the butt is boiled. You, of course, understand that during the process of boiling, the good meat will absorb the taint from the bad meat. We regret that you did not write us for advice before you began curing the hams, as we would have advised you to cure in brine. We will send you by mail, free of charge, our book, entitled "Secrets of Meat Curing and Sausage Making," which covers every point that its title indicates. The advice given in this book as to the handling of meats, you will find very valuable and covers the whole ground, from the condition of the animal before killing to the handling of the meat through the chill room and through the entire curing process. We call your special attention to the various articles for curing meats, which will give you the temperature for curing, how to overhaul the meat, how to pump the meat and how to make the brine for pumping. Full directions for curing the hams you will find carefully indexed. By following the advice given in these pages, you will have no loss from the souring of meats, but on the contrary, will be enabled to turn out meat of the highest quality possible.

BUILDING A COOLER.

Query.—W. G. H. writes: I have about completed a cooler except the floor and am undecided whether to make it of plank or cement. I thought you could give me the desired advice. One room is 16 feet square inside; 7 feet to joist with 7 feet of solid ice above, or about 50 tons capacity. The walls are 2 feet thick; 8 inches sawdust, 4 inches dead air space, 8 inches sawdust, with four thicknesses of one-inch boards, thus making the 2 feet. The building has these walls on all sides and partitions. I expect to use the drip from the above to cool another room, 8 feet by 16 feet inside, and will have the water run around this room in gutters (sheet iron) fastened to the wall. I want this as dry and as free from mould and dampness as possible and, therefore, am not sure as to whether a cement floor will be what is needed, though it was my intention to use cement. There is a 2-foot stone wall under the cooler which sets on sand—this sand having been washed up at times past by the lake. There are now fifty tons of ice over the cooler and back of this is an ice house, 16 feet square, inside filled with ice 14 feet high. This makes the building 20 feet wide by 48 feet long, by 20 feet studding. For ventilation a four-inch square flue will run from the bottom in one corner and from the top in the opposite corner of the cooler to the top of the roof, and above it, acting as chimneys. I want to use these coolers for fresh meats, packing hams and bacon, storing eggs and most anything that there is any money in, which requires to be kept in good condition. Your advice will be appreciated.

Ans.—You are building your cooler on very good plans. However, we would advise the use of cement for the floors. It will be found much better than wood, much purer and cleaner, and withal much drier. You speak about putting two ventilators in your cooler, which is all right, but you should be sure to provide these ventilators with slides, so you can shut them off and regulate the ventilation according to your wishes. Of course, you understand that it is not well to have the ventilators open all the time, as it would result in quite a loss of ice. The ventilators should be open only when the room needs ventilation, which will be at well-defined periods, or varying according to the amount of material in storage. Your plan of using the drip water of the ice and running it in pans will work all right. We have seen this method applied, and it was always satisfactory. Be sure to use galvanized iron gutters for the pans, not sheet iron, as it will rust easily.

WHY BOLOGNA "TAKES WATER" IN COOKING.

Query.—H. P. writes: "Sometimes I have bother with my bologna taking water when cooking them. Can you tell me what to do to prevent this trouble?"

Ans.—The difficulty you mention is caused by the sausage not being properly boiled. Ordinary round or long Bologna should be boiled in water of 160 to 170 degrees Fahrenheit for about thirty to forty minutes, and thick, large Bologna should be boiled in water of 155 to 160 degrees for from three-quarters to one hour, according to the size. If the sausages are very large, it will take from one and one-quarter to one and one-half hours to cook them properly. After sausage of any kind have been cooked, they should be handled as follows: Pour boiling water over them to wash off all the surplus grease that adheres to the casings, and then pour cold water over them to shrink and close the pores of the casings. This is very important and should be closely observed by all packers and sausage makers who wish to have their sausage look nice and keep their fresh appearance. The shrinkage and quality of cooked Bologna depends considerably upon the temperature in which they have been boiled. It is very necessary for every man who cooks sausage to use a thermometer.

WHY BOLOGNA SHRIVELS.

Query.—T. B.: Can you tell me the reason bologna shrivels when it is taken from the hot water? It looks fine until it gets cold.

Ans.—There are several reasons why your bologna might shrivel when taken out of the boiling water. First, it might be that you do not cure your meat right before the bologna is made, and second, you probably do not use the right kind of a binder, and third, you probably boil the bologna in too hot water. If when the meat is cured properly and you do use the right kind of a binder, the bologna shrivels when taken out of the boiling water, it is because you are boiling it at too high a temperature. Before making bologna you should sprinkle **Freeze-Em-Pickle** over the meat and leave it for a few days. We refer to our instructions for preparing bologna trimmings, which will be found in our book, "Secrets of Meat Curing and Sausage Making."

ADVICE ON CURING HAMS AND BACON.

Query.—E. A. S. & Co. write: I have taken a barrel of meat, hams and shoulders, which I cured in my ice box after your instructions, and I wish to say that it is as fine as was ever produced by anyone. My ice box holds well, standing at from 38 to 39 degrees, but it is small and only has room for one barrel in it. I have made arrangements to try packing in the house this winter. I have a closet made of brick on both sides and by proper ventilation in cold weather so as to keep it from 35 to 40 degrees. I think I can save hams all O. K. in tierces. I have about ten oak tierces for the purpose. (Is that all right?) I have an old ice box in the rear 8x8 feet with a good roof on it, walls filled with sawdust. I would like to know if I can fill this with hams and shoulders when the weather gets cold and just dry salt them. Can I save them by just letting them stay there all winter until next spring? I can put in a layer of hams and cover them with salt, then put in another layer and cover with salt, and so on until I fill it. I would like your opinion and advice as to these methods. I kept side meat this way last winter just leaving it in salt.

Ans.—If you keep the temperature of the small room which you mention at from 35 to 40 degrees it will answer the purpose for curing. The oak tierces for curing are all right provided they are new. We advise that you wash them out with scalding hot water, so as to get rid of the oak taste. If the tierces are not new, then you must make doubly sure that they are scalded out thoroughly and at the same time you should use our Ozo for cleansing them.

The old ice-box which you mention can be used for dry salting hams and shoulders when the weather gets cold, provided you do not let the meat freeze. You must not let the temperature get below 35 degrees, because at a lower temperature, meat will not take on salt. Hams can be dry salt cured just the same as side meats, but when hams are very thick, we would advise that you pump them. Our book, ''Secrets of Meat Curing and Sausage Making,'' will give you full information as to the pumping process and a formula for making the pumping brine. Hams are very seldom dry salt cured; they are nearly always sweet-pickle cured. A sweet pickle or sugar cured ham has a much finer flavor than the dry salt cured ham.

If you pack side meat properly and overhaul it regularly until it is fully cured, and if you keep the temperature of the curing room at about 38 degrees, you will have no trouble in keeping dry salt meat in salt all winter. Of course if you keep it in salt too long, it will get very salty. Our book on curing meats will give you full directions for dry salt curing. Hams, after they are fully cured in brine, can be rubbed with salt and kept in a cooler for several months, and if desired, all winter, but the shrinkage will be great and they will take on salt and might become too salty for your trade.

WHY OIL SEPARATES FROM LARD.

Query.—E. & W.: We are having trouble with our lard; the oil separates from the lard during the warm weather so part of the lard is really oil, and we cannot use it in that condition. Our business is too small to justify us in employing a practical man to take charge of our lard. We ask you for your advice.

Ans.—To keep the oil from separating from the lard, you should carry out the following directions: First, you should provide yourself with a lard cooler with an agitator attached, as the lard after it is rendered and when it begins to cool should be agitated until it becomes thick like cream, before it is run into the buckets. If lard is not agitated, when it is cooled the stearin crystallizes and the oil separates from the stearin, but by chilling the lard and by agitating it while it cools, the stearin does not get a chance to crystallize and the oil will not separate and the lard will keep better in this condition. Lard that is put up in winter for summer use is much improved by adding about ten per cent of tallow, but when this lard is sold, it should be sold as lard with ten per cent of tallow added. If you wish to treat the lard that you have on hand, we advise you to treat it as follows: For every 100 lbs. of lard, put 100 lbs. of water in your lard kettle; add to it four ounces of our Lard Purifier, and throw 100 lbs. of lard into this water. Start the fire and gradually heat it until the lard is melted and is as hot as it will stand without boiling over. Keep on stirring the lard until it begins to melt, so as to thoroughly wash it. After the lard is thoroughly washed, you will find a certain amount of scum will come to the top, skim this off and then allow the lard to settle for about two hours, so that all the water will separate from the lard and settle down at the bottom. Skim the lard off the top of the water and then let it cool, but keep on agitating it or stirring it while it is cooling, until it is thick like cream.

COATING BOLOGNA SAUSAGE NOT NECESSARY TO PREVENT MOULD.

Query.—E. D. writes: I would like to ask you if you have anything to coat bologna with after making? I think it is called Gloss or Lustre; have seen it used, but have not been able to find out where to get it.

Ans.—What you refer to is Bologna Varnish. The use of such a preparation has been practically discontinued as it does not conform to pure food laws; it is not proper that a varnish should be put on the outside of food of any kind. Bologna Varnish is made from shellac, and shellac is used in all kinds of furniture varnish, so you can readily see that it is not the proper thing to use on Bologna. In former years, the use of varnish was quite general, but it was finally discontinued, and is now practically a thing of the past. If you want to prevent your Bologna from getting mouldy, you should make them as follows: First, cure the meat with **Freeze-Em-Pickle** as directed in our book, "Secrets of Meat Curing and Sausage Making," and add Bull-Meat-Brand Sausage Binder to the meat, as this absorbs the moisture. Bologna made by the **Freeze-Em-Pickle** Process keeps fine and will not mold for a reasonable length of time.

MAKING SOAP FROM TALLOW.

Query.—F. B. writes: We have a little meat business and quite often have on hand a surplus of tallow. Now we have been thinking probably we could put this into a soap, something cheap that would not cost us too much to put on the market. Can you kindly give us any information in the matter, and if the idea is a practical one for a small shop like ours?

Ans.—It would not pay you to undertake to make a hard soap in a small way, as it would be necessary for you to compete with other soaps on the market, and you are aware that laundry soap sells at a very low price and is put upon the market upon a very small margin of profit. You would also find it quite a task to make hard soap, and the time required would hardly justify you to undertake it on a small scale. If you can dispose of soft soap in your locality, we would advise you to use your surplus tallow in that way, but, of course, this suggestion from a financial point of view would depend entirely upon whether there is a sufficient demand for such an article in your vicinity. Possibly you could work up a trade among private families and sell it to them for scrubbing purposes, also to hotels, stores and restaurants, but as your town is small, you might have difficulty in disposing of a sufficient quantity to make it pay you. On the other hand, it would not cost you much to make the experiment. You are surrounded by a good hog-feeding country, and it is possible that you could dispose of quite a quantity of soft soap to the farmers, as it is a very fine thing for hogs, and the truth of the matter is, their hogs would be much better off if they would feed it frequently. You might be benefited more by this suggestion than by sales from other sources.

The following is a recipe for making soft soap with potash: To 20 pounds of clear grease or tallow take 17 pounds of pure white potash. Buy the potash in as fine lumps as it can be procured, and place it in the bottom of the soap barrel, which must be water-tight and strongly hooped. Boil the grease and pour it boiling hot upon the potash; then add two large pailfuls of boiling hot water; dissolve 1 pound of borax in 2 quarts of boiling hot water and stir all together thoroughly. Next morning add 2 pails of cold water and stir for half an hour; continue this process until a barrel containing thirty-six gallons is filled up. In a week or even less, it will be ready for use. The borax can be turned into grease while boiling, and also 1 pound of rosin. Soap made in this manner always comes, and is a first-rate article, and will last twice as long as that bought at a soap factory. The grease must be tried out, free from scraps, ham rinds, bones, or any other debris; then the soap will be as thick as jelly, and almost as clear. To make soft soap hard put into a kettle four pailfuls of soft soap, and stir in it by degrees about one quart of common salt. Boil until all the water is separated from the curd, remove the fire from the kettle and draw off the water with a siphon (a yard or so of rubber hose will answer); then pour the soap into a wooden form in which muslin has been placed. For this purpose a wooden box, sufficiently large and tight, may be employed. When the soap is firm turn out to dry, cut into bars with a brass wire and let it harden. A little powdered rosin will assist the soap to harden and give it a yellow color. If the soft soap is very thin, more salt should be added

PLANS FOR SAUSAGE FACTORY.

Query.—O. C. L. writes: I am now in business again on my own hook, so please send me your book on Meat Curing and Sausage Making. I will, in the near future, equip my market with an up-to-date sausage factory. I have the following machinery: 1 six-horse power gasoline engine, silent cutter, Enterprise machine, 1 bone cutter, 1 steam boiler for rendering lard, cooking sausage, etc. The room I intend to place this machinery in is 15x25 feet; would like to hear some of your suggestions, and plans in placing the machinery; would appreciate this very much. Has the freezing of pork sausage any detrimental effect on the flavor of the sausage? Accept my well wishes.

Ans.—The machinery you enumerate will give you a sausage plant that is quite complete. We think, however, that your room is a little bit small in which to place so much machinery. If you could put the boiler and rendering kettle in another room, away from the sausage factory, it would be better. You would probably be able to make such an addition as would answer your purpose at a very small cost. This arrangement would make it much more convenient because the boiler and the rendering tank in your sausage factory will make it very hot. The arrangement or disposal of the machinery will not make material difference in a room of the size mentioned. You can arrange it most any way to best suit your convenience.

The freezing of pork sausage certainly has a most detrimental effect on the flavor. Freezing meat always tends, to some extent, to spoil the flavor of the meat. When the albumen of the meat is frozen, and is afterwards thawed out, the albumen leaves the cells of the meat and in that way the flavor is lost and the meat becomes insipid.

PURIFYING TALLOW.

Query.—T. W. C. writes: "I am tanking mutton and beef tallow together at 40 pounds pressure, and would like to know the best way to use your tallow purifier so I can use my tallow with cottonseed oil to make a lard compound."

Ans.—It would not be practicable to use our Lard and Tallow Purifier in the tank. It can be used to greatest advantage in an open jacket kettle. You can treat the tallow in the jacket kettle after it is rendered and comes from the steam tank.

HOW PACKERS BRAND THEIR HAMS

Question.—W. Z. writes: How do packers brand their hams.

Answer.—Packers brand their hams with Ink made from the following formula:

Glucose	2¼ lbs.
Lampblack	¼ to ½ lb.
Water	1½ lbs.
Grain Alcohol	½ pint

Place the Glucose and water in a dish and heat on stove until it becomes thin. Now take the Lampblack, put it in a separate dish and add enough of the water and Glucose so as to make a thick paste; work this paste up until all of the lumps are dissolved. Then take the Lampblack paste and gradually mix it into the water and Glucose until the desired shade of color is secured. After mixing thoroughly remove from fire and set aside to cool. When cool add the ½ pint of Grain Alcohol, mixing thoroughly. Keep in a corked bottle or can.

Spread a small quantity of the Ink thus made over a pad which is easily made by taking 10 thicknesses of cheese cloth and tacking them on top of a flat board. The branding itself is done with an iron brand containing such letters or other marking as you wish to appear on the hams. The branding should be done before the hams are put into the smoke house.

STARTING A BUTCHER BUSINESS

Query.—M. E. A. writes: Will you please forward me another copy of your desirable book, "How to Cure Meat and Make Sausage"? And if it is not too much trouble, I would like to have you advise how it is best to start in the butcher and pork packing business in a small way. I have about $700 capital and wish to ask how is the best way to fit up a retail store without too much expense and yet to have it look good, and also to fit up a sausage kitchen and have everything that a man needs to run the business successfully. I may as well state that I have had lots of experience, but after reading your book and the advice that it gives I am sure that even experienced men can learn a lot by reading it.

Ans.—With such a limited amount of capital, it would be advisable to buy second-handed fixtures. These can always be obtained much cheaper than new ones, and you can get good fixtures which will answer the purpose, but they must be neat, clean and in good repair. If you intend to do your own butchering, our advice is that you make arrangements with some butcher who has a slaughter house, and where you can do your butchering, and pay him a certain amount for each animal slaughtered. A very important point that we advise you to follow is to sell everything for cash only, as your capital is not sufficient to give credit to anyone. Were you to give credit and make a lot of book accounts, you would soon run out of money and would not be able to buy large stock and supplies for your market. We also advise that you induce your customers to take their meat home with them, and thus relieve yourself of the necessity of keeping a horse and wagon for delivery purposes. This would save quite an outlay in capital, and a great deal of expense and time. You can then announce with a small advertisement in the daily paper that you sell for cash only, and that you can afford to be more liberal with your customers than you could if you carried accounts, and because you do not incur the expense of delivery. Such an advertisement with placards in your store, no doubt, would result favorably. You must remember at all times that your capital is limited and that you must "trim your sails" accordingly. It is the over-reaching the limits of the possibilities of capital that make the most failures among tradesmen. We would not advise you to advertise meat at a cut price because you sell for cash; people do not want stuff that is cheap, for if you sell stuff at a low price, they imagine there is something wrong with it. Charge the same price that all the other butchers do, and in that way, keep their friendship. If a woman gets something that she doesn't like and brings it back, tell her that you are very glad she brought it back, if it did not suit her, because you never want any of your customers to keep anything that does not please them.

A sausage room can be rigged up very cheap; all you need to start with is a small Enterprise grinder, so that you can grind up your trimmings and work them into sausage, and by working the meat trimmings up into the different formulas that we give in our book, "Secrets of Meat Curing and Sausage Making," you will not have any loss, as all of your trimmings can be worked up to good advantage. You also should make a great display of your own cured corned beef and turn out fine corned beef, so that when your customers buy it, they are well pleased. The main thing in the success of running a retail market is that the butcher understands how to buy his live stock so that he gets the right quality of beef and gets it at the right price. If you have good meats to sell you will have no trouble in selling them, but if you have poor goods to sell, you may sell them to a customer once or twice, but the third time the customer will not come near you. The same thing holds good with you; if you were buying some of your supplies from the jobber and the jobber did not send you good goods, you may try him once more and if he again sends you poor goods, the third time you certainly will not buy from him, but you will go to some other jobber who will give you the best goods for your money. Your customers are just as smart and as sensitive as you are, and want the same kind of treatment that you like, so if you will always treat your customers as you would like to be treated yourself if you were buying meat at a market, you are bound to meet with success.

CUTTING UP MEATS—NECESSARY FOR EXPERIENCE.

Query.—J. J. writes: I have decided to go into the meat business and would like to know if you can advise me of some booklet or pamphlet on cutting up meat; also let me know the price of your book, and if you know of a good firm handling butcher supplies and refrigerators.

Ans.—We judge from your inquiry that you are inexperienced in the meat business, and if such is the case, we would advise that you go to work for some good butcher for a while before going into the business for yourself. You could there learn the practical side of the business, and provided you do not now understand how to cut up meat to the greatest profit, you could acquire knowledge upon these points which would be of more value to you than volumes that could be written upon the subject. We most emphatically advise you to learn the business thoroughly before embarking into it on your own account. We take great pleasure in sending you our booklet, ''Secrets of Meat Curing and Sausage Making,'' which you will find of great value to you in teaching you to cure meat and make sausage.

IMITATION FREEZE-EM PICKLE.

Query.—L. M. writes: "M——— & ———, from whom I buy most of my butcher supplies, handle an imitation of your Freeze-Em Pickle which they claim is the same as your preparation. I do not want it and will not have it. They tried to convince me that what they had is what I want, but I have used Freeze-Em Pickle for years and, knowing from your advertisements that there are imitations of it, I want to steer clear of them. Will you please send me the name of a jobber handling Freeze-Em Pickle near me?"

Ans.—This is a clear case of an attempt for a substitution of spurious goods for those of our manufacture. These dealers can not help knowing that our customers want **Freeze-Em-Pickle**, and nothing else, but for the sake of reaping an illegitimate profit, they misrepresent imitation goods as being the same as ours. We wish to state that there is only one **Freeze-Em-Pickle**, and all claims to the contrary are absolutely false. They are merely the tricks of illegitimate dealers to pirate the good reputation made by our preparations. In order to be convinced of the superiority of **Freeze-Em-Pickle**, it is only necessary to test it with any preparation purporting to be the same or similar to it and selling under similar names, which are calculated to deceive.

SOURING OF HAM IN SMOKE HOUSE.

Query.—M. P. M. writes: "I am having trouble with my hams souring in the smokehouse. They seem to get too much smoke. What can you suggest that will help me to avoid this trouble and to keep my hams sweet?"

Ans.—You are mistaken in supposing that your hams sour from getting too much smoke; that is not the trouble. Hams will not sour from such cause. Your trouble is owing entirely to the fact that the hams are not properly and fully cured before going into the smoke house. Smoke aids to preserve hams and will not cause them to sour. They sour because the portion that has not been thoroughly cured, which is generally close to the bone, has not been reached by the brine. In many cases souring comes from imperfect chilling of meat before putting it into the brine; then again you may not have overhauled the **meat** at the proper time and with the frequency which good curing requires. In the first place, the hog should not be killed when overheated or excited. Second, after they have been scalded and scraped, they must be dressed as quickly as possible, washed out thoroughly with clean water, then split and allowed to hang in a well ventilated room until partly cooled off. They should then be run into a cooler or chilling room as quickly as possible, where the temperature should be reduced to 32 to 34 degrees Fahrenheit. They should be allowed to thus chill for 24 hours for medium size hogs. When hogs are properly chilled, the temperature of the inside of the ham or shoulder will not be more than one to one and one-half degrees higher than the cooler. Those without ice machinery for curing, who are using common ice houses, can employ the crushed ice method for chilling the meat. By this is meant to put the meat on the floor and throw cracked ice over it, and thus allow it to remain over night. After being thoroughly chilled, the hams must undergo the various processes which you will find set forth in our book, "Secrets of Meat Curing and Sausage Making," which we take pleasure in sending to you free of charge. If you will follow the directions contained in this book you will never have trouble with soured hams from imperfect curing or other causes.

CLEANING CASINGS.

Query.—S. & H. write: "I would like to know if you have any preparations for cleaning casings. We clean all the casings we get and would like to get some chemicals to take the tallow and lard off of them."

Ans.—There is no preparation that will free the lard from casings. If you use something that is strong enough to take off the fat, it will eat up the casings as well. The only thing practicable that can be done is to wash the casings thoroughly and change the water a number of times. In the last washing water it would be advisable to put in some washing soda as that will soften the water and assist in cleaning the casings. The fat you will have to remove by hand. There are machines made for removing the fat from casings, but it will not pay you to go to the expense of making such a purchase unless you clean a very large amount of casings per day.

CAUSE OF "RUSTY" MEAT.

Query.—R. J. B. writes: "We keep our meat in an ice box 35 degrees cold and the barrels we used in curing it were galvanized, and we have used them for five years. We use the regular pickling salt. Our meat comes out rusty. What can you suggest?"

Ans.—If your cooler is kept at 35 degrees, you must have an ice machine instead of the regular ice box or cooler, and 35 degrees is too cold for curing purposes. An even temperature of 38 degrees is the proper one for curing meat, and all packers who use ice machines should endeavor to keep their coolers at a temperature not varying from 37 to 39 degrees, and they never should be allowed to get above 40 degrees. Meat will not cure in any brine or take on enough salt when dry salted if stored in a room that is below 36 degrees. If meat is packed even in the strongest kind of brine and put into a cooler which is kept at 32 to 33 degrees and thus left at this degree of cold for three months, it will come out of the brine only partly cured; it will, therefore, only keep for a short time and will start to decompose when taken into a higher temperature. If you have used galvanized iron tanks for five years, it is possible that the zinc or the galvanizing is worn off on the inside of the vats so as to expose the iron. Brine will rapidly rust iron and that will cause your meat to become rusty. Galvanized iron tanks for curing are all right until the galvanizing is worn off and the moment this happens, the tanks are useless for curing purposes. Salt that is rusted or salt that is shoveled with a rusty shovel will also cause rusty meat. It is absolutely necessary that the salt be pure and free from rust. If live stock is driven for some distance and slaughtered while it is overheated, the meat will not cure properly and will also turn out rusty. Stock that has been driven should always be allowed to remain in the pens over night. We send you our book, "Secrets of Meat Curing and Sausage Making," which you will find full of valuable information in reference to curing of meat. If you will follow the directions contained therein closely, you will always have good results.

SALT FOR BRINE—BOILING BRINE— ROPY BRINE.

Query.—W. M. writes: "Is common barrel salt or rock salt the best and cheapest to use for making brine? I have been using rock salt and I think it is sweet, but in using rock salt I have to boil it in order to dissolve the salt. Is it necessary to boil the water if it is pure? I am having trouble with my brine. It becomes jelly-like in summer and in winter. What is the cause of this?"

Ans.—Evaporated salt, or what is known as the ordinary barrel salt of a good quality, is generally approved by butchers for making brine. Rock salt is much used by the large packers, as it is a stronger salt, but their facilities for curing meat are altogether different from those of the butcher and the ordinary curer.

It is not necessary to boil the water for brine if you know it to be perfectly pure. If its purity is doubted, it should always be boiled and the impurities which rise to the top should be thoroughly skimmed off, or if they precipitate the water should be carefully drawn off. When brine becomes jelly-like, you mean that it gets ropy. This condition is owing to a great many causes; sometimes it is due to the sugar which may be of low grade or unrefined, or where molasses and syrup are used, it quite often results. The best grade of granulated sugar should always be used for brine. Sometimes the ropiness of brine is due to the packages in which the meat is cured. This is especially true when syrup barrels are used. One of the most common causes of ropy brine is owing to the fact that the meat is cured in too warm a temperature. If the curing temperature is kept from 38 to 40 degrees, the brine will remain thin and not get ropy, but there is always risk in a temperature higher than we have given. If the meat has not been properly chilled before putting it in pickle, ropiness will also result. Great care should always be given to meat before putting it in the brine, as it will become soft and spongy if not chilled through to the bone. When in this condition it becomes pickle-soaked and contaminates the brine.

PACKING EGGS.

Query.—D. B. writes: "I have been using your goods for some time back and they give the best of satisfaction. Can you give me a good recipe for packing eggs?"

Ans.—You will find the following very efficient for preserving eggs: To each pailful of water add two pints of fresh slaked lime, one pint of salt and one ounce of White Berliner Konservirungs-Salze; mix well and then fill a barrel half full of this fluid, put the eggs into it and they will keep for a long time. The eggs, of course, should be stored in a cool room. A cool cellar will answer, but the temperature should never be allowed to get too low—never lower than 38 degrees.

HOW TO TEST VINEGAR.

Query.—G. G. writes: "Do you sell a thermometer or gauge for testing vinegar? How am I to know the degree of strength of the vinegar without a gauge?"

Ans.—Vinegar is tested with a special apparatus called a Twitchel Tester. Unless you use large quantities of vinegar, it would hardly pay you to go to the expense of buying such an apparatus as they are rather expensive and cost about $15 each. If you buy the vinegar by the barrel from the wholesale grocers and specify the degree of strength, they will give you the article desired. If you have any doubts as to the purity of vinegar there are various ways to test its purity. The adulterant of vinegar is sulphuric acid, which increases its indicated strength. Sulphuric acid can be detected by placing some of the vinegar to be tested in a saucer. Put some white sugar in the vinegar and evaporate to dryness by placing the saucer on top of a boiling water kettle. After the water has evaporated if the sugar turns black, the vinegar contains an adulterating acid. In lieu of a saucer, a teacup can be used in which the vinegar and sugar can be placed. The cup can then be placed in a basin of hot water in which it can be allowed to float until the vinegar in the cup is evaporated. If the vinegar contains free sulphuric acid the dry sugar will be found to be blackened. These are simple methods and are claimed to be more accurate as a test than the use of the Barium Chloride Test. The Barium Chloride Test is as follows: Mix one **ounce** of Chloride of Barium with ten **ounces of water**. A little of this mixture dropped in vinegar will quickly test its purity. If the vinegar contains sulphuric acid, this mixture will make it turn flaky at once, but if it remains clear and shows no change, the vinegar is free from sulphuric acid adulteration. Sulphuric acid makes vinegar show a very high test when, as a matter of fact, it is of very poor real vinegar strength.

SEPARATING WATER FROM LARD.

Query.—C. W. writes: "I have my lard in such a shape that I don't know what to do with it. It seems that the water will not separate from the lard and the mixture stays about the thickness of cream and about as white. Can you give me any instructions or advice?

Ans.—To overcome your difficulty, we would advise you to remelt the lard and heat it quite hot, even up to 190 to 200 degrees, but do not let it come to a boil. Then let the lard settle. The water and impurities will settle to the bottom. The lard will rise to the top. If you heat the lard to the boiling point of water, that is, 212 degrees, it would do no harm except that the lard will then foam and you will have to be careful so that it does not foam over the top of the kettle. When it foams, it will bring the impurities to the surface, besides much of the moisture will evaporate. Either of these methods will remove your difficulty. You can dry the lard by heating it sufficiently or you can melt the lard and have it hot enough so that the water will settle to the bottom. After the lard is melted, dip it from the kettle, or if you have a lard cooler, run it into the lard cooler; be careful, though, that all water which may be at the bottom of the kettle is drawn off first if your intend to run the lard into a lard cooler. You will have to get rid of the water that is in the lard, so do not stir the lard while the water is still in the kettle. If you dip the lard out of the top of the kettle and place it in a lard tierce, when the lard begins to cool, you can stir it and keep on stirring it until it is thick like cream; it should then be run into buckets. You can readily understand that if there is a large per cent of water in the lard, it will keep the lard soft, which is the trouble you are now having.

COLORING SAUSAGE MEAT ARTIFI-CIALLY IS ILLEGAL.

Query.—J. R. B.: Will you send me a guarantee that your Rosaline for coloring sausage, etc., will stand the Pure Food Law? Also state particulars of Potato Flour, and whether it is guaranteed or not to be pure. I want to use the goods, and the house I deal with won't guarantee them to me.

Ans.—In reply to your inquiry we beg to say that Rosaline for coloring bologna or other sausage would not be legal under your state law. However, you can produce even a better sausage, both in appearance and taste, by using **Freeze-Em-Pickle** according to the directions given in the enclosed circular, "A New Way to Make Bologna and Frankfort Sausage." **Freeze-Em-Pickle** is legal in your state as well as all other states, as it does not contain any ingredient that has been ruled against under any of the food laws. We would urge you to adopt this method of making your sausage, not only because it complies with your law, but because you will make better sausage and will save yourself from loss of the meat juices which would be lost if you made your sausage in the old way. As regards potato flour, we do not handle this product and are not interested in it. Bull-Meat-Brand Sausage Binder, our guaranteed binder, is far superior to potato flour for this purpose, and it is legal in your state if used in the proportion of not to exceed 5 per cent, which will bind your sausage very nicely, and be greatly to your advantage. Bull-Meat-Brand Sausage Binder is a pure and wholesome article of food in itself; it tends to absorb the juices and fats and helps retain them in the sausage when it is cooked, thus making a more palatable and pleasing sausage than where no binder is used. Whenever a sausage in which a binder has been used is shipped out of the state, it is necessary to label the container to show that a binder was used, in order to comply with the National Meat Inspection Law, which controls the interstate shipment of all meat food products. **Freeze-Em-Pickle** and Bull-Meat Sausage Binder are guaranteed by us under the Pure Food Laws, and every package of these preparations leaving our factory, carry a label to this effect. Unless these preparations comply with the Pure Food Law, we could not afford to put our guarantee on the package. You will find **Freeze-Em-Pickle** a very valuable aid to you for other purposes than for making your Bologna, Frankfort and other sausage. By its use you can make very fine hams, breakfast bacon, shoulders, corned beef, etc. If there are any other questions you would like to ask, we shall be pleased to have you write us, and we hope you will order a case of **Freeze-Em-Pickle** and a barrel of Bull-Meat-Brand Sausage Binder, as their use will quickly convince you that you can not afford to do business without them.

WHITENING AND PURIFYING TALLOW.

Query.—Messrs. S. B. write: "We render our tallow and other slaughter house offal all together in the regular tanks, and we would like to inquire whether you have anything that will whiten it after it is rendered."

Ans.—You can treat the tallow and whiten and purify it after you have rendered it in the regular manner in your tank if you are willing to go to the additional labor of treating it in your open jacket kettle. The proper way to do is to fill your open jacket kettle or caldron, whichever you may use, about one-third full of hot water; dissolve in this a one-pound package of our Lard and Tallow Purifier, then on top of this put the tallow after you have rendered it. It will make no difference whether the tallow is hot or whether it is cold. Get the water boiling hot; stir the water and the tallow frequently, about two minutes each time. This stirring should be at intervals of about five minutes for from fifteen to twenty minutes; then turn off the heat and permit the tallow to settle; next skim off the tallow from the top. More tallow can be treated in the same solution in the same manner; in fact, you can use the same solution in the jacket kettle two or three times. It should then be renewed with a fresh solution because the water will become impure, as the impurities of the tallow remain in the water and contaminate it; while in this condition the Tallow and Lard Purifier will exhaust its strength. Of course, more Lard and Tallow Purifier could be added to the same solution, but it is advisable to change the water occasionally as it will aid materially in purifying the tallow.

MEAT MOULDING IN A COOLER.

Query.—M. & S. Co.: Please forward to us one of your brine tester hydrometers. Ought fresh beef to mould in a cooler where the temperature is 36 degrees, after being in there ten to fourteen days? We have lost meat this way in a cooler with three coats of white lead throughout and the temperature maintained by ice. Not only has meat moulded, but it has had a pine taste.

Ans.—As requested, we have sent you a hydrometer by express. You wish to know if fresh beef stored in a cooler ten or twelve days should begin to become mouldy. You say that your cooler is cooled by ice and that its temperature is 36 degrees. We are inclined to believe that your thermometer is not accurate. It would be very difficult to get the temperature of a cooler down to 36 degrees with ice. If an ice box is kept closed from Saturday night until Monday morning the temperature runs down to 36 or 37 degrees, but where it is in constant use, and opened from time to time throughout the day it is almost impossible to reduce the temperature to 36 degrees, unless the cooler is a very small one and a large amount of ice is packed in the ice chamber above. Try another thermometer. It is important to have one that is right. Do not buy a cheap thermometer for a cold storage tester. If your cooler is constructed properly it should be perfectly dry and all the drip water drained without entering the storage chambers. A cooler, even when cooled with ice, should be so dry on the inside that a match might be struck on the sides. If the cooler is moist, there is no need to search further for the cause of your meat moulding. If the cooler is perfectly dry then the beef will keep about two weeks without moulding, then it is liable to mould slightly, but not enough to do any harm. It is frequently stored three weeks before it is consumed, and when kept that long it is tender and juicy—in other words, it is "ripe." You say that your meat tastes of pine. You did not state whether or not your cooler was a new one or not. If it is a new one and has been properly constructed it should not give meat a taste; if it has been made from boards not thoroughly dry it will cause meat to taste of pine and it might even be responsible for some mould. Then again the walls may have been stuffed with green pine sawdust, and this will cause trouble. It may be that your cooler is a home-made one, not properly constructed; perhaps the circulation is not right. You merely state that the meat moulds and tastes of pine, whereas you should have given full details. If you will send us a drawing of your cooler and full details we will be able to give you the cause of your trouble and the remedy as well.

CAUSE OF FAILURE IN CURING BACON.

Query.—T. K. writes: "We have been having trouble with our bacon. We put it down in second-hand lard tierces which we got from the large bakers here. We thoroughly cleansed them with boiling water before using them, and have been careful to weigh everything and measure the water we made the brine out of. We used brown sugar, the same as we have always used previous to this time. Our bacon was thoroughly cooled out before it was salted, and was never frozen. After being put in the pickle, we let it stand in the back part of the shop, where the temperature was often below freezing, but never cold enough to freeze the meat in the brine. We repacked it by moving from one tierce to another, always putting the same brine on the meat. We usually let our bacon in the brine for six weeks, unless it is very heavy, then we let it in a longer time. We usually keep four tierces full, and by moving from one to another always have the last one ready to take out and smoke. We used just the common barrel salt and have always had good results until now; in fact, this time the meat is perfectly sweet, but the fat of it is very dark colored, while heretofore it has always been nice and white. We do all our own killing. If you can tell us what we have done wrong, we would like to know, as we are always trying to improve whenever we can."

Ans.—You have been very fortunate indeed to have escaped trouble if you have always cured your bacon as you explain. There are many things which you have done while curing which are likely to cause you serious trouble, and which should never be done in the future. You are lucky that some of the meat did not spoil completely. It is never advisable to use lard tierces for curing, as the the lard is run into the tierces while hot, and the fat naturally soaks into the wood. This fat in time becomes rancid, and is likely to contaminate the brine and also the meat, even though you scald out the tierces, you do not get the grease out of the pores of the wood. It is always best and safest to use new tierces for curing purposes; in fact, there is great risk in using anything else. You should never use brown sugar for sweet pickle, but the very best grade of granulated sugar. Brown sugar is always more likely to contain foreign substances detrimental to the brine, and in most cases causes the brine to turn ropy, sometimes even causing it to ferment. The purest of sugar should always be used for sweet pickle. You have deviated from one of the greatest essentials to successful curing by not observing the most important of all requirements and that is an even temperature of about 38 degrees during the entire period of curing. You state that your meat was sometimes in a temperature below freezing point, but never cold enough to freeze the meat in the brine. Such a degree of temperature is enough to ruin your meat, as the curing room should never be allowed to go below 36 degrees. The moment you get the temperature below 36 degrees, the meat ceases to take on salt and will not cure; besides, it is likely to spoil in the brine. It is all right to cure heavy Breakfast Bacon six weeks, but bacon from light or small hogs will cure perfectly in twenty to twenty-five days. The meat, however, at a temperature below freezing point would not cure in six weeks or even in a much longer time. We, of course, understand that the temperature in your curing room was not always below the freezing point, but it should never be that cold.

We are going to send you free of charge our book, ''Secrets of Meat Curing and Sausage Making,'' and we will ask you to read carefully all we have to say on ''General Hints for Curing Meats,'' which covers the entire process, including chilling, overhauling, pumping, packing, temperature, etc. You will also note that we advise against the use of molasses and syrup barrels, as they are liable to cause ropiness of the brine. Also note what we have to say in regard to the handling of meat in curing, the chilling room, the condition of the meat, and the proper time to slaughter. If you will read carefully all we have to say in reference to curing in this book and will follow our methods and instructions, you cannot fail to turn out the finest kind of mild cured sweet pickled meat, having a most delicious flavor and a beautiful appearance. We ask you to make the trial and report results.

HOW TO TREAT PORK WHICH IS TOO SALTY.

Query.—F. B. writes: "We have about twenty barrels of pork that have become very salty in the brine. What would you do and how can we get the brine out?"

Ans.—Salt pork is usually put down in very strong brine, therefore it is perfectly proper that pickled pork should be very salty. If it is desired to store the pork for a long time, it should be left in the strong brine and in order to freshen it so that it will not be so salty, the pork should be washed in fresh water. It is best to handle one barrel at a time as it is to be sold or used in the market. The water in which the pork is soaked should be as cold as possible; in fact, it would do no harm to put a little ice in it. By allowing the pickled pork to soak in the fresh water, a great deal of the salt will be drawn from the meat. The meat should be soaked twenty-four hours altogether, and during the daytime the water should be changed every six hours. After the meat has been soaked, it can be placed in a mild brine, which should not be over 40 degrees strength, but if the meat can be disposed of in a few days, it is not necessary to keep it in the brine at all. It will be sufficient to place it on a shelf in the ice box; at the end of three or four days, it might be necessary to wash it off with fresh water.

IMITATION BULL-MEAT-BRAND SAUSAGE BINDER.

QUERY.—G. H. F. writes: We recently ordered from a jobber 50 lbs. of Freeze-Em Pickle and 100 lbs. of Bull-Meat Sausage Binder. The Freeze-Em Pickle was not shipped but we received a barrel of what is claimed to be Bull-Meat Sausage Binder. We notice that the Bull-Meat Sausage Binder is not put up in the regular way. It is in a plain keg without any of your labels upon it. We are suspicious about its genuineness. Do you ever ship Bull-Meat Sausage Binder in this way? As yet we have not opened the package to test it.

Ans.—You can rest assured that you have not received our goods and you should return them at once. We never pack goods of ours of any description except in our well known packages with labels on the outside and circulars inside. We never sell Bull-Meat-Brand Sausage Binder in any other manner than in red drums, which are familiar to you and the trade generally. These drums vary only in size, otherwise they are identical in every particular. They have our large label on the

head and our long label on the side, just as you see
them illustrated in the cuts which you will find in our
circulars and advertisements. You have received some
substituted article which the shipper has sought to im-
pose upon you with the hope that you would not question its genuineness. We leave to your own ideas of
fairness as to just how such a firm should be regarded.
Our goods are the first and genuine of their kind and
have won great prestige among butchers all over the
United States. Unscrupulous parties in trade seek to
reap some advantage from our great reputation by
substituting worthless preparations upon which they
make a big profit. You should always be careful in
ordering your goods to specify the article wanted and
insist that the name of B. Heller & Co. shall be upon
the package and that you will accept no other. Upon
receiving the goods, you should always inspect the
labels and see that they are ours. Do not be misled by
similar names or packages resembling ours.

COMPLYING WITH FOOD LAWS IN CUR-
ING MEATS.

*Query.—F. K. writes: "We should like to have you
inform us what we can use in our state for curing meat
and at the same time keep within the restrictions of the
law. They have prosecuted butchers all over the state of
Pennsylvania for using preservatives of some kinds, and
it leaves everyone in the meat business at a loss to know
what to do. We can't keep meat or cure it without using
preservatives of some kind. What would you advise us
to do?"*

Ans.—We manufacture a preparation known as
Freeze-Em-Pickle, which can be used for curing purposes and fully keep within the requirements of all
food laws, both state and National, as well as laws
of foreign countries. This article can be used in
all kinds of sausage, fresh or dried. We guarantee
that the use of this article will not in any manner conflict with the pure food laws of your state, and you are
perfectly safe in using it. Its uses are so various
that it would be impossible for us to give full directions for using it within the limits of these columns,
but we take pleasure in sending you a booklet which
will give you all necessary instructions and much
other valuable information.

KEEPING CURED MEATS IN CELLARS DURING SUMMER.

Query.—We have not enough cooler room to cure meat during the summer time, and we want to know if there is any way we can keep cured meat in our cellar during June weather without it becoming too salty.

Ans.—Even if you cure the meat in the winter and keep the cooler at a proper temperature and then leave the meat in the brine during the summer, the brine will turn sour, or become ropy, or thick, and will spoil the meat. To store meat in brine, it is absolutely necessary to keep it at a very low temperature. In fact, it is necessary to have an ice machine to keep the temperature in the cooler or storage room as low as 30 degrees. You could get it as low as 28 degrees. The meat would not freeze, but by having the temperature so low, the meat would not take on any more salt. You seem to be of the opinion that if the pickle on the meat were reduced you could keep the meat in the brine and keep it in a warm temperature. That would be impossible. Of course, having the brine weaker, it would not cause the meat to become so salty, but nevertheless, the brine would spoil, and it would then spoil the meat. To store meat in brine it is absolutely necessary to have the proper facilities and that means an ice machine. Our advice is that you cure enough meat during the winter according to the **Freeze-Em-Pickle** process to carry you until the middle or end of May, and then about the first of May begin curing some more meat in your regular cooler where the temperature is low enough so that the meat will cure properly.

STRONG LARD FROM BOARS.

Query.—J. A. S. writes: "I have rendered 100 lbs. of lard made as follows: 75 lbs. from fat barrows, 25 lbs. from fat boars. I find that the lard is strong. Can you give me the cause of it?"

Ans.—The odor from boar fat is so strong that such fat should not be used in first grade lard. Boar fat will only make a second grade of lard. We advise that you always keep it separate and sell it at a discount as a second grade of lard to bakers. The strong boar odor cannot be removed from the lard and the only thing that can be done is to whiten and purify it. In future render your barrow fat and boar fat separately.

TO MAKE HEAD CHEESE AND NEW ENGLAND STYLE HAM SOLID

Answer.—To make Head Cheese sticky and solid without putting hog rinds in it, use Bull-Meat Brand Sausage Binder, putting from ten to twelve pounds of Bull-Meat-Brand Sausage Binder into 100 pounds of meat. The quantity used must be governed by the percentage proportion amount allowed by your State Pure Food Law. This will make a firm, solid Head Cheese, filling all the holes with a jelly-like mass. Bull-Meat-Brand Sausage Binder is an excellent binder for Head Cheese and other sausage products.

If you desire your New England Style Ham to be more sticky, you must take your pork trimmings and cut them about the size of an egg and mix with every 100 pounds of meat 1 pound of our **Freeze-Em-Pickle,** but do not put any salt with them whatsoever. Let the meat stand in the cooler for a week and you will find that the juices in the meat will have been thickened like glue and be sticky. Then take the meat out of the cooler; add 1½ pounds of salt to 100 lbs. of meat and season with Zanzibar-Brand Seasoning. Take a small quantity of this meat and grind it very fine and then mix the fine with the coarse pieces and stuff it. Cook it very carefully with slow heat, then put it in the cooler in a press or put boards on it and press it down with stones. Your New England Style Pressed Ham is then finished. Of course, you can use some Zanzibar-Carbon to color the casings. See directions for momentary dipping on page 117.

HOW TO PREVENT MOULD ON SAUSAGE, HAMS AND BACON.

Query.—L. B. writes: "Will you please let me know if there is anything to prevent the moulding of summer sausage, hams and bacon?"

Ans.—It is first necessary that you hang the sausage and meat in a dry, cool room. If you keep it in a room where the air is moist, it will mould rapidly. If lard is rubbed on the sausage and also the meat, it will aid materially in preventing moulding. When so used, it should be applied with a cloth and rubbed on both the meat and the skin side. If your meat has already begun to mould, it should first be washed with warm water and then permitted to dry for a few hours. When dry apply a little of the lard with a cloth.

SHARPENING KNIVES AND PLATES OF MEAT GRINDERS.

Query.—F. W. F. Co. asks how to sharpen knives and plates of meat grinders.

Ans.—If the plates are grooved and rough, it will be necessary to have them turned off in a lathe. Then the knives should be sharpened on the cutting-edge just like a scissors. We do not mean the flat side which runs against the plate. But if the knife is also rough on the flat side, then the flat side should be smoothed off a little on a grindstone, and after the plate is turned down the knife should be ground with emery and oil right on the plate to make a tight fit. If you have no lathe, it will have to be done in a machine shop, and in that event we would advise you to get into touch with some of the large concerns which supply butchers' cutlery, etc. We would be pleased to give you the names of some very good firms if you desire.

HOW TO CURE MEAT FROM FARM-KILLED HOGS.

Query.—C. A. J. writes: I have more or less trouble in curing hams from farmer killed hogs. The trouble I have is in the marrow. Would you please tell me the best way for farmers to kill and chill hogs and how is best to cure such meat?

Ans.—We take pleasure in sending you by mail under separate cover, our book, "Secrets of Meat Curing and Sausage Making." This book will give you all needed information with reference to meat curing and sausage making. You should study this carefully because it gives you the needed information for handling the meat before it is put in brine and during the time it is in the brine. It tells you how to pump the meats; how to make the brine for pumping; when to overhaul the meat; the temperature to cure in, etc. If you will follow all information given in these articles you will overcome the trouble you have had. You should also use **Freeze-Em-Pickle** for curing because by its use you will be able to turn out the finest mild-cured sweet pickled meats having a most delicious flavor, of good appearance. Moreover you would have a uniform cure and no loss from sour meats. You say that you have had trouble from hams souring at the marrow. Read carefully our article relating to the pumping of meats. By pumping you will overcome the souring at the marrow.

CAUSE OF FAILURE IN CURING MEATS.

Query.—H. B. writes: I have been trying to cure corned beef, but it has a very funny taste. If you can tell me what is the trouble and how to avoid it I will be greatly obliged. I boil the water for making it into brine and use refrigerated meats. I thoroughly cleaned the barrel with scalding hot water. I did not cure the meat in a cooler, but in a room where the temperature runs from sixty to sixty-five degrees. The brine was seventy degrees strength, according to the pickle-tester. I did not use either sugar or molasses in the brine. The curing is a failure. Will you please give me all the information you can?

Ans.—Your questions are their own answers. It is impossible to cure Corned Beef or any other kind of meat in a room where the temperature is as high as 60 degrees. It should not be higher than 45 degrees, and 40 degrees will be much better.

We refer you to our directions for curing Corned Beef in our book, "Secrets of Meat Curing and Sausage Making."

The directions contained therein should always be followed to the letter, if good results are desired, and when they are followed you will turn out the very finest Corned Beef; it will be in perfect condition and have the sweet taste so much desired. The brine for 100 pounds of meat should be made as follows: 8 pounds of common salt, 1 pound of **Freeze-Em-Pickle**, 2 pounds of granulated sugar and 5 gallons of cold water. The meat should be cured in this brine ten to fifteen days, according to the weight and thickness of the pieces. Use only fresh meats that have been thoroughly chilled.

LARDING NEEDLES—HOW USED.

Query.—F. P. C. writes: What are larding needles used for? I would like to receive a copy of your book.

Ans.—A larding needle is used for drawing fine or thin strips of bacon through beef tenderloins and other kinds of meat. Frequently small strips of dry salt pork are drawn through beef tenderloins, also through meat to be roasted. This makes the meat nice and juicy and also imparts to it a fine flavor. The strips which are to be drawn through the meat are cut very thin and usually square. They are about ⅛ to 3-32 of an inch in thickness.

WHY COOLER "SWEATS."

Query.—F. B. writes: "I would like a little information in regard to my cooler. In sultry weather it sweats terribly, almost changing its natural finish to white and the sweat rolls down from it. If you can give me any information as to how I can stop it, I will be very thankful to you. The inside of the cooler is perfectly dry; in fact, I could strike a match in it anywhere. Kindly let me know if there is any way of preventing this trouble."

Ans.—The trouble with your cooler is no doubt due to the moisture of the atmosphere and to some imperfection in insulation. The defect can be remedied by the manufacturers. You say the cooler is perfectly dry inside, therefore, its construction must be very good, but the outside insulation is not just right, so the outside becomes too cool and the moist air coming in contact with the cold surface readily condenses. If the cooler can be insulated in such a way that the outside will not become so cold, we have no doubt your trouble can be overcome.

LEGALITY OF WHITE BERLINER BRAND KONSERVIRUNGS-SALZE.

Query.—O. B. writes: "We notice in the Scientific Meat Industry that you claim White Berliner Konservirungs-Salze can be used as a preservative for meats and keep within the requirements of the food laws of Pennsylvania. We wish to inquire whether one is perfectly safe in using this preparation as a preservative in Pennsylvania. Of course it is well understood that butchers must use a preservative of some kind, but they are interpreting the law in this state very strictly. Please let us hear from you fully in regard to this."

Ans.—White Berliner Konservirungs-Salze, when used in the proportion of four to eight ounces to each 100 lbs. of meat, complies with the pure food laws of Pennsylvania. No one need hesitate to use it for all the purposes for which we have recommended it in these columns, as there would be no grounds for action against anyone for its use. It is perfectly harmless and is everywhere recognized as such. No objection has been made against its use. We advise all butchers in Pennsylvania to make use of this preparation, as it will fully meet their requirements and absolve them from prosecution for the use of a meat perservative.

COLD-STORINE IS NOW LEGAL.

Query.—L. B. S.: We notice that you have put Cold-Storine on the market again. Is this product now legal to use?

Ans.—In reply to your favor of the 10th inst. we are pleased to inform you that Cold-Storine is now made under a new improved formula and contains no ingredients that have been ruled out under the National Pure Food Law or the Federal Meat Inspection Law. It is therefore now legal to use everywhere.

As you undoubtedly know, Cold-Storine is used to keep sausage, tripe, tongue, poultry, etc., in a good condition, and it does this work most satisfactorily. Simply by storing the sausage, tripe and other meats in a solution of Cold-Storine, each night, they can be displayed on the counters during the entire day, and yet keep in a good condition for a week or longer. This preparation can save you considerable money by preventing losses from spoiled goods.

You undoubtedly have your greatest difficulty in keeping link pork sausage in a good salable condition after it has been exposed on the counter for several days. This difficulty is entirely overcome by storing them in a solution of Cold-Storine over night. It will prevent them from becoming slimy and enable them to retain their full weight and fresh appearance until sold.

You are of course anxious to cut down your percentage of losses from spoiled goods, as nothing else eats so large a hole into your profits as this. So we expect you will be glad to hear that you can again use Cold-Storine. Like all progressive meat dealers, you undoubtedly look upon the use of Cold-Storine, not as an item of expense, but as a big money-making proposition. We enclose herewith our folder entitled, "Put a Dollar Into Cold-Storine and Take Out Ten," which will give you further information on this product.

HOW TO GIVE A BRIGHT, RED COLOR TO BOLOGNA AND FRANKFORT SAUSAGE WITHOUT ARTIFICIAL COLORING.

Query.—I am trying to make Bologna and Frankfort sausage, and make it all right except the color of the meat. I cannot get a nice pink color.. I have tried Freeze-Em Pickle; it is all right, but it is too slow a process. I want to make my sausage out of fresh meat and smoke it in a smoke-house, but cannot get a nice pink color on the meat. It has a gray color and does not look right. I have a color on hand, but it don't give satisfaction. It makes the meat too red and does not look good.

Now, if you have anything that will overcome my trouble and will give my sausage a nice pink color, not red, and will comply with the National Pure Food Law, send it right along. I will remit on arrival. I would send the money now, but do not know the value of it. I make about twenty-five pounds of sausage at a batch.

Ans.—Your letter of recent date received. You say you are trying to make bologna and that you make it all right, but that the color of the meat is not a nice pink color. You say you tried the **Freeze-Em-Pickle** and that it worked all right, but that it is too slow a process. You further say you want to make your bologna out of fresh meat, but that you do not get a nice pink color when it is made that way. You say the meat is gray.

In all of that you are correct, and you will always have a gray sausage unless you make it with **Freeze-Em-Pickle** according to the directions in our circular. If you make bologna sausage out of fresh meat, it, of course, will be gray. If you roast a piece of beef, it will be gray. If you cook a piece of beef, it will be gray. It is the same with bologna. When bologna is made with fresh meat, it will be gray, just as though you take a piece of fresh meat and boil it. It is impossible to make bologna with a pink color and make it out of fresh meat. For that reason, we recommend you to use **Freeze-Em-Pickle** and prepare your bologna meat with **Freeze-Em-Pickle** beforehand. You can do that in about two or three days. It is better, however, to let the meat cure for a week.

All you have to do is to trim out the beef and pork trimmings with which you intend to make the bologna, cut the pieces up about the size of an English walnut and sprinkle on **Freeze-Em-Pickle** in the proportion of one pound **Freeze-Em-Pickle** to every 100 pounds of meat. Mix the meat thoroughly and then pack it tightly in a tierce or a box, in fact a shallow box where the meat is not very thick is better, but pack it in tightly, and then put it in the cooler and let it remain there for at least four or five days, or a week, if possible. Then when you make bologna, the bologna will be better in flavor, will be juicier, will have a fine red appearance, and will be perfect in all respects. This we positively guarantee.

If you want to make bologna and frankfort sausage properly and have it right in all respects, you must take the necessary time and prepare the meat accordingly.

Formerly when artificial colors could be used in bologna and frankfort sausage, then it was all right to make it out of fresh meat and use an artificial inside color, but now, however, the food laws are such that you cannot use an inside color and therefore it is necessary to make it according to the **Freeze-Em-Pickle** process and with our **Freeze-Em-Pickle**. Then you will have a nice pink color on the inside of your bologna and frankfort sausage. You say you have a color on hand but it does not give satisfaction. It is a good thing that it does not give satisfaction, because if you were to use it, you could be arrested and fined and it would cause you a great deal of trouble; in fact, your reputation might be ruined if your name got in the papers stating that you used coloring on the inside of your bologna and frankfort sausage, because the food laws prohibit that.

By using the **Freeze-Em-Pickle** process you will make sausage that will in every way comply with your state food law and will at the same time, have a fine inside color, and excellent flavor and splendid keeping qualities. This will overcome all the troubles you mention, and all that is necessary is for you to prepare your meats a few days before hand. In fact, you can prepare a quantity of the meat before hand and keep it and use it along as you need it, making up 25 pounds at a time whenever you wish to do so, and leave the balance until a later occasion. Meat will keep this way in a good cooler indefinitely. This is the only way we can recommend your making sausage that will comply with your law and at the same time have the color you desire. Of course, it is a little more trouble, but it is trouble that will well repay you, because your sausage will really be of better quality and it will make a much better appearance.

HOW TO REMOVE WOOL FROM GREEN AND DRY SHEEP PELTS

Question.— K. M. Co. writes: Can you give us a method for pulling the wool from green hides and also from dry hides? We get the dead carcasses from the feed and transit yards—a good many hundred pelts during a year. Lots of these pelts are torn. If we can pull the wool we will be able to realize more money out of handling these pelts.

Answer.—As a general rule, wool is pulled from pelts by concerns that make this work a business. The method used is sweating and steaming the pelts. The pelts are hung on racks in a room into which live steam is turned. The pelts are kept hot for a number of days and the heat loosens the wool. It can then be easily pulled from the skin. The wool is then dried and baled.

You could not adopt this method profitably on a small scale, but we will give you a method that you can use which will prove a satisfactory way for small handlers of pelts who desire to pull the wool.

Make a pile of your pelts, wetting the pelts as you pile them. Cover the pelts with blankets or gunny sacks and allow the pile of pelts to sweat. The wet pelts being covered up tight, will become hot and sweat. This will loosen the wool and it can be readily pulled off.

Another way of removing the wool from pelts is to spread the pelts upon the floor, with the wool down next to the floor. On the skin side of the pelts place crushed fresh lime and dampen the lime. This wetting of the lime will cause it to slake and soak into the skin. The wool will be loosened by this treatment of the pelts and it can be easily pulled. This method, however, will spoil the skins and render them of no value.

The simpler method of handling the green hides by a butcher or other dealer who has only a small business equipment is to use the sweating process. By this method both the wool and the skins can be saved and sold. Ordinarily, by the sweating method the pelts are piled one on top of the other, some water sprinkled on each pelt, and the piles made from two feet to three feet high, and allowed to sweat. Great care must be taken not to let the pelts sweat too much, otherwise the hide will decay and in pulling the wool

the hide will tear. As soon as the wool is sufficiently loosened from the pelt it should be pulled. The skins can then be salted and cured, or the skins can be put into a brine and cured. After the skins are thoroughly cured they are ready to be shipped to the tannery.

HOW TO MAKE PEPPERED BEEF

Question.—G. E. O'F. writess—Can you furnish me with a recipe for making (Postromer) Peppered Beef? I am a user of your goods and will be under obligations to you for this information.

(Copyrighted by B. Heller & Co.; Reprint Forbidden)

Answer.—We do not clearly understand your question. If you mean cured Briskets that are covered with red pepper, or Paprika Compound, and then smoked, you can proceed as follows:

Cure your boneless briskets in corned beef brine with garlic in it. You will find a formula for this in our book, "Secrets of Meat Curing and Sausage Making," a copy of which we are sending you. After the meat is cured, and before you place it in the smoke-house, rub our Chile Powder all over the outside of it, and then smoke it. Or, you can smoke it and cook it, and then rub the Chile Powder over it after it is cooked. In this way, you will use less Chile Powder.

If this does not fully answer your question write us again giving us more complete statement of what is desired.

UTILIZING FAT TRIMMINGS

Question.—H. A. writes: Please send me information as to how to use up my fat trimmings.

Answer.—The best way to make use of your fat trimmings is to work them up into Pork Sausage, using plenty of Bull-Meat-Brand Sausage Binder to absorb the fat. When plenty of Bull-Meat Sausage Binder is used the fat stays in the sausage when fried instead of frying out. This keeps the meat from shrinking.

For Curing Hams, Bacon, Shoulders, Corned Beef, and for Curing Beef and Pork for making all kinds of Sausage

Freeze-Em-Pickle is a preparation for Curing Hams, Shoulders, Bacon, Corned Beef, Dry Salt Meat, Pickled Pork and Meat for Making Bologna and other kinds of sausage, etc. The Freeze-Em-Pickle Process retards fermentation and souring of brine when used according to our directions. It gives a delicious, mild flavor, curing the meat more uniformly and with a fine color. By its use curing is made easier, and anyone, without being experienced, can cure meats successfully.

Trimmings and sausage meats treated with dry Freeze-Em-Pickle can be stored away for six months, or even longer, and will then make better sausage than will fresh meats. Dry curing meats for sausage by the Freeze-Em-Pickle

Process congeals the albumen in the meat, so that it and the juices do not draw out in the form of brine. It thus keeps more of the nutriment and flavor in the meat and sausage, making it more juicy and better when fried or otherwise cooked.

Those using the Freeze-Em-Pickle Process have an absolute guaranty in its use and can always depend upon getting good results when our directions are followed. It possesses the advantage which the curer of meat has been seeking for years, and it also fully complies with the State, National and Foreign Food Laws.

The Freeze-Em-Pickle Process of curing meats gives a mild, delicious flavored cure. Meats cured by it will not be too salty, but will have that sugar-cured flavor which is so much liked.

MAKING BOLOGNA AND FRANKFURT SAUSAGE

The Freeze-Em-Pickle Process is highly recommended for preparing meat for Bologna, Frankfurts, etc. When the meat for Bologna and Frankfurt Sausage is prepared by this Process, the sausage made will be juicy and delicious.

ELIMINATE MEAT-CURING TROUBLES

Packers, Butchers and Curers have many difficulties in turning out good, sweet-pickle cured meat. By adopting the Freeze-Em-Pickle Process these troubles are eliminated and the finished products are superior to those made in other ways.

Write for Lowest Prices

Our Guaranty

We guarantee that Freeze-Em-Pickle does not contain any ingredient that has been ruled out by any food law and we further guarantee that the Freeze-Em-Pickle Process of curing meats is in accordance with the requirements of the Federal Meat Inspection Law. We also guarantee that meats cured by the Freeze-Em-Pickle Process will have a fine flavor and a mild, sweet cure when our directions are followed in every detail. We guarantee that meats treated by the Freeze-Em-Pickle Process will not spoil nor sour if kept under proper conditions. Freeze-Em-Pickle is being used by many United States Government Inspected Packing Houses throughout the country.

B. Heller & Co.

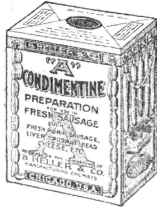
251

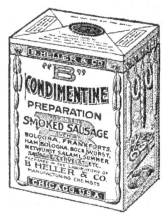

B. HELLER & CO'S.
HAM-ROLL-INE

A Meat Curing
Preparation
used in
Making
Prepared Ham
Rolls

Ham-Roll-Ine is a powdered preparation put up expressly for curing Ham Trimmings used in making Sausage or Ham Rolls. It produces a Fine, Mild Cure, and gives the meat a beautiful appetizing color and excellent flavor.

Ham or Sausage Rolls in which Ham-Roll-Ine is used are kept in a fresh, appetizing condition when displayed on the counter, thereby greatly increasing the sales.

Ham-Roll-Ine complies with the United States Government Meat Inspection Regulations, and its use is permitted in all Government Inspected Packing Houses. It is legal to use under the United States Pure Food Laws.

Directions for making Ham Rolls or Sausage Rolls will be sent on request.

Write for Lowest Prices

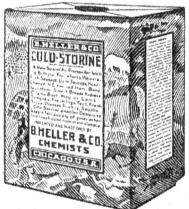

New Style Package Adopted Jan. 1, 1918

For many years Freeze-Em has been packed only in one and five-pound bottles. On account of the high freight rate on Chemicals in glass, we decided to change this package. From now on, our trade can procure it in cans if they so desire, although we will continue to supply it in bottles to those who prefer that style package. The cans will effect a saving in transportation for our trade that will be well worth considering.

The liberal use of Freeze-Em, in either style package, prevents the corrupting influence of decomposing meat particles in meat-block tops and other tools, utensils and machinery.

It is put up in 1-pound and 5-pound cans, 25-pound and 50-pound pails, 100-pound kegs, half-barrels of 200 pounds, and barrels of 500 pounds.

Write for Lowest Prices

257

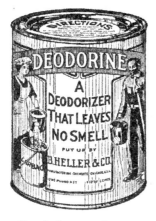

CHICAGO, U.S.A.

Your Customers are Interested in the Sanitary Condition of Your Place of Business

BY USING

Aseptifume

TRADE MARK REGISTERED

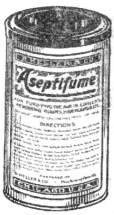

You will Secure their Confidence and make Sure of their Continued Patronage because your place will be Clean.

Aseptifume is used for Purifying the Air and Destroying Obnoxious Odors in Hide Rooms, Rendering Rooms, Slaughter Houses, and many other places.

It can be used in Refrigerators, Fruit and Vegetable Cellars, etc., by removing all Food Products and then Burning Aseptifume in them.

This method of Using Aseptifume will put Food-Storage Places in better and more Wholesome Condition.

Left over-night in a sealed room, it kills flies and all other insects there and destroys objectionable odors.

Write for Lowest Prices

BULL-MEAT-BRAND FLOUR

Highly Recommended as a
Sausage Binder and Meat Juice Absorbent

Sausage makers who have made a test of Bull-Meat-Brand Flour say that it is a most satisfactory Blender, Binder and Absorbent for Bologna, Frankfurts, Pork Sausage, etc.

Bull-Meat-Brand Flour is a Pure Cereal Product made from the Glutinous parts of selected grain and contains no adulterants of any kind. It possesses those absorbing and binding qualities which make it especially adapted for use in sausage making. It adds to the nutritive qualities of the sausage through its tendency to absorb and retain the meat

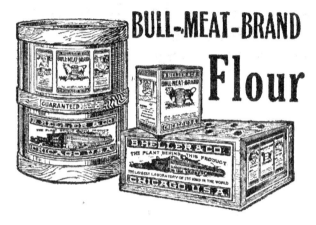

BULL-MEAT-BRAND

Flour

juices and fats. This makes the sausage more juicy and appetizing.

Bull-Meat-Brand Flour does not dry out nor become lumpy, but blends with the meat and fat when used according to our directions.

Bull-Meat-Brand Flour complies with the requirements of the Pure Food Laws. Being a wholesome and nutritious article of food in itself, it improves the sausage in flavor by holding the juices in the sausage. Our guarantee is attached to every package of Bull-Meat-Brand Flour leaving our factory.

Prices on Application

Don't Envy the Successful Sausage Maker

But Make Your Sausage Equal Any In Flavor
BY USING OUR

PREPARED SAUSAGE SEASONINGS
Be A Successful Sausage Maker Yourself
SATISFACTION GUARANTEED

In order to make Fine Sausage the Sausage Maker must use Fine Seasonings. It pays to use the very best Seasonings that can be obtained.

Zanzibar-Brand Prepared Sausage Seasonings are made from carefully tested and selected spices and herbs. Their use gives to Sausage a delicious and appetizing flavor The pleasing aroma arising from cooked Sausage containing these Seasonings adds zest to the appetite. Zanzibar-Brand Sausage Seasonings are 100% Spices and Herbs.

There are so called sausage seasonings on the market which contain 40% to 50% bread crumbs. Buy the all seasoning kind (Zanzibar-Brand) and be safe.

Our Zanzibar-Brand Sausage Seasonings cost a little more than the ordinary kind, but they are Guaranteed to be All Spice and Free from Adulteration.

The Formulas from which the Zanzibar-Brand Sausage Seasonings are made are old Secret Formulas the property of B. Heller & Co. These Formulas have been used in past generations in the Heller Family, and also by Mr. Adolph Heller, while in the Packing and Sausage Business. The added Perfection of these Formulas has been brought about through the twenty years of B. Heller & Co's experience as Experts and Consulting Packing House Chemists.

Zanzibar-Brand Prepared Sausage Seasonings impart a Fine Flavor as well as a Delicious Aroma to all kinds of Sausage. The ingredients used in the Zanzibar-Brand Seasonings are Pure, and of High Quality. The combinations impart to Sausage a Zestful and Piquant Flavor entirely their own, which is very Delicious and Appetizing and one which is exceedingly pleasing. Zanzibar-Brand Seasonings will help increase anyone's Sausage Trade wherever used, because the Sausage Flavored with these Seasonings will have such a Fine Flavor as well as an Appetizing Aroma.

Owing to the Zanzibar-Brand Seasonings being Free from Adulterations, and of High Quality, it is necessary to use only one-half as much of the Zanzibar-Brand Seasonings as of diluted and adulterated prepared Seasonings or Spices. It, therefore, can be seen that our Zanzibar-Brand Seasonings are Cheaper owing to the small amount required to give the Sausage the Desired Flavor. Any Sausage Maker who will try these Seasonings will always use them, not only because they give such a Delicious Flavor to the Sausage, but also owing to the economy in their use.

Following are the principal seasonings we put up, used by some of the most celebrated sausage makers:

Pork Sausage Seasoning, without Sage
Pork Sausage Seasoning, with Sage
Bologna, Smoked Sausage Seasoning
Frankfurt and Weiner Sausage Seas'ng
Liver, Blood, Head Cheese Seasoning
Swedish Style Sausage Seasoning
Polish Style Sausage Seasoning
Summer Sausage Seasoning
Pickled Tongue, Pigs Feet Seasoning
Corned Beef Seasoning
Hamburger Seasoning
Spanish Style Sausage Seasoning
Chile Powder, Zanzibar-Brand

They are put up in cans of 10, 25, 50 and 100 pounds and in barrels of 300 pounds.

Write for Lowest Prices

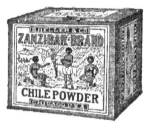

B. HELLER & CO'S

ZANZIBAR-BRAND

SAVORY JELL=JELL

Produces a Delicious Jell for Filling in Meat Preparations

For use in Meat Pies, Meat Loaves, Head Cheese, Souse, Jellied Pigs Feet, or any Meat Food Products where it is desired to have a nice jellied appearance when cold.

The flavors of the spices and aromatics used to produce Savory Jell-Jell are so thoroughly combined during our process of manufacture that no particular flavor is predominant. The flavors are evenly balanced and blended.

Use Savory Jell-Jell to fill Meat Pies, mix in with the Meat Loaves before baking and as a Jell Binder and Flavoring in Head Cheese.

The Flavor of Savory Jell-Jell Can Not be produced by a Mixture of Spices

Prices on Application

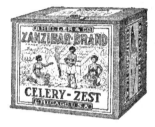
266

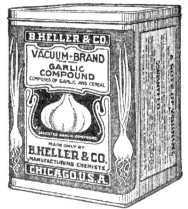

B. HELLER & CO'S
VACUUM-BRAND

Pure Garlic Powder

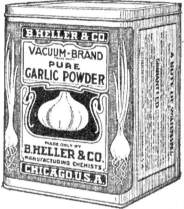

This is the Pure Garlic with the moisture extracted and then finely powdered.

Available and ready for use at all times in any climate; unvarying in its strength, goes farthest, and most economical in use.

Its powder form admits of a more even distribution.

Vacuum-Brand Pure Garlic Powder is suitable for Meats, Sausages, Meat Loaves, and other food products.

This Garlic is recommended for use in Sausage and other food products in which no cereal is used. In foods where cereals are used the Garlic Compound is the best and cheapest to use.

We guarantee Vacuum-Brand Garlic Powder to comply with the National and State Pure Food Laws, and our guarantee is affixed to each package.

It is put up in cans of various sizes, containing 1, 5, 10, 25, 50, and 100 pounds; also, in barrels containing 250 pounds.

Write for Lowest Prices

OUR GUARANTY

We hereby Guarantee that Zanzibar-Carbon-Brand Colors are Harmless, as the only Coloring Matters used are Certified Colors, which are permitted to be used by the United States Government. By this we mean that a sample of each batch of Zanzibar-Carbon Brand Casing Mixtures has first been submitted to the United States Government at Washington, D. C., to be tested and be passed on as permissible before any of it is shipped by us. The Government gives us a certificate number for each lot. The numbers and our Guarantee are on each can. It is therefore legal to use these Colors under the Government rulings in United States Government Inspected Packing Houses for Coloring Sausage Casings.

The genuine ZANZIBAR-CARBON-BRAND CASING BROWN and Casing YELLOW mixtures are sold in cans only, and not in bulk. Every can is sealed with a lead seal. The following is a facsimile of the seal we use for sealing all these cans.

Showing one side of lead seal

showing other side of lead seal

$1000.00 GUARANTEED WINDOW CLEANER

[Reg. U. S. Pat. Off]

$1000.00 Guaranteed Window Cleaner quickly and with little effort removes dust, Soot and Stains from Windows, Skylights, etc. Regardless of how long standing the accumulations may be, they quickly yield under an application of $1000.00 Guaranteed Window Cleaner. Also unexcelled for Cleaning Show Cases, Mirrors, Picture Glass, and Table Glassware.

Contains no grit, acids or other injurious substances. Will not irritate or injure the hands. In fact, It is unexcelled for cleaning and polishing Cut Glass. Recommended for cleaning and polishing eye glasses.

Its use admits more and better light, promoting the efficiency of workers, and saving artificial light. It makes it possible to show goods off to better advantage through windows, and to maintain a sanitary appearance where it counts for the most: namely, at the windows, show-cases and sky-lights.

It does the work quicker and better, leaving no unsightly streaks, smears, or film, and leaves a sparklingly clean, polished surface which does not so readily soil again.

Write for Lowest Prices

MALABOZA BRAND

Pure Food Casing Color

(Liquid)

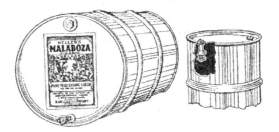

Malaboza Brand Pure Food Casing Color is used to color the outside of smoked sausage casings. It imparts to the casing a beautiful, rich smoke-shade color that is most pleasing. Sausages need only a light smoke when this color is used on the casings; this means less shrinkage and an inviting, appetizing appearance that is conducive to largely increased trade.

Malaboza Brand Pure Food Casing Color does not contain any coal tar or aniline colors. It complies fully with the Pure Food Laws and may be used with every confidence.

Packed in Steel Drums with faucet, as above illustrated.

Write for Lowest Prices

273

MALABOZA BRAND
PURE FOOD FISH COLOR
(Liquid)

Malaboza Brand Pure Food Fish Color is a purely Vegetable Color satisfactory in every way, for coloring Fish. It imparts a beautiful, rich smoke shade to the Fish, improving their appearance and increasing their salability.

It is economical, complies with Pure Food Laws and may be used with confidence. Packers of Smoked Fish will find Malaboza Brand Pure Food Fish Color indispensable.

Packed in Steel Drums as above illustrated.

Write for Lowest Prices

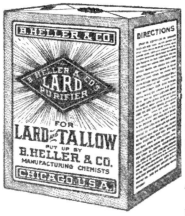

HELPS REMOVE THE DIRT AND THERE-
FORE WHITENS THE SKIN
OF THE HOGS

Hog-Scald softens the scalding water and aids in loosening and removing the hair; it also helps to remove the dirt and cleanse the skin of the hog.

Hog-Scald is a time and money saver. The small quantity required and its moderate cost is so little compared with the advantages obtained that every one slaughtering hogs should use it.

It prevents the souring of hog carcasses from remaining too long in the scalding water, as Hog-Scald reduces the time needed for scalding. It is very successfully used also in cleaning chickens.

Write for Lowest Prices

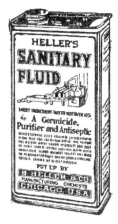

WHITE SWAN
WASHING POWDER

No Future Orders or Contracts of any kind will be accepted.

White Swan Washing Powder is both a Cleaner and a Purifier. It should be used freely as a sanitary precaution. Every place where articles of food are kept should be carefully and thoroughly cleansed with this preparation so that they may be kept in a clean, wholesome condition, thereby preventing decay and disease.

Packers, Butchers, Bottlers, Dairymen and Ice Cream Manufacturers will find this a very satisfactory and economical preparation for washing anything that is more or less greasy. It cuts the grease and dirt and leaves no smeary, greasy film on utensils washed with it as ordinary washing powders do.

Write for Lowest Prices

B.H.HELLER & CO.

$1000.00 GUARANTEED
OZO TOILET CLEANER
Removes Unsightly Stains, Incrustations, Etc. From Closet Bowls

$1000.00 Guaranteed Ozo Toilet Cleaner should be used regularly once or twice a week to keep closet bowls clean. It will prevent unsightly stains and the accumulation of rusty-looking incrustations.

$1000.00 Guaranteed Ozo Toilet Cleaner is a preparation intended solely for use in Toilet Bowls. It removes stains, incrustations, etc.. and when used regularly will keep the bowl looking clean and white.

$1000.00 Guaranteed Ozo Toilet Cleaner is of special value in removing long-standing stains and accumulated incrustations. It does its work quickly, easily and without injury.

$1000.00 Guaranteed Ozo Toilet Cleaner is easy to use—just pour from the can into the bowl.

DIRECTIONS

Pull chain, completely wetting sides of bowl. Dust $1000.00 Guaranteed Ozo Toilet Cleaner over the entire inside and into water. Let stand a few minutes. Rub off discoloration with a rag tied to a stick, or closet bowl brush. Then flush bowl.

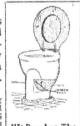

"It Reaches The Unseen Trap"

When discoloration is of long standing repeat operation, letting $1000.00 Guaranteed Ozo Toilet Cleaner remain in bowl 20 or 25 minutes. Accumulated incrustations and long-standing stains can be removed by sprinkling $1000.00 Guaranteed Ozo Toilet Cleaner freely into the bowl and letting it stand over night.

Write for Lowest Prices

ROYAL MARBLE CLEANER

Preparation for Cleaning and Renewing Marble

Royal Marble Cleaner quickly removes all stains, grease and scum from Marble, Porcelain and Enameled Basins, Bath Tubs, Sinks, Tiling, etc., and revives in them their natural appearance. It is not gritty and will not scratch or injure the finest surface. In those localities where the water contains iron, sulphur, etc., stains are produced in the basins, tubs, etc., which can easily be removed with this cleaner.

Butchers and Packers will find Royal Marble Cleaner indispensable in cleaning the linings of Refrigerators, Ice Boxes, etc. It cleans quickly, easily and satisfactorily.

Royal Marble Cleaner is in powder form, easily applied directly from the sifter-top can. It does not injure the hands.

Write for Lowest Prices

B. HELLER & CO.

Here is Something All Butchers Need
Has the 'O. K.' of Successful
Dealers Everywhere

B. HELLER & CO'S

VARN-I-GLO

(REG. U. S. PAT. OFF.)

A LUSTROUS POLISH FOR ALL KINDS OF
FINISHED SURFACES

VARN-I-GLO gives a Brilliant and Lustrous Polish to all Varnished and Lacquered Surfaces. It also Cleans these surfaces very thoroughly, removing Grease, Dirt and Ugly Spots that mar the Beauty of Fine Furniture.

VARN-I-GLO Burnishes up Old Furniture, Ice Boxes, Counters, etc., in fact, all Varnished and Lacquered Surfaces. One of the many strong points of VARN-I-GLO is that it gives a high polish to Finished Surfaces without leaving a greasy or cloudy after-effect.

Write for Lowest Prices

292

$1000.00 GUARANTEED

LIQUID BED-BUG KILLER

$1000.00 Guaranteed Liquid Bug Killer is guaranteed to kill Bed-Bugs. When thoroughly applied it is sure to kill them. This Liquid Bed-Bug Killer can be sprayed freely into all cracks and crevices. It does not injure fine fabrics, wall paper, etc. When sprayed freely into all cracks, in the corners of beds, dresser drawers, etc., and in the seams and tufts of mattresses where bugs congregate, it does its work thoroughly.

Liquid Bug Killer gives the best of satisfaction and does exactly as is claimed for it. One trial will prove how thoroughly it works.

To make the application of Liquid Bug Killer thorough and economical, an inexpensive special atomizer has been designed with which a penetrating, fine spray-like mist can be injected into corners, cracks and crevices.

Write for Lowest Prices

295

$1000.00
GUARANTEED
ANT-BANE

(A POWDER)

Of all the insect pests to which a household is subject, none are more troublesome or more difficult to get rid of than Ants. When once they have invaded the premises it is almost impossible to get rid of them by ordinary methods.

$1000.00 Guaranteed Ant-Bane is prepared especially for getting rid of Ants.

It is a Guaranteed remedy and rids premises of these troublesome insects.

Write for Lowest Prices

$1000.00 GUARANTEED RAT AND MICE KILLER

(IN PASTE FORM)

Rats and Mice are among the most destructive of all pests, and when once a building has become infested with them it is a hard task to get rid of them. They are not only destroyers of food and property, but are known carriers of disease.

$1000.00 Guaranteed Rat and Mice Killer is prepared expressly as an effective aid in removing Rats, Mice and other Rodents from butcher shops, packing houses, etc.

When used according to our directions the results will be satisfactory.

298

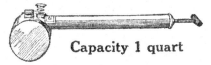

B. HELLER & CO.

COMBINED WRITING AND COPYING FLUID

ZANZIBAR-BRAND

Flows Readily and Dries Quickly, Leaving a Strong, Permanent, Legible Blue-Black Color

Zanzibar-Brand Combined Writing and Copying Fluid flows freely and easily from the pen, does not bead nor drop; penetrates the paper readily and dries quickly. It produces a rich, deep blue-black color, making a permanent, readable, lasting record. It does not smear or smudge from handling, nor fade out by exposure.

It does not clog the most delicate mechanism of complicated fountain pens.

When the ink dries up in the well, refill with water and it will still be an intensely black ink.

Write for Lowest Prices

ZANZIBAR-BRAND
INDELIBLE INK
For Marking Laundry Work

An Indelible Ink so permanently indelible that its markings could not be effected even if steeped in concentrated bleach for several hours. Its deep jet black shade is really deepened by washing, rather than weakened. It flows smoothly from the pen, dries immediately on the goods and does not spread through the fibre.

ZANZIBAR-BRAND
INDELIBLE INK ERADICATOR
For Removing Indelible Ink Stains

This Eradicator gives satisfactory results in dissolving and removing Indelible Ink Stains and marks made with Zanzibar-Brand Indelible Ink. Its use is insurance against loss caused by ink stains on the laundry work due to accident or careless handling of the marking ink. It should be kept on hand for these emergencies. This Eradicator will not injure the most delicate colors or fabrics.

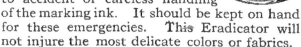

Write for Lowest Prices

CPSIA information can be obtained
at www.ICGtesting.com
Printed in the USA
BVOW06*2138230217

476869BV00010B/119/P